LANGUAGES ARE
GOOD FOR US

SOPHIE HARDACH is the author of three novels,
The Registrar's Manual for Detecting Forced Marriages,
Of Love and Other Wars and *Confession with Blue Horses*.
Confession with Blue Horses was shortlisted for the Costa
Novel Prize 2019. Also a journalist, she worked as a
correspondent for Reuters news agency in Tokyo, Paris
and Milan and has written for a number of publications
including the *Guardian*, *BBC Future* and *The Economist*.
Languages Are Good for Us is her first non-fiction book.

Languages
Are Good
For Us

SOPHIE HARDACH

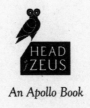

An Apollo Book

This is an Apollo book, first published in the UK in 2021 by
Head of Zeus Ltd
This paperback edition first published in 2021 by
Head of Zeus Ltd

9 7 5 3 1 2 4 6 8

A catalogue record for this book is available from
the British Library.

ISBN (PB): 9781789543995
ISBN (E): 9781789543940

Maps by Jeff Edwards
Typeset by Adrian McLaughlin

The Cuneiform font was developed by S. Vanséveren and is hosted on the
hittitology portal https://www.hethport.uni-wuerzburg.de/cuneifont/

Printed and bound in Great Britain by
CPI Group (UK) Ltd, Croydon CR0 4YY

Head of Zeus Ltd
First Floor East
5–8 Hardwick Street
London EC1R 4RG

WWW.HEADOFZEUS.COM

For Dan and Aaron, and all the world's language teachers,
with gratitude.

Contents

Across the Water

Longing and Belonging

LANGUAGES ARE
GOOD FOR US

Prologue

We are born into a world filled with thousands of languages and dialects. In our earliest months, we can perceive and mimic all the sounds that make up these languages. We can make out fine tonal shifts that may later be lost to us, and distinguish between consonants that many adults would perceive as the same. If our hearing is impaired, we can learn through vision. We can master any of the world's many sign languages, simply by watching adults using them, copying them with babbling hands, and perfecting these gestures until we become fluent. If we can neither hear nor see, we can acquire language through touch. The speaker can tap different parts of our hand to spell out letters, or we may place our hands on theirs, as they talk in sign language.

This vast ocean of sounds, signs and touch is ours to explore. Even in our first months, however, we tend to specialize in the language that matters more to us than any of the others: our mother tongue. We listen more attentively when something is said in the familiar melody and rhythm of that language, long before we learn the meaning of words and sentences. We even mimic its melody, which becomes our guide through language. Individual sounds and syllables follow, then words and sentences. Through the constant back and forth with the people who look after us, we become better and more precise at putting our thoughts, desires and feelings into words. Babies who use sign language move from so-called manual babbling to ever more rhythmic sign sequences.

This process is sometimes characterized as a loss, a turning away from the world's openness. But the intense focus on the languages that are most important to us allows us to analyse and make sense of an immense amount of information in a very short time. In that first year we gradually build a native repertoire of sounds, words and expressions, which allows us to pick out patterns from the endless noise around us.

Young children are sometimes presented as uniquely open and flexible when it comes to language-learning, and adults as hopelessly entrenched in their familiar sounds. But when you look at children closely, you will see that they make countless mistakes, and sometimes take much longer than adults to learn certain aspects of a language. After all, adults have the enormous advantage of already knowing how the world works, which languages are spoken where, how they relate to each other, and so on.

Neither do we necessarily hone in as infants on just one language. Babies who regularly hear two or more languages can distinguish them by their different rhythms and melodies. Gradually, they sort sounds and words into different channels, but they can also mix and switch between these channels.

Even after we specialize in one or two native languages, we can still acquire many others. The history of the world is a history of people communicating with each other, often in ways that run counter to common ideas around languages and language-learning. Multilingualism is neither a new nor a rare phenomenon, nor is it traditionally the preserve of the elite. People have enjoyed and experimented with different words and sounds throughout history, across all levels of wealth and education.

Some four thousand years ago, children and teenagers in the scribal schools of ancient Iraq learned to read and write in two languages. One was Sumerian, humanity's oldest written language. The other was Akkadian, which is related to Arabic and Hebrew. Around the same time, Iraqi traders settled in ancient Turkey and married local women. These husbands and wives learned each other's languages just by being around each other, and raised bilingual children. In their letters, written on clay tablets, they used one of the oldest words for interpreter, *targumannum*.

This word hopped from place to place, and language to language. It was mentioned in Akkadian clay accounts that recorded payments to interpreters. It even surfaced in a tablet found in Turkey that is written in several languages, including an ancient Indic dialect that is related to modern Hindi. Through Arabic and Latin, the word later travelled to Europe. It appeared in sixteenth-century Ireland in the form of *truchman*, an interpreter between Irish and English.

There is an even older recorded word for interpreter, the Sumerian *eme-bala*, from *eme*, tongue or language, and *bal*, to cross or turn over. The word literally means 'language-turner' or 'language-crosser'.[1]

When the Spanish conquered the Americas, they needed people who could cross back and forth between languages that had never been in contact before. They did this initially by kidnapping locals, including children, and forcing them to learn Spanish. Later, shipwrecked Spanish sailors captured by indigenous communities learned American languages through immersion. Indigenous interpreters continued to translate for the Spanish throughout the conquest, often because they had no other choice.

Royal polyglots are particularly well documented, though we'll never know how much of their linguistic prowess is myth. Šulgi (pronounced 'Shulgi'), who reigned in ancient Iraq around 2000 BCE, claimed that he was fluent in five languages. When he met 'an Amorite, a man of the mountains', he was able to 'correct his confused words in his own language'. Plutarch claimed that Cleopatra could turn her tongue to whatever language she pleased, 'like an instrument of many strings', and very rarely needed an interpreter.

William the Conqueror tried to learn English, but gave up because of his advancing age and many duties, according to a monk who chronicled the Norman Conquest. The monk thought it was a bad decision, one that lay at the root of many tensions between the English and the French occupiers. The invaders' language crept into all corners of English life. In a medieval monastery in Canterbury, an Anglo-Saxon monk called Aethelweard was possessed by a terrifying demon who made him speak French.

For many people throughout history, however, multilingualism was nothing to boast or worry about. It was simply part of their everyday reality, and a convenient skill when it came to asking for directions, or getting a better deal on a donkey-load of tin.

Guthlac, an Anglo-Saxon hermit who lived in a hollowed-out burial mound around 700 CE, spoke Celtic because he'd spent some time living among native speakers of the language. He probably didn't use it much, given that he was a hermit. But he recognized the sound when some Celtic burglars clambered all over his burial mound, chattered away in their language, and woke him up from his nap.

Other interesting linguistic innovations happened as a by-product of humans living together and getting along.

On Martha's Vineyard, an island off the coast of New England, sign language became a common means of communication from the eighteenth to the early twentieth century, due to a pattern of hereditary deafness. When the anthropologist Nora Ellen Groce visited the island in the 1970s, she noticed an unusually high concentration of deaf people in family histories. She asked a man how the deaf used to communicate with the hearing people around them – by writing everything down? No, the (hearing) man replied: 'Everyone here spoke sign language.'

'You mean the deaf people's families and such?' the anthropologist enquired.

'Sure,' the man said, 'and everybody else in town too – I used to speak it, my mother did, everybody.'[2]

Groce discovered that on some parts of the island, the entire hearing community was bilingual in English and sign language. Deaf and hearing people used it to talk to each other. Hearing people also ended up using it among themselves when they wanted to chat across a distance, discuss private matters in a discreet, silent cluster, or converse on a loud, windy beach or boat.[3]

A basic sign language also emerged among monks in Canterbury who'd taken a vow of silence, but still needed to communicate with each other. They developed a relatively small but colourful vocabulary, with signs for useful everyday items such as pepper, oysters, and underwear.

In mountainous, thinly populated or densely forested areas around the world, people have even invented whistled languages, derived from their ordinary spoken ones, as a means of talking across a distance.[4] Whistled speech has been documented in language communities as diverse as Akha (spoken in mountain villages in northern Thailand), Mixtec (in Mexico), Siberian Yupik (in Alaska), and Tamazight (a whistled Berber language recorded in the Atlas mountains of Morocco).[5] From about the fifth century BCE, Greek historians described North African people who 'spoke like bats' or 'didn't have a language but instead used acute whistling.'[6] Ancient Chinese texts mention whistling as a way of reciting spiritual or philosophical verses, and communicating at long range.

Some languages were born out of crisis and necessity. In a colonial-era German children's home in the Pacific, boys and girls who had been torn from their families created a new language, Unserdeutsch. It was passed on for generations, and continues to be spoken by a small community to this day.

We know of all these stories thanks to an extraordinary technology: writing. Invented in ancient Iraq some five thousand years ago, writing has profoundly shaped languages ever since. People have used it to record magical spells, angry letters, royal decrees and everyday worries. Many old texts are visible evidence of language contact through the ages.

A more than three-thousand-year-old Egyptian papyrus features magical spells in languages from the island of Crete and the Near East. A two-thousand-year-old tombstone found in the ruins of a Roman fort at South Shields, England, is inscribed in Latin and Palmyrene, a language spoken in ancient Syria. It was put up by Barates, a Syrian who came to England with the Roman army, for his late wife, Regina, a Celtic woman. In Galle, Sri Lanka, a stone slab was discovered with a trilingual inscription in Chinese, Persian and Tamil. It was carved in China around 1400 CE and presented as a gift to celebrate trade between the countries.

Writing did not just preserve languages, it changed them. In the first millennium CE, Korea, Japan and Vietnam adopted Chinese characters to write their own, completely unrelated languages. They also imported a wealth of Chinese loanwords. These remained in use even after Korea, Japan and Vietnam diverged from Chinese literacy, modified the characters and came up with their own scripts, or, in the case of Vietnamese, switched to the Latin alphabet.[7]

Even today, literacy continues to affect our pronunciation. The English word 'nephew', for example, used to be pronounced more like the French *neveu*, with a soft 'v'. Today, most English speakers take their cue from the 'ph' on the page and pronounce it more like 'neffew'.

★

Languages come to us above all through people. In his book on languages in early modern England, the historian John Gallagher coins the term 'invisible educators' to refer to the unacknowledged language teachers of the world, such as servants and family members. Merchants, travellers, refugees, and ordinary people giving directions to a near-unintelligible stranger, also act as such informal language teachers.

I only properly recognized the crucial importance of such invisible educators after my son was born. My British husband and I are raising him bilingually, in English and German. When you are the only one speaking to your child in your native language, you suddenly become acutely aware of how much we rely on a broad community of speakers to keep all our languages alive. For one thing I have learned is that languages never stand still. The more we speak them, the more they grow. When we turn away, they lose strength. Even our own native language skills continue to expand over a lifetime, as we add new expressions and find words to describe new experiences.

This book is about languages and the people who love them. It is about the strange and wonderful ways in which humans have used languages since the days of the earliest clay records, and about the linguistic threads that connect all of us across time and space. Above all, it is about pleasure. We all have an innate ability to learn and shape the languages of this world, to find joy in them, and to keep them alive for the next generations.

FIRST SOUNDS,
FIRST SIGNS

Early Sounds

During our last three months in the womb, when our ears have matured enough to pick up sound, we can hear all sorts of fascinating noises. Some startle us: barking dogs, a roaring engine. Others are calming and reassuring: the whoosh of our mother's blood circulating, the sound of her breathing, of her body digesting food. After our birth, such fuzzy background noise will often still lull us to sleep, for example when we lie in a car seat, soothed by warmth and the vibrating engine. Even as adults, the gentle rocking and chugging of a train tends to make us sleepy.

Within that comforting sensory experience, made up of sound and movement, the dominant voice is that of our mother. It's the only one that reaches us directly, internally, travelling down her vocal cords, through bone, tissue, amniotic fluid, and into our ears. We can feel this voice as a vibration. Other voices reach us, too, in a muffled way, like someone speaking through a pillow. We can't hear the details of speech, but we can hear its music, its underlying melody and rhythm.[1]

How do we know the soundscape of the womb? In some studies, researchers placed microphones in the wombs of pregnant sheep, but an experiment from the 1980s specifically looked at what human babies can hear. French researchers inserted a microphone into the wombs of women who were about to give birth, close to the baby's head. The mothers were then asked to recite 'La Pendule', 'The Clock', a French nursery rhyme. In the resulting recording, only about a third of the individual sounds that make up the rhyme – l, a, p, en, and so on – could be heard. But the rising and falling intonation of the rhyme made it through with perfect clarity. And the mother's voice was much more intense than the voices of others around her.[2]

Melody, rhythm and tone shape our first experience of human language, regardless of whether we hear them in the womb, or, in the case of deaf babies learning sign languages after birth, see them as a visual pattern of rhythmic gestures and facial expressions. Linguists call this underlying melody of a language its prosody. It varies from language to language, and gives us helpful cues that allow us to tell one word from another, and one phrase from another. When we speak to babies, we tend to naturally amplify prosody, and make it easier to hear.

English, for example, follows a pattern of **stress**ed and **un**stressed **syll**ables. It also maintains a regular beat. Any unstressed syllables that get in the way of that beat are dropped or compressed. **Dropp**'d or com**press**'d. Handily, a stressed syllable often marks the beginning of a word, and allows us to hear meaningful, individual units of speech. Without prosody, language would come to us as one long, monotonous stream of sound.

Onelongmonotonousstreamofsound.

French doesn't have the same kind of stressed/unstressed pattern as English. Instead, words and phrases are cut up by lengthened sounds at the end of every unit. The final syllable of an individual word – say, bon*joouur* – is lengthened. The syllable at the end of the whole phrase or sentence is lengthened even further. If you say 'Bon*joouur*!', and then 'Bonjour Mar*iie*!', and then 'Bonjour Marie, ça v*aaa*?', you can hear how the lengthening moves right to the end, like a heavy stone rolling down the phrase and stretching out that final sound.[3] French is also characterized by a rising melody, while in German the melody falls towards the end of a phrase.[4]

In Mandarin, tones can change the meaning of a word. 马, *mǎ*, said with a falling-then-rising tone, means 'horse'. But 妈, *mā*, said with a high tone, means mother. The character for 'mother' hints both at the ma-like sound, by including a little horse (马), and at the female-related meaning, by including a little symbol for woman or female (女).

Lamnso, a language spoken in Cameroon, is even more tonally complex, with eight tones.[5] One is high-pitched and downward gliding, another is low-pitched and downward gliding, another rises, then falls, and so on. Depending on the tone, the Lamnso word 'kay' can mean eaves, charcoal, rat, person or fence.[6] To outsiders, such a wealth of tones can feel incredibly daunting. Adults in particular can struggle with mastering tones, and often have a much easier time remembering words. I for one am pretty hopeless at them. But one way to make friends with tones is to remember how incredibly useful they are, helpfully singling out syllables, and conveying different meanings.

Sign languages also use prosody, in a visual form. There is a visual rhythm to the way speakers of sign languages move their hands. To outsiders, this is particularly noticeable in fingerspelling. Fingerspelling, or spelling out words with finger shapes, can be used in sign language to spell personal names or place names for which there is no sign. Matt Malzkuhn, a sign language teacher at Gaulladet University in Washington, D.C., asked different fingerspellers to spell out the phrase 'zombies quickly drank jugs of very holy elixir'. He filmed them and playfully compared their fingerspelling to different visual fonts. One fingerspeller's fast, precise signs were 'almost like a typewriter, click, clack, click, clack'.[7]

Visual intonation, delivered through nods, shrugs or a raised eyebrow, can affect the meaning of individual signs. In Irish Sign Language (ISL), the sign for 'false' – a doubtfully wavering hand –

turns into the sign for 'disbelief', or 'unsure', when accompanied by a smile.[8] In British Sign Language (BSL), furrowed eyebrows can indicate a question, while a smile signals an affirmation.[9]

Parents can exaggerate that visual prosody when they teach their babies sign language, just like parents who do this with spoken language. They may emphasize certain movements, repeat signs, or underline the meaning of a signed phrase through facial expressions. 'Mummy likes that!', signed with a delighted expression, is more easily understandable to a young child than the same signs delivered neutrally.[10]

An uncertain or speculative tone can also be delivered through touch, by spelling out words such as 'perhaps' or 'maybe' in a meaningful context. In 1887, Annie Sullivan, a teacher, taught Helen Keller, a blind and deaf child, to communicate by spelling out words into each other's palms. Sullivan gradually expanded the vocabulary towards more emotive terms and subtle tonal cues, including 'perhaps'. She illustrated her method with a conversation that took place when they came across a little boy:

Helen. What is little boy's name ?

Teacher. I do not know; he is a little strange boy; *perhaps* his name is Jack.

Helen. Where is he going?

Teacher. He *may* be going to the common to have fun with other boys.

Helen. What will he play?

Teacher. I *suppose* he will play ball.[11]

Helen then began using 'perhaps' and other subtle tonal indicators herself.[12]

Whistled languages also make use of prosody, and may mimic either the tone or the rhythm of the base language.[13]

A *secret weapon*

Throughout our life, prosody allows us to understand the sounds or signs made by other people. It's fundamental to languages, and language-learning. It is the whole tone of a language, its very essence. Getting it right can make someone sound very native-like, even if their vocabulary is quite basic. Getting it wrong can make someone appear halting and uncertain, even if they're extremely proficient on paper.

When I started learning English, native English-speakers sounded completely unintelligible to me. And yet, at some point, the fog parted, and I could hear what they were saying, could hear the words and phrases. How did that happen? If someone had asked me at the time, I would have said that I'd memorized enough English words to recognize them in speech. But that was only one part of it. The other was prosody. My mind had tuned into the music of the English language.

Danijela Trenkic, a specialist in second language development at the University of York, experienced something similar when she first arrived in England to start a master's degree at the University of Cambridge. She'd graduated in English language, linguistics and literature in Serbia, her home country. She'd not only read her way through the English literary canon, including Chaucer's *Canterbury Tales* in the original Middle English, but had translated parts of it. A language test for applicants to UK universities judged her native-like. And yet, at Cambridge, her book-based English left her stranded. 'Frankly, I felt stupid in English,' she wrote to me in an email. She couldn't keep up with fast conversations. Worse, she couldn't understand her lecturers.

Disheartened, she went to see her supervisor and confessed that she might have to drop out as she couldn't follow the lectures. Her supervisor turned out to be an expert on listening to spoken English. She laughed, and told her to listen to the **stressed syll**ables.

'And that did the trick,' Danijela Trenkic recalled. Suddenly, her ears could hear English.

You may have experienced this when on holiday in a new country. Initially, the language there may sound like gibberish. After a few days, you can probably pick out a few common sounds or phrases, even if you have no idea what they mean. That's because your mind has started to understand the foreign prosody, and can use it to chop up speech into words and sentences. It can then search for patterns, such as repetitions, within the noise. This works best in settings where certain words are repeated over and over. If you spend time with a parent of a small child, in any language, you'll soon learn the words for 'sweetie', 'darling', and so on.

Prosody, then, is a secret weapon. Our mind can activate it, without us even realizing it. Many writers consciously tap its power, by reading pages out loud to see if they flow. We can also use it when we learn languages, for example by listening to foreign songs or news broadcasts with our eyes closed, allowing ourselves to absorb the unfamiliar melody.

Newborn sounds

As useful as prosody is to adults, it's even more useful to babies. That's because babies come into the world without any explicit information about what language is, what it does, and how it works. Figuring it out, learning to understand it, and, eventually, using it themselves, is crucial to expressing their needs and having them met.

Thanks to the microphones in the womb that picked up the muffled sound of 'La Pendule', we know that babies hear the melody of human speech. If their mothers speak two languages on a regular basis, they will hear both of these distinct melodies. Researchers have found that they're not just passively surrounded by those melodies, but are actively influenced by them. They grow used to the melody of their mother tongue, and when they are born, they even begin to mimic it.

Kathleen Wermke, a biologist and medical anthropologist, has spent several decades recording and analysing the sounds of newborns and babies. She is the founder of the Center for Pre-Speech Development and Developmental Disorders at the University Clinic in Würzburg, Germany. I visited her there in 2019, and spent a day listening to the recorded waah-waah-waah of dozens of babies. Only it's not actually waah-waah-waah. Wermke and her colleagues have found out that even in the first days of life, newborn cries are highly nuanced. They are shaped by the language the baby heard in the womb.[14]

French babies cry with the rising melody of French, and German babies with the falling melody of German. The newborns of Mandarin-speaking mothers produce particularly varied and complex cries, mimicking the tonal variations of their native language. The most accomplished verbal artists are born to Lamnso-speaking mothers. Lamnso newborns experiment with very advanced melodies even in their first week of life, reflecting the many tones they heard in the womb.[15]

Recognizing this melody has several advantages. It allows newborns to gradually recognize patterns in their native tongue, and pick out individual words and sentences. In English, for example, a stressed syllable will usually direct the baby to the beginning of a word, and to individually important words: '**Mum**my **likes** that!'

Prosody also helps the babies differentiate between languages. Monolingual newborns can already tell the difference between their mother tongue and other languages, and prefer their native language over others. They do this through prosody. Using the same tool, bilingual babies can also tell the difference between their two languages.

Krista Byers-Heinlein, a specialist in early language development at Concordia University, pointed out to me that a newborn in a multilingual home doesn't even know the concept of 'language'.

'They're just born into this environment and they don't know if there's going to be one language, two languages, there could be three languages, four languages,' she said. 'It's different from acquiring a second language some time after you've mastered your first language. If you've mastered your first language, you have a way of getting into that second language, and you know: "Oh, that language is something else." If you're an older child or an adult, someone's telling you, ok, now you're going to learn French, now you're going to learn Spanish. As an infant, you don't have access to that information at all.'

One might think newborns would just decide that all the sounds in the home are part of one big speech-lump, and maybe later divide that lump up into languages. But that doesn't seem to be the case. Instead, they can differentiate between languages from the start.

In 2010, Krista Byers-Heinlein, at the time a PhD student with Janet Werker, an expert on early language development at the University of British Columbia, and Tracey Burns, at the Organisation for Economic Co-operation and Development in Paris, tested the language preferences of two groups of babies. One group was born to English-speaking mothers. The others were born to mothers who spoke both English and Tagalog, a language from the Philippines, during their pregnancy. The study showed that in both groups, the babies could distinguish between Tagalog and English. However, the English-only babies were more interested in English, while the bilingual babies were equally interested in both Tagalog and English.[16] These babies didn't yet know what 'English' or 'Tagalog' meant, they didn't have a concept of Canada, or the Philippines. But they knew that the people closest to them sang in these two distinct ways.

Tokyo, London, rake, lake

Babies enjoy hearing the familiar prosody of their mother tongue, or mother tongues, and they also use it in very practical ways for their next task: learning words, and understanding how they can be combined into sentences.

In Italian, prepositions and articles precede nouns: *a Roma* (to Rome), *il gatto* (the cat). In Japanese, the order is the other way round: *Tokyo ni*, literally, 'Tokyo to', means 'to Tokyo'. Judit Gervain, a senior research scientist at the National Centre for Scientific Research in Paris, showed in a study that eight-month-old Japanese and Italian babies already preferred the word orders of their native languages. They did this partly by recognizing certain patterns to do with the frequency of words. In Japanese, the relatively infrequent word (Tokyo) is followed by an extremely frequent word (*ni*, meaning 'to'). In Italian, it's the other way round. *A*, 'to', is an extremely frequent word in Italian. *Roma*, less so. Prosody also helped: the melodic pattern of 'a **Ro**ma', 'il **gat**to', from a soft syllable to an emphatic one, is the opposite of '**To**kyo ni', which goes from an emphatic syllable to a soft one.[17]

In our first months, we also specialize in the sounds that make up our mother tongue.

At birth, we can hear all the sounds that make up human languages. But if we maintained that universal repertoire, it would be extremely difficult to learn words. We would constantly be wondering about each individual sound: is this a d, or more like a dh, or a dd, or a dt? In a language with many finely graded d-like sounds, this would be an important decision. In English it would be a waste of time, because there aren't many d-like sounds. If someone happens to pronounce a 'd' differently, it may just be because they're talking with their mouth full, not because they are saying a totally new word. By stopping to look for meaning where there is none, babies can focus on the differences that matter. In English, for example, 'ra' and 'la' are distinct sounds, even though they're quite similar.

As a result of this specialization, we gradually become less sensitive to sounds that don't exist in our native language.

By the time we reach adulthood, we may not even be able to hear, let alone imitate, the difference between certain consonants or vowels. For example, two different d-sounds exist in Hindi but not in English. One of them is the d as in *dal*, Hindi for lentils; the other is the d in *dal*, Hindi for branch. Native Hindi speakers can distinguish between those sounds, while monolingual English speakers typically can't. Research suggests, however, that young babies of all linguistic backgrounds can hear that difference before they start narrowing their range. In the 1980s, a study led by Werker showed that English-learning babies at six to eight months, but no longer by ten to twelve months, were able to distinguish between the two d-sounds.[18]

Research by Patricia Kuhl, another specialist in early language acquisition, showed a similar pattern in a group of American and Japanese babies. At six to eight months, around 64 per cent of babies in both groups could distinguish between the American English 'r' and 'l' consonants, which don't exist in the same way in Japanese. By ten to twelve months of age, American babies had tuned into this difference even more; over 70 per cent could now hear the difference. The proportion of Japanese babies who could tell the difference, however, had dipped to just under 60 per cent.[19]

What's interesting is that the English-learning babies had become more sensitive to the difference. That's to say, this process is not just a long downward slide, a waste of a wonderful, polyglot gift. Babies turn away from the sounds they don't need, but they also emphatically turn towards the ones they need and will use. Janet Werker says she discourages her students from describing the process as a loss. Instead, she prefers to see it as a specialization. Once babies have built a stable repertoire of sounds, they can learn words and figure out their referents, i.e., the objects or people those words refer to.

'An English-learning baby is very sensitive to ra and la, they become more sensitive to it, then they can use that to direct word learning,' Werker told me. 'They hear mum say rake, they hear mum say lake, and they are like, gee, those must be different words, I should look for different referents. Whereas an English-learning baby, if they hear mum say doll, and they hear mum say doll [with a different d-sound], they're like, I'm not easily hearing that difference, that must be one word. Whereas a Hindi-learning baby – oh, dal, dal, those must be two different referents in my environment, and indeed, one is a branch, and the other is lentils.'

This doesn't mean those foreign sounds are lost to us forever. As shown by the many adults who learn a language later in life, we can resensitize ourselves by listening to them and practising them.

Through cooing, babbling, and eventually speaking, we get ever better at our own language. Babies who learn British Sign Language go through a very similar process, known as 'manual babbling'. They use their hands to imitate the rhythm and shapes made by the signing adults around them, and develop increasingly precise and sophisticated gestures.[20]

Everyday music

Once you've been made aware of the music of everyday speech, it can become quite addictive. I'd never been very conscious of the lengthened vowels that mark the end of French words and phrases, for example. But once you hear them, you can't un-hear them.

A few weeks after my conversation with Janet Werker, I was sitting in a restaurant in Paris with my friend James. James grew up in Wales, but speaks fluent French and German, and I was keen to find out what he'd make of the concept of prosody. I told him about the lengthened vowels, and we sang random French sentences back and forth to each other, experimenting with those subtle cues. At one point the waiter asked us if we wanted to see the dessert menu. As soon as he was out of earshot, we repeated, eyes wide with delight: '... *la carte des desseeerts?*' There it was, the final lengthening, the real world conforming to linguistic theory!

Then James said something that really resonated with me. To sound native-like in French, he said, you basically have to put on a totally exaggerated French accent. The point at which you sound completely ridiculous to yourself is the point at which you start to sound native to French people. I knew exactly what he meant, because I'd experienced the same when I first learned English. The weirder I'd sounded to myself, the more normal I sounded to English people. And then, at some point, I tipped across the line, let myself fall into that different prosody and those different sounds, and now English feels normal to me.

These days, most of us come to foreign languages through writing. Books, apps, written exercises and words on a whiteboard or screen tend to dominate our experience of them. Writing and reading have also shaped languages and language-learning throughout history, from the moment when the first signs were pressed into clay some five thousand years ago. Literacy is a wonderful gift, deepening our love of a language and making it easier to learn new languages later in life. But the reason I started this book with a chapter on prosody is that it's an absolutely fundamental aspect of speaking and learning languages, and yet it's often rather overlooked.

Prosody is hard to learn in a hurry. It requires spending some time with a language and its speakers, and really listening to them, rather than just grabbing a list of words. Once you can hear it, it will stay with you, and convey beauty and meaning. I've come to think of it as something like the soul of a language, the part that remains when everything else is taken away.

I learned one more lesson about prosody. Not from a researcher, but from my son.

One day, I picked him up from nursery. As I was chatting to him in German, he looked up at the bright blue sky and suddenly said in English: 'It's a *lovely* day today!' It completely took me by surprise, because he sounded so quintessentially English, and not just in terms of his accent. Presumably he'd picked it up from a nursery worker, mimicking her. Later that day, I met up with two friends, one French and the other English. I told them about my son's comment, and how much it had surprised me.

'It's just not something a German child would say,' I said. 'Or a German adult, for that matter.'

The English friend quizzed me about this. Didn't Germans talk about the weather? Yes, I replied, but not in that delighted, animated, sing-songy way. I tried to explain to her what I meant, but it was difficult. We do talk about the weather; but not in that voice.

Eventually I said: 'It's like… when English people talk about the weather, their whole pitch rises.'

'They do that when they talk about dogs, too,' the French friend chimed in. 'Someone brought a dog into the office the other day, and basically, the pitch of the entire room went up.'

So there you have it. Prosody. A convenient tool for telling one word from another. A key to foreign languages. A subtle tonal shift that can give a word or phrase a whole new meaning.

And, in British English, a means of conveying the unexpected delight of a sudden burst of sunshine, or a friendly visiting dog.

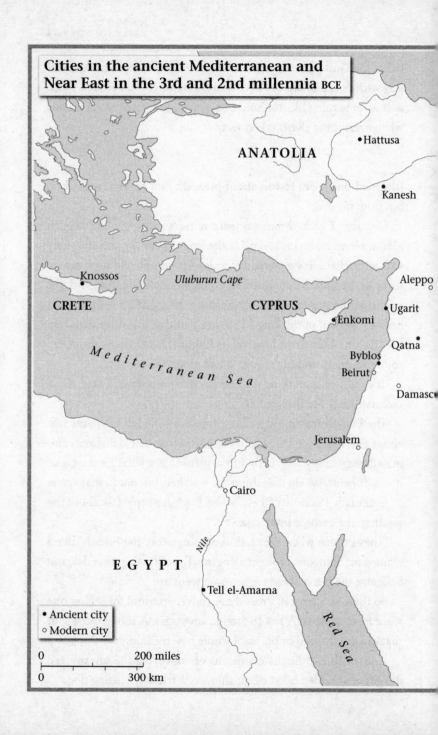

Cities in the ancient Mediterranean and Near East in the 3rd and 2nd millennia BCE

ANATOLIA

•Hattusa

•Kanesh

•Knossos

Uluburun Cape

Aleppo ○

CRETE

CYPRUS

•Ugarit

•Enkomi

Qatna ○

Mediterranean Sea

Byblos

Beirut •

Damascus ○

Jerusalem ○

•Cairo ○

Nile

E G Y P T

•Tell el-Amarna

Red Sea

• Ancient city
○ Modern city

0   200 miles
0   300 km

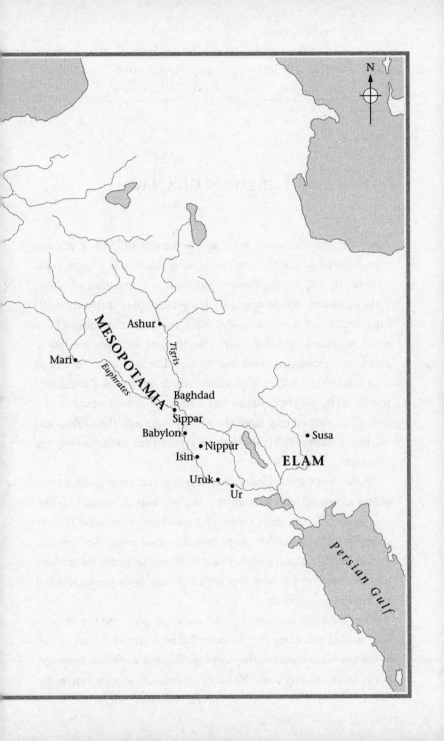

Language on Clay

More than five thousand years ago, in the city of Uruk in ancient Iraq, a group of people invented writing. Uruk was a large, prosperous city on the Euphrates river, with a population of about forty thousand, and an imposing temple complex at its centre. Its inhabitants had been using clay balls and little clay tokens for a while, to record food deliveries to the temples and issue receipts as part of the growing trade in this region.[1] The balls were impressed with seals or the tokens themselves, which represented numbers.[2] Increasingly, people replaced this with a more sophisticated system. They shaped clay from the nearby river into flat tablets and inscribed them with symbols, using styluses cut from the swampy reed beds.

Those early tablets looked like ancient comic strips, with frames drawn around groups of numbers and symbols. A round indentation made with the end of the stylus stood for the number ten, for example. Paired with a simple picture of a vessel, it signified 'ten clay pots of oil'.[3] Daily and monthly rations of beer or barley for workers were recorded in this way, too, with a picture of an open-mouthed person meaning 'ration'.

Over time, the accounts became more complex, and the pictures were turned into more abstract signs that represented sounds as well as things. From then on, the script spelled out a specific language, the oldest one in recorded history: Sumerian. It was spoken by the

Sumerian tablet with an account of barley distribution, c.3100–2900 BC.
Credit: The Metropolitan Museum of Art (Image: Public Domain)

inhabitants of the region between the Tigris and Euphrates rivers, which would later be known as Mesopotamia (from the Greek *mesos*, between, and *potamos*, river). The Sumerians themselves called their language *eme-ĝir*, native tongue, from *eme*, tongue, and *gir*, native.[4] Sumerian has no surviving relatives, and is not related to any known language from the past, either. It may be the last descendant of an even older language family that existed before the invention of writing. Today the Sumerian signs are known as 'cuneiform', from the Latin for 'wedge-shaped'.

The leap from mere pictures to sounds transformed writing from a basic administrative tool into a rich and nuanced form of communication. Cuneiform became a recording device for songs, poems, prayers, and anything else humans might want to say to each other, to future generations, or to their gods. It covered the full range of human emotion and experience.

The early tablets from Uruk typically said something like '150 litres of barley, a field of 6 hectares'.[5] Compare that to the depth and lyricism of a Sumerian tablet from a thousand years later, around 1800 BCE, bearing a lament by the priestess Enheduanna of Ur, which was copied in scribal schools:

> He stood there in triumph and drove me out of the temple. He made me fly like a swallow from the window... He made me walk through the thorn bushes of the mountains. He stripped me of the rightful crown. He gave me a knife and dagger and said: 'Here are your ornaments.'[6]

Eventually, cuneiform was adapted to capture many languages spoken in and around Mesopotamia. The first was Akkadian, part of the close-knit Semitic family, which is still going strong. Modern members of the Semitic group include Arabic and Hebrew, as well as Amharic and Tigrinya, spoken in Ethiopia.

Bilingual clay tablet inscribed with a hymn in Sumerian and Akkadian, 1st millennium BCE. Credit: The Metropolitan Museum of Art
(Image: Public Domain)

*

The Sumerians had their own version of how and why writing was invented: by Enmerkar, a legendary hero, during a contest with his rival, the Lord of Aratta.

At the start of the story of Enmerkar, humanity speaks in three voices, Sumerian, Akkadian and Amorite, another Semitic language. A god switches all humans to one language, Sumerian, to simplify matters for the contest.

As the competition drags on, Enmerkar and the Lord of Aratta send each other spoken messages through envoys who are initially full of energy, 'like a young donkey, braying as it is freed from the chariot's tongue'.[7] But as the years pass, the messages become too long for the exhausted messengers to memorize. So Enmerkar 'patted some clay and wrote the message as if on a tablet. Formerly, the writing of messages on clay was not established. Now, under that sun and on that day, it was indeed so.'[8] The messenger hands the tablet to Enmerkar's rival, asking him to read it and give him his reply. 'The lord of Aratta looked at the tablet. The transmitted message was just nails, and his brow expressed anger.' Humiliated, he unleashes a thunderstorm and an earthquake, but ultimately acknowledges his defeat. Enmerkar arrives in triumph, wearing a colourful turban, dressed in a garment made of lion skins.[9]

Of gods and stars

Cuneiform was in use for about three thousand years, until the last wedge-shaped signs were pressed into clay around 75 CE. How did a collection of basic numbers and pictures evolve into such a sophisticated and long-lasting script? Some cuneiform signs still look like the thing that inspired them in the first place, and help us understand this journey from mere symbols to literacy. Among the most ancient and memorable of these is the cuneiform sign for god, which is based on a drawing of a star.[10] It looks like this:

The Sumerian word for god (or goddess) is *diĝir* (the ĝ represents an ng-sound, as in 'thing'). The word for sky or heaven is *an*. The ⋇-sign can be read as *diĝir*, or as *an*. In a line from a myth written around 2000 BCE, 'the goddess Inanna, queen of heaven and earth', '*(diĝir) Inanna nin an-ki-ke*', it appears twice, with both these readings. First, it is read as *diĝir*, goddess, to mark the divine nature of Inanna. In its second appearance, it is read as *an*, heaven.[11]

The Sumerians were not precious about their sacred symbols, and used them for all sorts of practical purposes. The god sign appears in the Sumerian word for iron, *anbar*, which has nothing to do with spirituality. It's spelled ⋇⌐, with the ⋇ sign representing the sound *an* and the ⌐ sign representing the sound *bar*, meaning 'outside'. Put together, the signs don't mean heaven-outside. They're just used for their sounds, *anbar*, 'iron'.

This principle is very similar to the English-language text messages of the early 2000s of our era, where 'see you later' is sometimes spelled as 'C U l8r'. In Italian texting, an equivalent shortcut involves 'x', a mathematical symbol for multiplication. It's read as 'per' in Italian, which can also mean 'for'. For example, 'x me', 'per me', means 'for me'. Humans seem to have enjoyed playing these complex games with signs and sounds throughout history, and across cultures.

The more standardized cuneiform became, the more scribes were able to read and write it quickly and effortlessly. This freed up mental energy to focus on the texts themselves. The oral tradition remained an essential part of this evolving literary culture, as students were expected to memorize texts. Masters recited hymns and lists, which the students then copied as they heard them. Memory, fine motor skills, mental and oral composition, and visual pattern recognition all worked in concert to produce writing. As the archaeologist Karenleigh Overmann puts it, 'it was the cumulative effort of countless small tinkerings by average people in mundane activity that led to the development of literacy'.[12]

Mesopotamia's modern words

Through Akkadian, the ancestor of Hebrew and Arabic, an unbroken chain connects ancient cuneiform to the languages of today. Akkadian gradually pushed out Sumerian as the language of daily life after the rise of Sargon of Akkad, who conquered the Sumerian city-states and established the Akkadian empire around 2330 BCE. The term 'Sumerian' is based on the Akkadian name *šumeru*, which refers to the Sumerian language, region and people.[13]

In Akkadian, the god sign ✳ is simplified and read as *Ilu*, the Akkadian word for god.[14] Similar words existed in other ancient Semitic languages, such as Ugaritic, spoken in the wealthy trading city of Ugarit on the Syrian coast. In Ugarit, 'El' was a cosmic god worshipped alongside other deities, such as the storm god Baal. From about 1500 BCE he is mentioned in cuneiform texts from Ugarit, and statues of him were found along the Near Eastern coast.[15]

Ugaritic is similar to Hebrew, and 'El', along with variations such as 'Elohim', is one of several Hebrew words used to refer to God. It appears in the first line of the Hebrew Bible, *Bereshit bara Elohim et ha-shamayim v'et ha-aretz* ('In the beginning, God created heaven and earth').[16] Astonishingly, the word Ilu/El stayed intact through the shift from cuneiform to the completely different Aramaic and

Hebrew alphabets that replaced it, and through the even more dramatic shift from a polytheistic world of many gods to monotheistic
faiths that recognized only one God.

From there, it reached even more languages and worshippers. In
the 1530s CE, Martin Luther translated the Bible into German. He
rendered the first line as *Am Anfang schuf Gott Himmel und Erden*.[17]
Around the same time, William Tyndale produced the first English
translation: 'In the begynnynge God created heaven and erth' ('erth'
is not a typing error, but the original spelling).[18] Both translations
gloss over an interesting facet of the original text. In Hebrew, the '*-im*'
ending generally denotes the masculine plural. In another context,
'Elohim' would be translated as 'gods'. This would obviously sit
oddly with the monotheistic principle of Judaism. In any case, *bara*,
created, is in the singular in that biblical opening line, suggesting
that it is about only one divine being. Jewish and Christian scholars
have tended to interpret the plural ending of 'Elohim' as a symbolic
form, perhaps expressing the creative power of many forces bundled
into one.

The biblical saying 'an eye for an eye' first appears in an Akkadian
cuneiform inscription from around 1750 BCE ('If a man has blinded
the eye of another man, his eye shall be blinded').[19] Some Akkadian
deities have lost their sacred status, but persist in other forms. The
Akkadian sun god was called Šamaš (pronounced 'Shamash'). He
shines on as *shemesh* in Hebrew, and *shams* in Arabic, both of which
mean 'sun'.

In the fourteenth century BCE, Akkadian cuneiform functioned
as a diplomatic lingua franca all over the eastern Mediterranean
and beyond. Rulers in ancient Cyprus, Anatolia, the Near East and
Egypt sent each other Akkadian clay tablets across long distances,
asking each other for so-called peace gifts, to cement diplomatic ties. A king in ancient Iraq wrote to an Egyptian pharaoh
reminding him that their fathers had been great friends who had

sent each other 'lovely peace gifts'. He complained that the pharaoh never sent him any truly lovely peace gifts, such as gold, which he happened to need because he was building a temple.[20] The Akkadian word for 'peace gift', *šulmu* (or *šulmani* in the plural), is a variation of the Akkadian word for peace, alliance or friendly relations, *salamu*.[21] It lives on in modern-day words for peace: the Hebrew *shalom* שלום, the Arabic *salam* سلام and the Tigrinya *selam* ሰላም. Across the Semitic language family, this word doubles as a greeting.

In London, many different Semitic scripts and languages grace shop signs, restaurants and places of worship. In my own neighbourhood, I often walk past an Ethiopian hair salon called 'Selam'. The owners proudly display the name on the shop front both in English letters and as ሰላም. A long and continuous linguistic thread connects this purple-and-white sign by a busy road to ancient clay tablets sent between kings and pharaohs.

A drinking song

As cuneiform spread across the Near and Middle East, people used the script as they saw fit. Some composed elaborate hymns and incantations. Others told their scribe to dispatch a quick note about a late shipment of beer or sheep. Some merchants and royals learned to write themselves, and sent clay letters to their spouse, business partner, daughter or son with the next donkey caravan. They mastered fewer signs than professional scribes, but enough to express themselves competently. Tens of thousands of tablets and inscribed stone slabs have been found in the ruins of homes, palaces and temples all over Iraq, Syria, Turkey, Iran and as far south as Egypt. They capture a chorus of voices that remains as vibrant as when these texts were first written:

'*Gakkul-e gakkul-e! Gakkul-e lam-sa-re! Gakkul-e nig ur, sag-sag-ge!*'
The brewing vat, the brewing vat! The brewing vat, the beer vat!
The brewing vat, which puts us in a happy mood!

> (Sumerian drinking song, copied in scribal schools)[22]

Is there garlic? Let him pay six shekels of silver. Behold, fresh garlic
has been gathered. Send me a boat, that I may send up garlic and
dates. Speedily let me hear news about the garlic and dates.

> (Akkadian merchant letter)[23]

Sleep come, sleep come, sleep come to my son, sleep hasten to my
son! Put to sleep his open eyes, settle your hand upon his sparkling
eyes.

> (Sumerian lullaby)[24]

My father, now the ships of the enemy have been coming. They
have been setting fire to my cities and have done harm to the land.

> (Akkadian diplomatic letter sent
> by the ruler of Ugarit)[25]

Your slave girl Dabitum sends the following message: What I have
told you now has happened to me: For seven months this child
was in my body, but for a month now the child has been dead and
nobody wants to take care of me. May it please my master to do
something lest I die.

> (Akkadian private letter)[26]

In the land where you dwell, there are many ostriches; why have
you not sent me ostriches?

> (Akkadian letter from Zimri-Lim, a king in the city
> of Mari in Syria, to his sister, Liqtum, in the town
> of Burundum in northern Syria)[27]

I cannot sleep at night on account of worrying about you.

(Akkadian private letter)[28]

Multilingual kings

Cuneiform faded from use as shorter and arguably more convenient scripts took over in the Near and Middle East. They were derived from a consonantal alphabet of twenty-two letters invented by the Phoenicians in ancient Lebanon around 1000 BCE (Phoenician is a dialect of Aramaic, another Semitic language). It's the ancestor of the letters I am typing right now. Just like the god sign in cuneiform, some of them carry within them an echo of the ancient pictures that inspired them. The 'A', for example, was originally written on its side and based on a drawing of a horned ox head.[29]

Cuneiform slid into obscurity to the point where no one could remember how to read it. Only in the nineteenth century did modern scholars crack the mystery of these wedge-shaped signs, working their way from cuneiform texts in languages with close modern relatives, such as Old Persian and Akkadian, to texts in completely unfamiliar ones, such as Sumerian and Hittite.

The cuneiform tablets not only preserve these ancient languages, they also tell us how people felt about them at the time, how they learned them, translated between them, and argued over them.

'I can do service as a translator with an Amorite, a man of the mountains,' claimed King Šulgi, who ruled around 2000 BCE. 'I myself can correct his confused words in his own language. When a man of Subir yells, I can even distinguish the words in his language, although I am not a fellow-citizen of his.'[30]

Šulgi said he could provide justice in five languages – Sumerian, Akkadian, Amorite, Elamite and the language of Subir: 'In my palace no one in conversation switches to another language as quickly as I do.'

It's impossible to know whether Šulgi was actually able to speak all these languages, or could barely say hello in Amorite. But clearly, multilingualism was seen as a symbol of superiority and intellectual prowess. It was a skill that powerful kings such as Šulgi, and the mighty Ashurbanipal of seventh-century BCE Assyria, boasted about along with their claims of unparalleled strength and success in the battlefield.

'I will learn Amorite!'

Other ancient discussions around languages reflected human concerns over belonging, status and identity that may feel very familiar to modern readers.

Around 1780 BCE, the nomad king Šamši-Addu had an argument over languages with his son, Yasmah-Addu, who lived in a palace in Mari, central Syria. They wrote to each other in Akkadian, but their dispute was over two other languages, Sumerian and Amorite.

Sumerian remained a very prestigious language even after it fell out of common use, comparable to Latin in the Middle Ages (and indeed today). It represented culture, memory, and the accumulated knowledge of many generations. It was also closely linked to urban culture, to the great cities of Mesopotamia.

Amorite was the ancestral language of the nomadic tribes of Syria, the Amorites. Their name stemmed from the Sumerian word *Amurru*, meaning 'west', because they originated west of the Sumerian city-states. Their main god, the divine herder Martu, was often depicted with a shepherd's crook, and a sheep or goat in his arms. Amorite was a Semitic language, closely related to Akkadian, and spoken across a large area. But it was not written down, except in the form of personal and place names, and a few scattered words.

The boundaries between settled people and wandering nomads were not all that clear-cut. After all, the Sumerians themselves had descended from nomads and herders. Settled farmers often migrated as part of their seasonal activities. Urban merchants also travelled widely. Still, in Sumerian myth, the voices and habits of the city dwellers tend to be presented as superior to those of the roaming nomads. As one character in a Sumerian story says about the Amorites, 'their ideas are confused; they cause only disturbance'. In this view, the nomad 'is clothed in sack-leather, lives in a tent, exposed to wind and rain, and cannot properly recite prayers. He lives in the mountains and ignores the places of gods, digs up truffles in the foothills, does not know how to bend the knee, and eats raw meat.'[31] Nomads were also seen as somewhat horse-mad, which alienated urban populations that were unfamiliar with horses.

As the Amorite nomads settled, many tried to assimilate into urban ways. In their stronghold at Mari, they surrounded themselves with luxuries. They kept a harem, were entertained by acrobatic dancers, singers, harpists and drummers, and ate their way through elaborate feasts accompanied by bread baked in the shapes of hedgehogs, fish and naked women.[32]

When the Amorite king Zimri-Lim conquered Mari, he reluctantly agreed to letting himself be carried into the city by underlings, like an urban ruler, instead of riding into town on his horse.[33] Later, he gave into his old passion and imported rare white horses from the city of Qatna, keeping them in a shady, painted courtyard in front of his royal apartments.[34] Still, he enjoyed urban comforts, too. He had an icehouse built, where ice was stored in the winter and in the summer chipped off, clinked into glasses of wine and beer, and mixed with pomegranate juice.[35]

In the case of Šamši-Addu's family, assimilation meant shedding their ancestral language, Amorite. Šamši-Addu himself still spoke it and used it to negotiate with other nomadic chieftains.[36] But he didn't pass it on to Yasmah-Addu, who grew up like a true urban prince, speaking Akkadian, and admiring an even more prestigious language, Sumerian.

Šamši-Addu frequently scolded and lectured his son in his letters, telling him to spend less time on women and fast chariots, and more on being an effective ruler, like his brother.[37] One day, Yasmah-Addu wrote to his father asking for a Sumerian scribe. It's not clear why; perhaps he wanted someone to read him Sumerian literature, or perhaps he simply thought a Sumerian scribe would be a fine thing to have. The king wrote back in fury:

> You have asked me to send you a man who can read Sumerian. What? Instead of asking me for a man who can read Sumerian, you should learn to speak Amorite! Anyway, which of the men in my service can read Sumerian? Sure, there's Šu-Ea, he can read Sumerian. Am I going to send you Šu-Ea? But he (is busy). Iškur-zi-kalamma can read Sumerian, but he's working in the administration. Is he supposed to leave his post and join you? Nanna-palil can read Sumerian. But he's absent... You wrote to me "May my lord send me a man from Rapiqum who can read Sumerian". There's no one among the people from Rapiqum who can read Sumerian![38]

You can hear the father's exasperation echoing through the millennia. He'd been quite content to let the language of his ancestors wither away, but now seemed to regret that choice.

There was in fact an urgent matter that the family needed to address, and for which Sumerian was utterly useless. The king was planning to take a census of various nomadic tribes in his realm, possibly in order to conscript them into his army. The problem was that these tribes spoke Amorite, and approaching them in a different language was unlikely to win them over. When Yasmah-Addu suggested he would just go and count them, his father urged him to stay away:

> You can't speak Amorite with them! Don't go! Send La'ûm, Mut-Bisir and Mašum instead, so that they can count them![39]

Yasmah-Addu replied that there was no need for that:

> Without exaggeration, I will learn to speak Amorite! Three days after this tablet, I will count the nomads.[40]

No one knows how Yasmah-Addu's Amorite classes turned out. Did he really master Amorite in three days? Did it help him count the nomads? Did he give up and summon Iškur-zi-kalamma, the Sumerian scribe, instead, and discover the beauty of literature? All we know is that the family's dominance was short-lived. When Šamši-Addu died, Yasmah-Addu was driven out of his kingdom. Some say he was executed.

'Speak of me in awed amazement'

Stories of such spontaneous, informal language-learning are relatively rare in the old clay records, simply because most people wouldn't have written about it. Most of what we know about ancient language-learning comes to us from a more structured environment: scribal education.

Cuneiform literacy was typically passed on in the family. Priests, exorcists and professional scribes taught their sons (and sometimes their daughters) to read and write. Unusually from a modern point of view, this training was routinely bilingual. From childhood, scribes acquired complete fluency in two languages, Sumerian and

Akkadian. Even after Sumerian was no longer commonly used, they were expected to write but also to speak both to a high standard.

Many of these school texts date from the Old Babylonian period, around 1900–1700 BCE. At that time, Akkadian had become the language of daily life, but Sumerian was still revered in scribal schools, temples and palaces. Any half-educated merchant could scratch out a letter in Akkadian. But only those proficient in Sumerian could study the old hymns and myths, benefit from the wisdom of gods, kings and priestesses, and preserve it for the future. Knowing Sumerian elevated a person, and embedded them in a long chain of memory.

Remembering and being remembered was important to the people of Mesopotamia. Kings buried inscribed bricks in their monumental buildings, promising great rewards to future rulers who would honour them, and threatening to curse those who forgot or tarnished their memory. Language, and especially the Sumerian language, formed an eternal link between the generations. Šulgi imagined a future king being overwhelmed by the beauty and wisdom of his hymns: 'he will speak of me in awed amazement... and himself beget heavenly writings'.[41]

Thousands of tablets were found in the foundations of scribal schools. They reveal an entire historical legacy created by children. Their ordinary exercises and habitual slip-ups became immensely valuable over time.

To a modern researcher trying to reconstruct an ancient language, it's extremely useful to see a misspelled word in a practice text. If the student wrote it down as they heard it, they inadvertently reveal useful clues to its pronunciation. Repetitive bilingual word lists and writing drills can, with hindsight, function as accidental dictionaries. It's partly thanks to these discarded, error-strewn practice tablets that scholars have been able to piece together the scripts of the ancient world, and discover what daily life was like in history's first language schools.

The Secrets of House F

Some four thousand years ago, in the sacred city of Nippur between the Tigris and Euphrates, a boy was learning to write. His school was in an ordinary family home, in a crowded neighbourhood close to the temple. Priests, astrologers and dream interpreters hurried past, off to purify a new house, oversee an offering, or investigate the meaning of a worrying omen. The teachers were probably his own father, uncles or older brothers, or a neighbour who took on apprentices. The home was small but comfortable, with three rooms grouped around a courtyard, a bread oven, a board game for their breaks, and a recycling bin where discarded practice tablets were soaked in water, to be reshaped and reused the next day.[1]

No one here was precious about their tablets. A junior scribe, called *dub-sar tur* in Sumerian, would write thousands of signs until he reached proficiency. There was no point being sentimental. Tablets that were not thrown in the recycling bin were broken up and used to reinforce walls. However, the act of writing itself was important. You had to get it right, or risk being scolded or beaten. The scribe, like the other children at his school, signed his longer texts with his name, and a heartfelt 'praise to Nisaba', the goddess of writing.

Thousands of years later, when archaeologists dug up the ruins of Mesopotamia, they were especially keen to find schools and libraries, places that can reveal not just what people thought and knew in the past, but also how they acquired this knowledge. A school or library is often celebrated as a sensational find.[2] Initially, some European and American teams were led astray by their own ideas of what a classroom looked like. The Assyriologist Dominique Charpin tells the story of a team of archaeologists who thought they'd discovered a school in the palace at Mari, Syria. It fitted their expectations: a room with parallel rows of brick benches. Later, it turned out that it was in fact a warehouse, and the 'benches' had been used to hold up large jars of wine, which were slotted between them.[3]

In Mesopotamian images, scribes don't sit on benches anyway. They tend to stand, or squat. After all, a hard clay tablet doesn't need to be supported by a desk, unlike soft paper. Nor were ancient classrooms likely to be indoors. Cuneiform is written by pressing the stylus into fresh clay, creating a three-dimensional inscription that is best read in direct sunlight. Given that scribes couldn't switch on a lamp, they probably worked in courtyards. Gradually, scholars adjusted their view of education in Mesopotamia.

At the little school in Nippur, they found the bread oven, the board game, the recycling bin, and all those broken practice tablets. Some of them had the teacher's neat example on one side, and the student's clumsy copies on the other. Some had fingerprints on them, or wipe marks from a wet cloth, because the student had erased their efforts over and over. One tablet had been wiped so often that the student's side had worn dangerously thin. Because some were signed, we know the names of several students. One was a boy called Ninurtamushtal.[4]

The archaeologists named all the ruins alphabetically. This one became House F. It gave the world a wealth of ancient literature, because so many copies were found here, made by schoolchildren learning to write. Eleanor Robson, a Professor of ancient Middle Eastern history who has analysed the tablets from House F, calls it a 'deliberately traditionalist' school that promulgated Sumerian even as Akkadian had already taken over the world of business, administration, and the law. She notes that the literature taught in House F was almost entirely in Sumerian, and the poems students copied celebrated a ruler who'd already been dead for two hundred years.[5] Robson's description brings to mind modern elite schools that pride themselves on their Greek and Latin. The scribes of Nippur were clearly very proud of their association with a great culture of the past. Several household documents found in Nippur were written in Sumerian, suggesting that scribal families treasured the classical language even in their private lives.

The exorcists at No 7, Quiet Street

In other cities, similar small, private schools were found. Students tended to use a common set of core exercises and texts, with some variation between cities and houses.[6] This is remarkable given that there was no central educational authority or official curriculum in the modern sense. After all, teaching was mostly a family affair.

At No 7, Quiet Street, in the ancient city of Ur, an exorcist called Ku-Ningal taught his sons to read and write in Sumerian and Akkadian, alongside his routine duties of expelling bad spirits and appeasing the gods.[7] One of the sons was apparently dyslexic, based on the mistakes in his tablets.[8] The family even composed a jokey Akkadian story about a launderer.[9] It was a satire on their own trade of exorcism; launderers and exorcists worshipped the same patron god, since they were both in the business of cleansing things.

Ku-Ningal's family kept their little home-school going for about eighty years, passing on the art of exorcism and the art of writing. Their private archive tells the story of a large and lively household. At one point, Ku-Ningal listed the expenses for his daughter's wedding, which included 300 fish and 4 turbans along with oil, flour, butter, sheep, silver, wine and bread; plus a ritual bath and a jug of beer for the groom's mother. One of Ku-Ningal's sons followed in his footsteps as an exorcist, and trained his own sons.[10]

If you are surprised to find a family of Mesopotamian exorcists living at such a quintessentially English address, it is because Leonard Woolley, a British archaeologist, led the excavations at Ur in the 1930s. He named the streets after familiar ones back home. There's Quiet Street, Quality Lane, Church Lane, and so on. As a result, when you look at a map of ancient Ur, you could think yourself in an English market town, but one that's badly haunted.[11] Rather fittingly, one of Woolley's collaborators was married to Agatha Christie, the crime writer. Christie spent time at the digs, and even stuck a sign in cuneiform on her office door there. It spelled out 'Beit Agatha', Akkadian for 'Agatha's House'.

A scribal sisterhood

Some girls trained as scribes, too. Accounting tablets from around 2500–2000 BCE mention rations paid to female writers, including one called Nin-un-il.[12] In the centuries that followed, literate women were mentioned more frequently. At the palace in Mari, female scribes were given oil and wool for their services, and some worked specifically as kitchen scribes.[13] A female scribe called Šima-ilat served Šimatum, the daughter of the Amorite king Zimri-Lim.[14]

In a walled neighbourhood in the city of Sippar, a community of celibate priestesses lived and ran their own businesses. They negotiated real estate deals, adopted children, and served the gods and goddesses with daily hymns and offerings. Several tablets signed by women were found here, including writing exercises by a girl from around 1750 BCE.[15] Their training followed the same lines as the boys', was also bilingual, and probably mostly took place in the family. Inana-amamu, a scribe in Sippar, may have learned the craft from her father.[16]

Some women in royal families also learned to read and write. The wife of Ashurbanipal, an Assyrian ruler in the seventh century BCE, received a clay letter from her sister-in-law, who scolded her for not doing her homework: 'Why do you not write your tablets and recite your exercise?'[17]

As relatively narrow as it was, the female scribal tradition continued in the Middle East long after cuneiform faded from use. In medieval Muslim and Jewish communities, as in ancient Mesopotamia, some women became acclaimed scribes. Miriam Bat Benayah, the daughter of a Torah scribe in fifteenth-century Yemen, added a personal comment to one of her manuscripts: 'Please be indulgent of the shortcomings of this volume; I copied it while nursing a baby.'[18] In the Muslim Middle Ages, a scribe called Fatima wrote out a peace treaty between the caliph of Baghdad and the Byzantine emperor. At least one female writer, a Jewish woman in medieval Iraq, taught the art to her son.[19] In the Jewish merchant community of medieval Cairo, almost all boys and girls learned to read and write, and were taught by female teachers.

The trainee scribes of Mesopotamia therefore didn't just leave a historical legacy in terms of scripts and languages. They also started an educational tradition, a way of passing on knowledge in families or small classes and ensuring that children learned to become fluent in two or more tongues. How they did that is not all that different to how we still learn languages today.

From homework to history

It's partly thanks to these children and teenagers, and their daily coursework, that so much of our earliest history is preserved. They left us texts in Sumerian, in Akkadian, and, crucially, bilingual texts written in both Sumerian and Akkadian. They created lists of words in Sumerian and Akkadian, along with a pronunciation guide to each Sumerian word, spelled out in Akkadian (like writing the French word *merci* as 'mare-see' in English). Scholars consulted these lists when they began to reconstruct the sound and structure of Sumerian, which has no living descendants, and would otherwise have been difficult, if not impossible, to revive.[20]

The education of a scribe started with learning how to cut a reed stylus and shape an even tablet, which is not as easy as it sounds. Some tablets were folded and flattened in quite elaborate ways. Next, they mastered the individual wedges and syllables, and once they could do this competently, moved on to word lists.

Sumerian word lists form a literary genre of their own. They are catalogued by theme, such as jobs, animals, gods or trees, and are strangely mesmerizing, because they follow a logic from some four thousand years ago. This logic is intensely familiar in parts, as in a list of mouth-related vocabulary, with the words for bad breath, vocal cords, tongue, breath, interpreter, stammerer, and so on.[21] Other categories, however, feel very familiar at first glance and then suddenly veer into the territory of magic and fantasy, or just into things and habits that are firmly in the past.

One Sumerian list of animals starts out with sharp-eyed descriptions of ordinary animals: 'a sheep stung by a scorpion, a sheep for a banquet, a sheep for a prayer, a sheep for a bridal payment, a sheep used for bait for a wolf, a ewe that has given birth, a ewe with arthritic hips, a ewe that had a miscarriage…' Gradually, the animals become increasingly exotic and terrifying: 'fierce snake, stone snake, water snake, furious snake, dragon, snake with seven heads…'[22]

In a list of Sumerian jobs, some also sound rather ordinary: fisherwoman, apprentice singer, perfume maker, weed remover, thief. Others are more colourful and mysterious: sorcerer, snake charmer, senior snake charmer, exorcist, a 'priestess of the journey', a 'prostitute wearing sandals', a 'habitual fornicator'.[23] The mind can't help but be drawn to these characters as they strap on their sandals and venture out into a world of dragons and seven-headed snakes. They're both distant and close.

The painstaking precision of the Sumerian lists makes them very evocative. They are snapshots of an ancient world and all the people, animals, plants and things in it, down to the tiniest detail. Thousands of years ago, someone looked very closely at their surroundings, and left behind words that can make us see those surroundings, too.

One list follows the entire life cycle of a tree, from its beginnings in the forest to the things it can be turned into: 'Olive tree, almond tree, cedar, a forest consumed by fire, a forest consumed by insects, a thorny tree from Meluhha, a quince tree, an apricot tree, a pomegranate tree, a juniper tree, a date palm, a harness for climbing date palms, a cut-off branch, a sign, a plow, a three-toothed hoe, a wagon wheel, the peg of a wagon wheel, a wagon seat, a wagon bed, a footstool, a footstool decorated with ivory, a woman's chair, a man's chair, a bed with a wool mattress, a bed with legs shaped like an ox's hoof...'[24]

'Hurry! It's urgent!'

Scribal students diligently learned a broad and deep Sumerian vocabulary, much of which would have had no practical application whatsoever. They also learned to write in Akkadian, at times in a more businesslike fashion, as in this model letter taught in scribal schools (slightly condensed here for clarity):

May (the sun god) Šamaš keep you in good health! Concerning the field of so-and-so, which you had taken away and given to someone else: so-and-so went and petitioned the king and the king became very angry. Hurry! Before the officer of the king reaches you, return the field to its owner. It is urgent![25]

Sumerian and Akkadian are not related at all. But as different as they were, the two languages complemented and inspired each other. Akkadian borrowed many Sumerian words for things invented by the Sumerians, such as writing. The Sumerian word for tablet, *dub*, entered Akkadian as *tuppu*.[26] The Sumerian *sar*, to write, was adapted into Akkadian as *šatāru*.[27] A *dub-sar* is a Sumerian 'tablet-writer', or scribe; Akkadian borrowed this as *tupšarru*.[28] A *munus dub-sar* is a female scribe, and a *dub-sar tur*, a junior scribe (*munus* means woman or female; *tur* means young). *Edubba*, 'tablet-house', is the Sumerian word for school. Akkadian half borrowed, half translated this term as *bīt tuppi*.

Bīt, *bītu* or *bētu*, the Akkadian word for house, has remained almost unchanged since the days of clay tablets and scribal schools.[29] It lives on in the Hebrew *bayit*, the Arabic *bayt*, and the Ethiopian Amharic *bet*, all of which mean house or home.

Akkadian speakers went to the *bīt dīni*, the 'house of judgement', to argue their court cases over stolen sheep or silver, and prayed to Šamaš, the sun god, for a good verdict.[30] In present-day Hebrew, *beth din* still means 'house of judgement'. It refers to a rabbinical court that rules on matters such as religious conversion. There are several *beth din* in London, ranging from traditional to progressive, all linguistically connecting leafy English suburbs to the ancient Middle East.

Nor is Sumerian necessarily a language of the past. Preserved in clay, it has a better chance of surviving in the really long term than English, which is now written on increasingly ephemeral media. As Charpin puts it: 'Clay possesses one considerable advantage: it is resistant to fire, water, and magnetic disturbances. In short, in a few thousand years, our photographs, books, and hard disks will no doubt have disappeared, but our collections of cuneiform tablets will still be there.'[31]

'You can't even shape a tablet!'

The schoolchildren of Nippur, Ur and Sippar didn't know how valuable their Sumerian exercises would be to future generations, and probably enjoyed them no more than the average modern-day Latin student sweating through a grammar test. The Assyriologist Konrad Volk argues that their teachers faced an unprecedented challenge: 'For the first time in human history, a didactical concept was needed that could appropriately convey a dead language.'[32] One solution was to bring the language to life through dialogues. Many of them are set in schools, such as an argument between two boys called Enkimasi and Girnishag, who insult each other's Sumerian skills:

'You dolt, numbskull, school pest, you illiterate, you ignoramus of Sumerian, your hand is terrible; it cannot even hold the stylus properly... You are the laziest of scribes.'

'What do you mean... Me, I was raised on Sumerian, I am the son of a scribe. But you are a bungler, a windbag. When you try to shape a tablet, you can't even smooth the clay... Yet you claim to know Sumerian like me!'[33]

Arguments form a popular genre of Sumerian school texts, and not just between people. Objects and even seasons argue with each other, too. Summer tells winter that it's a lazy season. A tamarisk tree insults a date palm, boasting that its own wood is used for statues of gods, whereas dates are just laid down as offerings. A plough taunts a hoe:

'Hoe, digging miserably, weeding miserably with your teeth; Hoe, burrowing in the mud; Hoe, putting its head in the mud of the fields, spending your days with the brick-moulds in mud with nobody cleaning you, digging wells, digging ditches, digging!'

To which the hoe replies:

'Plough, what does my being small matter to me? I fill all the meadows with water.'[34]

There is an entire story set in a fictional scribal school, composed by an unknown teacher around 2000 BCE:

'School boy, where did you go?'
'I went to school.'
'What did you do in school?'
'I read my tablet, ate my lunch,
Prepared my tablet, wrote it, finished it, then
My lines were prepared for me ...
When school finished, I went home,
Entered the house, where my father was sitting.
I told my father about my hand copies, then
Read the tablet to him, and my father was pleased ...'[35]

The next day, the boy marches off to school again, cheerfully carrying his packed lunch and looking forward to another successful lesson. But this time, he can do nothing right. He is beaten for being late, for chatting, for handing in poor work. His Sumerian exercise is found wanting: 'My Sumerian teacher asked: "You call that Sumerian?" and beat me.'

Eventually, his father bribes the teacher with beer, meat and fragrant oil. At the end of the feast, the teacher showers the boy with blessings, and asks Nisaba, the goddess of writing, to look after him: 'May you rank highest among schoolboys!'[36]

This method of teaching Sumerian through funny stories was still in use more than a thousand years later, in 600 BCE. By then, Sumerian had become an even more distant linguistic memory. It lived on in stories, like this one about a high priest and a vegetable vendor (which I have edited for clarity). The story is bilingual and plays on the reputation of Nippur as a centre of learning, so infused with tradition that even ordinary people knew Sumerian, while the rest of the world had moved on to Akkadian:

A man from Nippur is bitten by a dog. He goes to see Amel-Baba, a high priest in the city of Isin, who cures him with an incantation. The patient invites him to Nippur, promising a feast of meat and two jugs of beer. He gives Amel-Baba clear directions: 'Enter Nippur through the High Gate, walk down Sila-dagala street, leaving Tilla-zida street and Sila-Nusku-u-Ninimma street to your left. You'll see Nin-lugal-abzu, daughter of Ki'aĝ-gi-enbilulu, daughter-in-law of Nišū-ana-Ea-taklā, who usually sits in the area of Tilla-zida street and sells vegetables. Ask her and she will show you.'

Amel-Baba travels to Nippur and follows his patient's directions through the High Gate, down Sila-dagala street, past Tilla-zida and Sila-Nusku-u-Ninimma street. He spots a woman selling vegetables. 'Nin-lugal-abzu?' he asks.

'Lugal-gu?' she replies in Sumerian. ('My lord?')

The high priest, despite his prestigious job and years of training, doesn't speak Sumerian, and is frightened by the strange sounds.

'Why are you cursing me?' he asks in Akkadian.

The vegetable vendor, educated Nippur woman that she is, easily switches from Sumerian to Akkadian: 'Why am I cursing you? All I said to you was "bēlī"!' ('My lord' in Akkadian.)

Amel-Baba is still slightly bewildered, but keen to make his way to the feast. He asks Nin-lugal-abzu to show him the house of the man who invited him: Ninurta-sagentarbi-zae-men, brother of Ninurta-mi-zideš-ki'aĝani, brother-in-law of Enlil-Nibru-kibi-gi. But he's barely finished speaking when she replies, again in her cultured Sumerian: 'He's gone out.'

'Why are you cursing me?' the startled high priest asks again, in Akkadian.

'Why am I cursing you? All I said to you was, "He's gone out"!' Nin-lugal-abzu replies (in Akkadian).

This linguistic quarrel goes on for some time. He asks her in Akkadian where his host went. She replies in Sumerian that he went to *e diĝir-be šuzianna*, to the house (or temple) of the goddess Suzianna, to make the usual offering. He thinks she is cursing him; she wearily insists that she'd only said *bīt ilišu šuzianna*, Akkadian for 'the house of the goddess Suzianna'.

Finally losing her patience, she exclaims: 'What a fool this one is! Let the students from our schools get together and chase him out through the High Gate with their tablets!'[37]

You don't need to know much Sumerian to get the point of the original text, which is mainly in Akkadian. The few Sumerian sentences are quite simple and feature words that are very common in Sumerian inscriptions, such as *e*, house, and *gal*, big. Even a Sumerian beginner could have read the story and had the pleasant feeling of being in on the joke.

Indeed, the basic words in the story are as useful to a modern-day Sumerian student as they would have been in ancient times, because they come up in many Sumerian compound words.

Lugal, lord, is such a compound. It literally means 'big man', from *gal*, big, and *lu*, man. A great ruler is a *lugal-gal*, a 'big-big-man'.

E can mean house, but also temple, room, or estate. A palace is an *egal*, a 'big house'.[38]

A dragon is an *usum-gal*, literally, a big snake. King Šulgi called himself a 'fierce-looking lion, begotten by a dragon'. In a tablet from around 2500 BCE, another ruler is described as the son of a *munus usumgal*, a dragon woman (*munus* means woman or female).[39]

These two simple words, *e* and *gal*, combined with a few more basic, common words like 'woman' or 'man', suddenly open the gates to a more than 4,000-year-old world of dragons, palaces, rulers and temples.

Sun gods and sesame

Languages don't just live in tablets and manuscripts. They also travel from port to port, kitchen to kitchen, spice cabinet to spice cabinet.

The Sumerians flavoured their meals with a spice called *gamun* in Sumerian. In Akkadian, it was called *kamunum*, which we know from bilingual lists. We still use this spice, and still know it by an almost identical name, cumin. The Akkadians enjoyed the tasty, nourishing seeds and oil of the sesame plant, called *šamaššammu*. The name is thought to mean sun-oil, or sun-plant, and is the ancestor of our word, sesame.

In the evening, the scribes sat on their rooftops and looked west, in the direction of the sunset, *erabu* in Akkadian. The region that lay in that direction would later be called Europe.

This long reach of language can be easy to forget when we look at scribal students. Their immediate universe may have been quite small: the family home, the neighbourhood and temple, perhaps a few trips to other sacred cities. But the words they wrote down did not stay in one place, or even one language. They hitched a ride on boats and caravans, to places where other scribes wrote them down; hitched a ride to yet another place, and were again written down by scribes. This is how some of these words reached us in the present day. We can, in fact, trace the journey of a single spice, cumin in English and *gamun* in Sumerian, around the world, across time, and into our kitchens.

Cumin: A Travelogue

Gamun is first mentioned in Sumerian tablets around 2300 BCE. In bilingual lists from scribal schools, this is translated into Akkadian as *kamunum*. Typically, the spice is sold and used in combination with others. A Sumerian tablet from around 2100 BCE records deliveries of 16 shekels' worth of crushed gamun and 14 shekels' worth of crushed sumac, lumped together with deliveries of salt and crushed coriander.[1]

An Akkadian tablet written sometime between 1900 and 1600 BCE suggests that to treat someone afflicted by the 'asu disease', 'you crush kamuna and you mix it in one litre of fine-quality oil, recite an incantation, and make him drink it'.[2]

According to a tablet in Akkadian and Sumerian from around 900–600 BCE, an Assyrian king inaugurated his new palace with a feast that included, among many other animals and plants, 100 grain-fed oxen, 1,000 lambs, 500 antelopes, 500 ducks, 500 geese, 10,000 turtle doves and thousands of other birds, as well as 10,000 skins of wine, hundreds of pots of sesame, shelled pistachios, onions, garlic, honey, ghee, sumac, cheese, dates, olives, '100 containers of hinhinu seeds', and 10 donkey-loads of 'gamun'. Thousands of dignitaries arrived from all over the region, from ancient Turkey, from the Near Eastern coast, and the king had them all bathed and anointed, then fed them for ten days.[3]

Cumin and a honeybee hieroglyph

To the south, the Egyptians also revered the little brown seeds, though they called them by a different name, *tpnn*. They used *tpnn* to treat stomach problems, coughs, tongue, ear and tooth infections, and 'heat in the anus'.[4] *Tpnn* appears in a recipe on the side of a cup: *tpnn smi bit*, 'cumin, set milk, honey'. In the original hieroglyphic inscription, the recipe looks like this, read from right to left (note that the little bee and the pot form the Egyptian hieroglyph for 'honey'):[5]

The Egyptian word, *tpnn*, doesn't seem to have caught on in other languages. But the Akkadian word, *kamun* or *kamunum*, did. It moved westwards, with merchants who took their donkey caravans to the Near Eastern coast, to the great trading city of Ugarit. There, goods were loaded onto ships and dispatched to Cyprus, and even further north-west, to Crete, and mainland Greece.

Several spices are mentioned in tablets written in Linear B, a script used on Crete and the Greek mainland from about 1400 to 1200 BCE, to write Greek. They were probably used as perfume, and to season food. Among them are *korijadono* (coriander, in the Linear B spelling) and *kumino* (cumin).[6]

Stewed Roman pumpkin

Around 400 BCE, *kúminon* is mentioned in a medical treatise written by the Greek physician Hippocrates, who recommends it as a laxative. About three centuries later, *cuminum* appears as the star ingredient in a Roman cookbook known as the Apicius manuscript. The author suggests adding *cuminum* to dishes of stewed pumpkin with onion, pepper and lovage; to sliced beets with leeks and coriander, seasoned with raisin wine, oil and vinegar; to boiled and sliced carrots, stewed with a little oil; to boiled brains with cucumber; to mashed parsnips and vegetable pies; to peaches or pears, sweetened with raisin wine; and to many other kinds of mouth-watering dishes. There are also recipes for *cuminum*-seasoned sausages, cumin sauce for oysters and shellfish, and a laxative made from *cuminum*, honey, ginger, pepper and dates.

In its homeland, the Near and Middle East, the spice continued to be enjoyed. The Akkadian *kamun* or *kamunum* entered Arabic as *kammun*. Medieval Arab recipes were quite similar to the Roman ones, and make liberal use of cumin.[7] A cookbook from medieval Baghdad includes particularly tempting cumin dishes. One recipe suggests serving aubergines with garlic, sesame oil, coriander and cumin. In another, leafy greens are stripped of their ribs, boiled and dried, then sautéd in sesame oil with garlic, cumin, coriander and cinnamon.[8]

Minus the cinnamon, and switching sesame oil for olive oil, this is still a popular dish, and has spread from the Middle East to Europe and North Africa. My Moroccan-born mother-in-law makes it frequently, using Swiss chard and following the identical process of boiling/steaming, drying, and sautéing the greens in garlic, oil and cumin, with a pinch of chilli for heat.

Muslim conquerors brought cumin to Spain. From around the eleventh century, it was grown in Spain, and exported to northern European countries.[9]

A girl called 'Little Cumin'

Cumin connected traders, cooks and writers with different mother tongues. It popped up in translations, in literary metaphors, in spontaneous expressions, and even nicknames.

In Fustat (Old Cairo), a community of Jewish merchants and their families thrived on the spice trade, setting up ventures with Muslim business partners, and investing in trading ships. They imported spices from India to Egypt, and sold them all around the Mediterranean. In return, they dispatched books, soap and other goods to the East. The community included famous sages and physicians, such as Maimonides, who used spices as medicines. Cumin tinctures were applied to sore eyes and ingested to soothe colics. The families even nicknamed girls and women after spices and vegetables. The nicknames Sumsuma (sesame), Sumaysima (little sesame), Shuwaykiya (little artichoke, a frequent nickname), Hiltīt (asafoetida, a pungent, onion-like spice) and Kammūna, cumin, were all mentioned in letters.[10]

Cumin caused some confusion to translators. In the early eleventh century, Ibn Ganah, a Jewish doctor living in Spain, wrote an Arabic treatise on drugs and plants. His sources were Greek, Arabic and Persian medical texts. In one of these texts he had found an intriguing reference to a Persian dish called *zirabag*. Apparently, this was some kind of yellow soup. But what exactly did zirabag mean? Ibn Ganah decided to ask one of his contacts, Abu l-Futuh, and recorded his reply: 'Abu l-Futuh told me that its meaning is "laun kammūn" (cumin soup). He said: "The Persian name of kammun is zira."'[11]

Ibn Ganah had stumbled across a very interesting phenomenon. West of ancient Mesopotamia, cumin is usually known as *kamun*, *kumin*, *kumino*, *comino*, and so on. East of ancient Mesopotamia, in languages such as Persian (Farsi), Hindi and Urdu, it tends to be called *zira*, *jira* or *jeera*. In China, where it may have arrived with traders or pilgrims returning from India, it is called *zhi ra*.

*

'Lycorys and eek comyn'

In Europe, Greek and Roman recipes were copied widely, and with them, *kuminun* and *cuminum* entered many languages. In the ninth century, a team of multilingual monks at a monastery in Fulda, Germany, copied the Apicius cookbook. The monastery had been founded by missionaries from the British Isles, and was abuzz with many scripts and languages. Around that time, *cuminum* was also mentioned in a plan for a garden at the monastery of St Gall, in Switzerland. The monastery was built in honour of an Irish monk, Gall, who'd lived in the place as a hermit. It was still a magnet to Irish missionaries and pilgrims, and was the hub of a vibrant, Europe-wide language exchange.

From around 1000 CE, cumin is mentioned in Old English plant lists as *cimen*. Later, it would be known in England as *comyn*, or as cumin, the name still used for it today. In the Middle Ages, between the twelfth and the fifteenth centuries, English tenants even paid their rent in pepper and cumin.[12] England imported cumin from Spain and Portugal, along with pepper and ginger. Many of the traders who shipped these spices were Italian.[13]

In England, cumin was used as a seasoning and medicine. It's a myth that spices were used to mask the taste of rotten meat. Spices were much more expensive than meat, and it wouldn't have made sense to waste them that way, especially when meat usually came from freshly slaughtered animals.[14] Instead, their use was about well-being and pleasure. Medieval English cuisine, as enjoyed by the elite, was influenced by the flavours of the Middle East. Copies and translations of the Arabic cookbooks mentioned earlier arrived in England via Italy. Susan Francia, who wrote an extensive study of cumin in medieval England, described the food of that era as highly spiced, enjoyed for its varied flavours as well as medicinal or preventative properties.[15] One recipe suggests combining boiled egg yolks with milk, cumin, saffron, rice flour and more chopped egg, as well as cheese.[16]

Cumin also spiced up English literature. A thirteenth-century satirical play mentions impoverished, wandering preachers in tattered old cloaks, who carry 'more bags than dealers in pepper and cumin'.[17] One of the characters in Chaucer's *Canterbury Tales*, Sir Thopas, feasts on 'lycorys and eek comyn With sugre', 'liquorice and also candied cumin seeds'.

This kind of indulgence became a rather ambiguous literary motif. On the one hand, gluttony was one of the seven deadly sins. Medieval European artists and writers painted gory scenes of excessive eating and drinking, and showed gluttons in hell being forced to eat live animals.[18]

On the other hand, culinary abundance was celebrated in folk tales of the Land of Cockaigne, which existed in many languages (Cokaygne in Anglo-Irish, Cocagne in French, Cuccagna in Italian, Schlaraffenland in German, Luilekkerland in Flemish; along with many other variants).[19] In the Italian version, a river of white wine flows past a mountain of Parmesan.[20] In the French 'pays de Cocagne', the rivers flow with red wine from Beaune and white wine from Auxerre. In a fifteenth-century Dutch poem, one of the rivers of Cokaengen is made of beer.[21]

Exotic spices perfumed these fictional landscapes, and turned mere gluttons into gourmets. In a fourteenth-century story from Ireland, a tree grows in Cokaygne that is made up of ginger, nutmeg, cinnamon and cloves.[22]

The French word *gourmand*, referring to someone who enjoys eating a lot, expresses that kind of carefree indulgence. The French food historian Florent Quellier describes being a gourmand as an 'instinctive, primitive joie de vivre', sensual, generous, and life-affirming.[23] Unlike 'gourmet', someone who appreciates fine food, 'gourmand' doesn't seem to have made it into any languages as a loanword, which is a shame.

Spicy stories 'con comino'

Cumin and its fellow spices inspired fabulous nicknames, fairy tales, satires and poems in their host languages. But because some of them were so tied to certain cultures, their status could quickly decline.

This happened, for example, after the expulsion of the Muslims and Jews from the Iberian peninsula. European Christians had long had a complicated relationship with Muslim food. They appreciated its delicious flavours, borrowed Muslim recipes and employed Muslim cooks, but increasingly, some of them worried that all of this represented an inappropriate level of religious contact.[24] By the fifteenth century, Christian scholars argued that Christians should not share meals with Muslims and Jews, and the Spanish Inquisition agreed.[25] In the sixteenth and seventeenth centuries, some Muslim- and Jewish-associated spices, including cumin, slid further from grace. The little brown seed went from being a friendly condiment grown by pious monks to a symbol of moral degradation.

Comino (cumin) appears as a metaphor for excessive sensuality in a racy sixteenth-century Spanish novel, *Portrait of Lozana: The Lusty Andalusian Woman* (*Retrato de la Loçana andaluza,* in the original Spanish; *lozano* or *lozana* can mean vigorous and healthy, but also exuberant, or lusty).[26] The main character, a prostitute from Seville, boasts about the recipes she learned from her grandmother and the fervour she puts into her dishes, a metaphor for her sexual prowess. The dishes are all typical Muslim-Spanish fare, such as couscous with chickpeas, meatballs with coriander, fried croquettes, stewed aubergines, cakes flavoured with almond paste and sesame seeds, and *zahinas y nabos sin tocino y con comino,* 'porridge and turnips without pork and with cumin'.[27]

*

A journey to the Cloud People

The Spanish conquerors brought cumin to the Americas, where it entered indigenous languages. One of them was Mixtec, a member of the Otomanguean family.

The name 'Mixtec' derives from a word in Nahuatl, which was spoken by the Mexica who dominated Mexico before the Spanish conquest. They called the Mixtecs 'Mixtecatl', meaning 'Country of the Clouds', a reference to their mountainous homeland. The Mixtecs call themselves Ñuu Savi, meaning something like 'The Rain Nation', and more generally 'Na Savi', 'People of the Rain'.

Their language, 'Ndusu Tu'un Savi', 'Words of the Rain', is still spoken by some half a million people in Mexico, mainly in the states of Oaxaca, Puebla and Guerrero.[28] The language is linked to a beautiful hieroglyphic writing system, painted on paper made of bark or deerskin. The Spanish destroyed many of these documents, but some survive and tell us of powerful kings, such as the eleventh-century Mixtec ruler Eight Deer Jaguar-Claw.[29]

After the conquest, the Mixtecs added Spanish ingredients to their traditional diet of tortillas and beans, and Spanish food words to their language.[30]

The result are hybrid dishes such as *mole negro*, black sauce, made of fried onions and garlic (brought by the Spanish, replacing wild native onions), chilli (native), tomatoes (native), cinnamon, cloves and cumin (all brought by the Spanish), and chocolate (native), as well as a host of other ingredients.[31] The Mixtecs translated some of the spice names. Ginger, *jengibre* in Spanish, became *ñami yatu*, 'spicy sweet potato', in Mixtec.[32] But they continued to refer to cumin as *comino*, keeping intact the long, long chain that stretches all the way back to the ancient civilizations of the Near and Middle East.

Comino has become a central ingredient of Mexican cuisine, along with coriander, also originally from the Middle East. It's also been more broadly associated with Mexican culture and Mexican identity. Visiting the US border town of Brownsville, Texas, in early 2020 for the *New York Times*, the food writer Priya Krishna describes driving along the steel barrier put up to keep out Mexican immigrants: 'Suddenly the air starts to smell of smoke and cumin.' Brownsville turns out to be a taco hot spot, where Mexican-Americans have set up some of the best taco restaurants in the US. Tacos and cumin, and the Spanish language, defiantly continue to mark the Mexican presence on both sides of the wall.[33]

Both the Akkadian-rooted *kamun* or *kamunum* and the Persian-rooted *zira, zeera* or *jeera* made their way into many African languages. Trading communities sprang up in different parts of Africa and brought spices and dishes from home. Jeera chicken, an Indian dish, is popular in Kenya (and from there, has made another geographical leap: the Regency Club, a restaurant in London, features Jeera Chicken on its menu of 'Indian cuisine with Kenyan roots').

Of course, these two versions, the Arabic *kammun* and the Persian *zira*, can happily coexist in the same place. I have a jar of cumin in my spice cupboard here in London. My neighbour Sabeeha, who lives across the road and grew up speaking Urdu, calls it *zeera*. The Indian restaurant down the road, run by a Hindi-speaking family, serves a very tasty dish called *jeera aloo*, cumin potatoes.

The scribe in your spice rack

Are all these different kinds of cumin the same, and identical to Sumerian *gamun*? It's hard to say. The ancient clay tablets mention white and black cumin. Black cumin is actually more likely to be *Nigella sativa*, the black nigella seeds. That would chime with archaeological finds of remains of nigella seeds, for example, in the hold of a trading ship that sank in the eastern Mediterranean around 1300 BCE.[34] But ancient remains of cumin, *Cuminum cyminum*, were also found.

In these recipes, plant lists and treatises, there is sometimes a bit of a confusion around cumin. Some people say cumin when they mean caraway, or nigella, or even aniseed. German scholars first translated Egyptian hieroglyphs as referring to caraway, when actually they were about cumin (it was possibly a case of cultural bias – in German kitchens, caraway is a lot more common than cumin).

Still, even with all this confusion, a dotted line connects the kitchens of Nippur and Ur to a wandering prostitute in a Spanish novel, to monks in a chilly German monastery, to Jewish nicknames in Old Cairo, to Rain People cooking stews in Mexico, to the supermarkets and spice racks of the modern world. I have to say that knowing this has made it a little more exciting to open my kitchen cupboard and see that jar labelled 'cumin'. It's like having a tiny scribe in my kitchen, busily copying the words of the past.

The God Sign

On a warm day in October, I join the queue snaking through the courtyard of the Louvre in Paris, all the way to the enormous glass pyramid that houses the entrance. Once we enter the pyramid and pass the security gates, our paths diverge. Everybody else hurries towards the *Mona Lisa*. I am headed in the opposite direction, making my way through a maze of quiet, strangely empty corridors and exhibition rooms, until I reach what feels like a forgotten corner of the museum.

Here, only a handful of other visitors are shuffling across the cool marble floor, past black stone statues and display cabinets filled with tablets. We're among the Louvre's collection of Near Eastern artefacts, an assembly of exquisite objects from ancient Iraq, Iran and Syria.

The main attraction in the section is a tall black basalt stele inscribed with the Code of Hammurabi, the world's oldest legal code, written in cuneiform. The wedge-shaped script is everywhere in this collection: on the tablets in the display cabinets, on the backs of statues, on monumental carvings of battle scenes. But to the vast majority of visitors, including myself, it's completely unintelligible, and that makes it strangely invisible. Usually, I would only briefly glance at the inscriptions, then move on to more relatable exhibits. Today, however, I'm here on a mission. I'm looking for the god sign.

It was the trainee scribes of Nippur and Ur who inspired me to try and learn some Sumerian cuneiform myself. Granted, I was unlikely ever to become a true *munus dub-sar*, a female scribe, or even a *dub-sar tur*, a junior scribe. But might it not be possible to master a few basic signs?

I'd walked many times through the Mesopotamian rooms of big museums, barely noticing the clay tablets and royal inscriptions because the script was just too alien. I'd felt like the Lord of Aratta, standing there in grim incomprehension. It was all just nails. And unlike the Egyptian hieroglyphs, which are totally baffling but at least contain some visually attractive birds and little people, cuneiform doesn't offer the casual observer a helping hand. You could stare at it and stare at it, and it would still all be lines of nail-like strokes. It's not intuitively guessable.

I began to wonder how it would feel to be not quite so shut out, to sense the human hands behind this script, to find a point of connection. To experience it as a real language, not just cryptic wallpaper. I decided to start by learning just one sign, one that was beautiful, and easy to remember. I chose the god sign, shaped like a star.

Man, house, dragon, tongue: how Sumerian works

Sumerian can appear very forbidding at first sight. Once you spend some time with it, however, certain features can feel familiar and helpful. For a start, Sumerian uses compound words, as in *lu-gal*, 'big man' (literally, man-big), a lord or king. This makes it a little easier to learn new words, or even guess their meaning if you know the individual building blocks. Also, some cuneiform signs contain useful clues to their meaning and pronunciation.

The word *eme-ĝir*,[1] 'native tongue', as the Sumerians called their language, is written like this, with two signs: 〈cuneiform〉. *Eme* means tongue; *ĝir* means native. The tongue sign is derived from the sign for mouth, *kag* in Sumerian, but written with a tiny additional sign inside, which is read as *me*. In other contexts, this sign can mean 'to be'. But here it is simply used to give a clue to how this sign is pronounced: not like *kag*, mouth, but more like *me*, i.e., *eme*.

Kag (mouth) 〈cuneiform〉

Plus:

'Me' syllable 〈cuneiform〉

Equals:

Tongue (also, language) 〈cuneiform〉

The sign is thousands of years old, but based on a reasoning we can still follow today. I find the god sign even more relatable, because I can picture humans at the dawn of history looking up at the night sky, at the many stars, and seeing the gods in them.

The god sign retained its shape over a very long time, and across adaptations of the cuneiform script. It looks like this 〈cuneiform〉 around 3000 BCE, and still looks like this in Sumerian inscriptions that appear a thousand, or even two thousand years later. In Akkadian, the sign is eventually simplified to 〈cuneiform〉. This sign, *ilu*, survives in the texts until the very last dated cuneiform tablets from around 75 CE. And *ilu*, as we've seen, links today's global religions with many millions of followers to the very beginning of human history. All of this makes it a very appealing sign to learn.

★

Gods and stones

Before visiting the Louvre, I'd studied the god sign in dictionaries, sign lists, and some online pictures of particularly legible cuneiform inscriptions. My worry was that I wouldn't be able to spot it in the wild. After all, there is often a gap between the textbook, where everything is clear and easy, and the real world, where nothing makes sense. At first, that's exactly what happened to me at the Louvre. The tiny scribal clay tablets in the display cabinets looked like squashed waffles. I couldn't even tell one line from another, let alone see individual signs. Then I noticed a smooth stone slab inscribed with big, clear signs. There it was, in the second line:

The thrill, the rush of the discovery, took me by surprise. This object was so ancient, so seemingly austere and abstract. And yet, it was alive. It was filled with the spirit of the people who'd created it, who'd wanted it to be read. That was why they had chosen such a durable material, inscribed it so clearly, and carefully buried it in the foundations of their royal buildings. They wanted the people of the future to connect with this message; and here I was, connecting. A hand had written this god sign, and my eyes were reading it. Two humans, thousands of years apart, linked by a stone tablet.

For the next hour or so, I walked through the Mesopotamian rooms of the Louvre and played Spot the God Sign. It was an enormously satisfying game, because the sign for divinity is everywhere in the cuneiform world. It is written on stone and clay, on the backs of statues, on steles and obelisks. I spotted tiny versions of it on cylinder seals made of colourful precious stones. There it was, engraved between pictures of gods and people.

The giant, bearded Akkadian warriors who glared fiercely from monumental stone carvings didn't look quite so dead and distant anymore.

As I squinted at one of the steles, I noticed two women standing next to me, looking curious but a little baffled. I showed them the god sign in the middle of the text, and they became very excited. Cheered by this friendly encounter, I wandered into the next room to look at a royal obelisk from Susa in ancient Iran, dating to around 2270 BCE. Just as I was identifying all the god signs on it, an elegantly dressed woman strode into the room, walked up to me, and put her hand on the obelisk.

'This belongs to us!' she exclaimed, sounding agitated. She said she was from Iran, and felt quite upset to see this room full of things taken from her country. I could see her point, but was mainly worried that an alarm would go off any minute now.

'I know one of the signs,' I said. 'Would you like me to show it to you?'

She nodded, took her hand off the stone, and together we found a couple of god signs. She thanked me in a tone that managed to be both regal and warm, like the priestess Enheduanna thanking a junior scribe for drawing up an unexpectedly advantageous land contract. Then she walked off to look for more god signs.

I decided to leave it at that. But just then, a father and his young son came into the room, both dressed in camouflage. Something about them was different from all the other visitors, and it wasn't just the camouflage outfits. It was the excitement. They sounded American, and were bouncing around as if this was just the best adventure ever. Shouts of 'Awesome!' and 'Cool!' rang through the quiet gallery.

It occurred to me that I had found the perfect recruits for a game involving a cryptic sign in an ancient code.

While I was still hesitating, the father asked me if I could take a photo of them. I took a few, then asked if they wanted to see something really amazing, one of the oldest symbols ever written by humans. Of course they did! The dad was nearly hopping with excitement.

I showed them the sign in one inscription, and with that, they were on fire. The father spotted it on various statues, and took pictures with his mobile. We agreed that it would be totally awesome if the museum were to put up a huge explanation of the god sign, and then everyone could look for it, and it would be so cool, and people would just love it. When we eventually parted ways, they both gave me firm military handshakes. The god sign game had won two very solid players.

NAMING THE WORLD

The Narrow Track

Some time in the nineteenth century BCE, in the town of Kanesh in ancient Anatolia, central Turkey, a woman called Kunnaniya broke open a clay envelope. She pulled out a cuneiform letter from her husband, Aššur-mūtappil. He was writing to her from Aššur, a city in northern Iraq that was six weeks away by donkey. Aššur-mūtappil sounded deeply worried, panicked almost. He urged her to bribe some officials, and then leave the city:

> Buy for the officials half a litre of cumin (kamunum)', he wrote. 'Get going and come here. Leave (our daughter) Šāt-Aššur in the good care of Walawala, the slave... as soon as the situation in the trading post has calmed down, get going. Šamaš-taklāku should sleep by the door (to guard the house).[1]

Kunnaniya spoke an Anatolian language. Aššur-mūtappil's mother tongue was Assyrian, a northern dialect of Akkadian. They wrote to each other in Assyrian. Their enslaved childminder, Walawala, would have spoken an Anatolian language, and perhaps some Assyrian, too. Šāt-Aššur, the little girl, would have been proficient in at least two languages and perhaps more, because the neighbourhood she lived in was very multilingual.

In the busy, thriving Assyrian merchants' quarter of Kanesh, there were many mixed families like this one. The neighbourhood was known as the *kārum*, the Akkadian word for 'quay', used here to refer to a trading outpost. Overland caravans docked at the *kārum* like ships sailing in and out, unloading tin and lapis lazuli from Iran and Afghanistan, and fine textiles from Assyria and elsewhere.

The foreign merchants lived in two-storey houses, collected bronze weapons and gold jewellery, and came together in a council of *rabiūtum*, 'big men', to deal with administrative matters.[2] Carts rumbled past on paved roads. Porters, food vendors and donkey drivers thronged in the marketplaces, bakers sold bread and sweet pastries, and there was an Assyrian temple.[3]

Mostly, they lived comfortable lives, though as Aššur-mūtappil's letter shows, there were periods of upheaval. Nor were the foreign traders always law-abiding. Some tried to skirt Anatolian taxes by smuggling their goods along a route known as the 'narrow track', an unofficial path through the mountains. At other times, the different communities learned from each other, swapped new technologies, and prospered together.

In the ruins of the merchants' quarter at Kanesh, more than 20,000 clay letters, contracts and other documents were found that tell the stories of the families who lived there. Their content ranges from ordinary domestic issues to dramatic adventures. Together, they present a picture of the first well-documented multilingual families in human history. As Cécile Michel, who has studied and translated many of these tablets, puts it: 'Some Assyrians married Anatolian women, while Assyrian widows occasionally married Anatolians, and communication between such couples was presumably no problem, the children of such unions being exposed to both languages, so that the succeeding generation would have been bilingual.'[4]

*

Clay tablet from Kanesh, stored in a private home, c.2000–1836 BCE. Fire destroyed the city and hardened the tablets. Credit: The Metropolitan Museum of Art (Image: Public Domain)

Language-mixing in the home

Multilingual families have probably existed for as long as humans have expressed themselves through speech. Analysis of bone fragments from a cave in Siberia has shown that a woman lived there 100,000 years ago whose mother was a Neanderthal, her father a Denisovan.[5] Whether these early humans could speak is a much debated issue. What is clear is that the different groups intermingled and cohabited at least to some extent, and continued to do so over tens of thousands of years, as they developed ever more complex speech sounds and melodies, and ultimately, the spoken and written languages we know today.

And yet, historically speaking, we know relatively little about multilingualism in the home. We can infer that mixed families existed, but they're typically not much written about. The letters from the Kanesh trading post help us understand the daily reality of such families. Somewhat unusually for the time, both women and men wrote to each other in this community. As a result, we can form a particularly detailed and emotionally nuanced view of their marriages and home lives. They discussed everything from child-care to business matters. In the process, they borrowed words from each other's languages in ways that must have seemed unremarkable at the time, but had a linguistic and cultural impact that can be felt to this day.

Trading, settling, marrying, speaking

The multilingual clans of Kanesh emerged somewhat by accident, as a consequence of long-distance trade. Merchants living in Aššur, northern Iraq, initially traded in and around their own city. Gradually, they expanded their reach. They pooled money to fund caravans of up to a hundred donkeys, and eventually covered the 1,000 kilometres from Aššur to Anatolia, in modern-day central Turkey.

Typically, a caravan trek began with a group of merchants in Aššur persuading investors to fund the next voyage. Once they had the money, they bought hardy black donkeys in a corral on the outskirts of the city, along with harnesses, saddle rugs and bags. They hired donkey drivers and of course purchased the goods themselves, often from foreign traders coming to Aššur, haggling in many languages. Tin came in from Afghanistan, via Susa in ancient Iran.[6] Lapis lazuli arrived along the same route. Fine textiles were also in high demand. When the donkeys were packed and the investment contracts signed (written in cuneiform on clay), the caravan set off north, to Kanesh.

During their six-week journey, the caravan crossed rickety bridges over wild rivers, trudged along treacherous mountain paths, and passed through several Anatolian kingdoms, obeying the cuneiform treaties they'd signed with Anatolian rulers. The rulers offered them some protection, but demanded taxes in return. In their letters, the Assyrian merchants habitually discussed alternative smugglers' routes, which were tax-free but came with the risk of bandit attacks and snowed-in mountain paths. Some merchants, including Aššur-mūtappil's father, were caught and thrown into jail.

Once they arrived in Kanesh, the Assyrians sold the tin, lapis lazuli and fine textiles, and sometimes the donkeys, too, if the planned return caravan was smaller. The profits were divided among the investors. Then the whole routine began again in Kanesh, as gold, silver and cheap local textiles were packed onto a fresh line-up of donkeys, ready to trot off.

At first, the merchants stayed in Anatolian inns, sold their goods, then returned to Iraq. But from about 2000 BCE, they began to settle in Kanesh and other trading outposts.[7] Some seemed quite happy to cut ties with their old home. A group of Assyrian creditors wrote to a debtor in Kanesh: 'Thirty years ago you left the city of Aššur... Our tablets have been going to you with caravan after caravan, but no report from you has ever come here.'[8]

A small number of merchants brought Assyrian wives with them. Others married Anatolian women. Others again had two wives, one in Kanesh, and another back in Iraq. Assyrian widows arrived in Kanesh from the south, attracted by laws that were more favourable to women, and married Anatolian men. With trade and mobility came greater freedom for women, to a certain extent. When the husbands were travelling, the wives ran their businesses. Anatolian and Assyrian women travelled, too, either with their husbands or on their own. Some bought houses, issued loans and invested in caravans.[9] One Assyrian woman joined her widowed mother in

Kanesh, and refused to go back to her husband in Aššur.[10] In another Anatolian trading post, an Amorite woman ran an inn.[11]

Multilingual clans

These new ways of trading, marrying and travelling brought languages into contact in an unprecedented way. Most of the merchants were Assyrians, like Aššur-mūtappil. Passing trade from southern Iraq and Syria also brought Babylonian and Amorite speakers to the *kārum* at Kanesh. These foreign languages were all quite similar, as they belonged to the Semitic family. But the native Anatolian languages, such as Hittite, Luwian and Hattic, were completely different.

Hittite and Luwian belong to the Indo-European language group, and are distantly related to modern European languages such as English (they only share a few obvious features and words, though, such as the Hittite *uatar*, water). Hattic was in a category of its own.

With families now stretched out over vast distances, writing took on a new importance.

Unusually for the time, a number of Assyrian merchants learned to read and write, and taught the skill to their wives and children.[12] They may not have wanted to share their smuggling plans with hired scribes. Perhaps they also struggled to recruit competent cuneiform writers in Kanesh, where the script was not used before the arrival of the Assyrians. This practical decision had far-reaching linguistic consequences.

Merchants wrote very differently from professional scribes. Their letters were more colloquial and informal (and had more mistakes in them).[13] They are a snapshot of how languages were actually spoken in the streets, rather than taught in scribal schools.

Klaas Veenhof, a specialist in the Assyrian trading networks, highlights the linguistic creativity these letter-writers used as they described new business deals and forms of investment that had probably never been written about before.[14] Their letters are also peppered with Anatolian loanwords for textiles, food and furniture that didn't exist back in Aššur.

The opposite was also the case: in his letter, Aššur-mūtappil urged his Anatolian wife to buy some *kamunum*, cumin, to bribe the officials. With that hastily scribbled letter, the word *kamunum* left its Semitic language context, and entered the Hittite- or Luwian-speaking world. Presumably, such wandering words had already circulated in markets and caravan stops for a while, but now they were written down and physically dispatched from one place to another.

Meanwhile, Anatolian rulers learned the cuneiform script from their Assyrian visitors. A century later, Anatolians adapted the script to their own languages.[15] What had started as a trip to Anatolia to sell some tin turned into an accidental cultural and linguistic phenomenon that transformed how languages were spoken and written. Some of the words coined or popularized in this multilingual setting are used to this day. Rather fittingly, one of them is the word for 'interpreter'.

Flour, beer and dried fish: the life of an interpreter

Historically, interpreters and translators are first mentioned in the Sumerian tablets from about 2500 BCE. In Sumerian, *eme-bal* means to translate or interpret, and *eme-bala*, translator or interpreter. A seal has been found that belonged to an interpreter of a language from Meluhha, in the valley of the Indus. Some tablets record payments of flour, beer and, in one case, dried fish, for the services of interpreters working in languages such as Gutian (a lost language, thought to have been spoken in the Zagros mountains of ancient Iran) and Amorite, spoken by nomads in ancient Syria.[16]

The word *eme-bala* is derived from *eme*, tongue or language, and *bala*, to turn over, or to cross.[17] It literally means something like language-turner, or language-crosser. Another Sumerian word, *iminbala*, 'word-crossing', also means to translate, but more in the sense of clarifying or revealing an underlying meaning. It's used when people speak to gods, or when they try to interpret a dream or an omen.[18] The word 'translate' has similar roots, being derived from the Latin *trans*, across, and the past tense of *ferre*, to carry or bring. However, in Akkadian, a totally different word was used for interpreter: *targumannum*.

This difference is surprising, given that Akkadian borrowed quite a few Sumerian words to do with writing and education. One might have thought that translating would fall into this category. But it seems that *targumannum* sneaked into the Akkadian language through a far less formal route.

The word's first appearance isn't in the tidy school tablets of Ur and Nippur, but in the scribbled letters from Kanesh. The merchants may have adopted it from the Anatolians. In Hittite and Luwian, *tarkumma* or *tarkummai* means to report, announce, or translate between languages.[19] Interpreters helped Anatolian royals speak to the Assyrian merchants and other foreigners.[20] In their letters and contracts, the Assyrians called these interpreters *targumannum*. Considering the multilingual context, interpreters are mentioned surprisingly rarely, which suggests that the Assyrians learned enough Hittite (and the Anatolians, enough Assyrian) to communicate. Intermarriage would have accelerated that process, especially as the children of mixed couples learned all the languages in the family.

The word *targumannum* spread through the Akkadian-speaking world, and beyond. Around 1770 BCE, the nomad king Zimri-Lim travelled to the trading city of Ugarit, on the Syrian coast, where he dispensed gifts of tin to a delegation of merchants from the island of

Crete.[21] The Cretans had with them an interpreter, a *targumannum*, who is mentioned in an accounting tablet covering the trip. He was given 20 shekels' worth of tin for his services.[22]

From Akkadian, the word *targumannum* made its way into Arabic and Hebrew. Around the first century BCE, interpreters called *meturgemen* live-translated Torah readings from Hebrew into Aramaic, which had replaced Akkadian as the region's lingua franca. In Judaism, the *targum* refers to a collection of Aramaic translations of the Hebrew Bible.[23]

In Classical Arabic, *turjuman* or *tarjaman* means translator or interpreter, and *tarjama* means translation. Variations of this word entered Persian, Turkish and Urdu.[24] *Turjuman al-ashwaq*, 'Interpreter of Desires', is a famous mystical Sufi poem, written in Arabic.[25]

European travellers in the Middle East and Asia took the word back to their home countries. Francesco Balducci Pegolotti, a Florentine merchant in the early fourteenth century, composed a global guide to markets, goods and trade routes extending as far as China. Writing in Italian, Pegolotti recommended that overland travellers to China hire a *turcimanno*, a translator and guide.[26] Ideally, this *turcimanno* would be complemented by two servants and a female companion who all knew *la lingua Cumanesca*, the Cuman language, spoken by Turkic nomads.[27] Pegolotti also said it was a good idea to grow a beard along that route. The effort and expense were worth it, for the traveller would return with a precious commodity, Chinese silk.

In the fifteenth century, William Caxton brought the first printing press to England. He also translated many works from French into English, including a French novel, *Paris and Vienne*. Set during the crusades, it tells the story of Paris, the son of a knight in southern France, who loves the aristocratic Vienne, who is far above his station. They eventually elope and live through all sorts of adventures. At one point a *tourcheman* appears, an interpreter who understands the 'Moorish language'. While the novel has sunk into obscurity, it was a big hit with the reading public in its time, and published in many languages. In 1572, the schoolboys at Westminster School in London staged it as a play.[28] The word *tourcheman*, *tourchemen* or *truchman* proved popular. Elliott Colla, reflecting on the history of Arabic-English translation, mentions some interesting variants of this word, such as 'truchwoman', a female interpreter, and 'truch sprite', a spirit-messenger.[29]

In sixteenth-century Scotland and Ireland, a trunchman, truchman, truchwoman, truncheman or trenchman was an interpreter proficient in English and Irish, and sometimes French and Spanish, too.[30]

The *Diccionario de la lengua española*, first published in the eighteenth century by the Royal Spanish Academy, defines *trujamán*, *trujamánna* or *turguman* as meaning interpreter, agent or middleman. The term entered Spanish through the Muslim occupation. It coexisted with another old Spanish word for interpreter, *la lengua*, 'the tongue', which was used by the Spanish conquerors of the Americas.[31]

European travellers in the Ottoman empire were accompanied by a *dragoman*, an official interpreter who doubled as a guide and minder. A dragoman could do very well for himself. In eighteenth- and nineteenth-century portraits, they appear dressed in elegant robes, wearing elaborate turbans or fur-trimmed hats. A watercolour portrait from 1750 shows the wife and children of a dragoman working for the sultan in Istanbul, standing in a silk-lined room with a European-style marble-topped table.[32] The younger child, a little boy, is galloping around on a cane used as a horse. He is dressed as a miniature dragoman, in a fur-trimmed red hat and robe, the distinctive uniform of the court interpreters. The mother is thought to be Greek or Armenian.

Working as a dragoman could bring wealth and prestige, but it came with a risk. A Christian dragoman for the Turkish authorities built a beautiful townhouse and garden on the island of Cyprus.[33]

Later, he fell into disgrace, was accused of embezzlement, and executed. A similar fate was shared by many interpreters in other cultures and time periods, who lived under a permanent cloud of suspicion, as if their multilingualism made them inherently unreliable or duplicitous.

The word *dragoman* was eventually applied to objects as well as people, as mass-printed dictionaries allowed every traveller to keep an interpreter in his or her pocket. In nineteenth-century German, *dragoman* pops up as a type of phrase book used by travellers in the Middle East and Africa. One of them was a 'Suaheli-Dragoman', a Swahili-German dictionary and phrase book, published in 1891.[34]

It is astonishing that a word used in a small, long-gone community of multilingual merchant families ended up travelling so widely, and for such a long time. But one can see why. Before online dictionaries and automatic translation, being able to ask for and hire an interpreter would have been the fastest way of establishing a channel of communication. That basic need remained the same, whether the foreign language in question was Hittite, Cuman or Irish.

Language on the narrow track

Just as the Assyrian traders spread and collected new words north of Mesopotamia, so other merchants toured the languages of the south. The Akkadian word *hašmanu*, meaning amethyst or an amethyst-like shade of blue, is thought to be based on the Egyptian word *hsmn*, amethyst. It was probably imported by gemstone traders.[35] The Egyptian word *hbny*, referring to a black wood from Africa, is thought to be the ancestor of the English 'ebony'.[36]

These are the unofficial paths that languages take, away from the textbooks and dictionaries. In family homes and marketplaces, amid the noise of braying donkeys and gossiping traders, a new expression arises; someone picks it up and passes it on to the next person. It's the narrow track of linguistic innovation; the smugglers' route. This kind of innovation is driven by a mix of curiosity and necessity. Often, it emerges from a situation where people have to talk about something they have never encountered before: a blue gemstone, a fragrant brown spice, or, as we'll see in the next chapter, a very big, strange animal.

Naming the World

When the Sumerians first encountered a horse, they decided it looked like a big, strange donkey. They called it *anše-kurra*, 'donkey from the foreign land'.[1] As with so many other Sumerian inventions, this set a historical trend. Many different language communities have invented names for new animals, plants or objects by comparing them to already familiar things.

The horse is a particularly good illustration of this particular kind of linguistic innovation, because its arrival in a culture tends to make a big impact. Horses are big, fast and potentially quite frightening, but when tamed and trained, they can be extremely useful.

Around 1350 BCE in Hattusa, a city in Anatolia, a horse-trainer called Kikkuli set about training these 'foreign donkeys', as he called them, using the Sumerian loanword. Kikkuli was from the land of Mitanni, a mysterious empire east of Anatolia. Its exact location is unclear, and its capital has not been found. The rulers there spoke an Indic language similar to Sanskrit, the ancestor of modern Hindi. The general population of Mitanni spoke Hurrian, which has no surviving relatives. From clay letters between the Mitanni elite and other kings in the region, we know that they were feared and admired for their highly skilled warriors in horse-drawn chariots.[2] Their warhorses gave them an enormous advantage in warfare, and it appears that Kikkuli's new masters in Anatolia were keen to learn more about this.

Kikkuli composed a horse-training manual that covers four clay tablets, each written by a different scribe. Their language skills vary from proficient to hapless. You can't help but feel for the scribe who is archly described as 'burdened neither by a knowledge of Hittite, nor by diligence' by Annelies Kammenhuber, who translated the tablets in 1963.[3] The translation process itself was rather dramatic. An earlier translation from around 1940 by Johannes Potratz, a German doctoral student in Leipzig, was destroyed when his publishing house was hit by a British bomb.[4]

'Thus speaks Kikkuli, a horse-trainer from the land of Mitanni', the first tablet begins. It goes on to spell out a detailed, day-by-day training routine: 'When he takes the horses to the meadow in the autumn, he harnesses them. He lets them trot and gallop for three miles, then across seven fields. On the way back, he lets them run across ten fields. Then he takes off their harnesses, rubs them down, and gives them water. He takes them into the stable...'[5]

The Hittites were keen innovators in their own right. They are among the first known cultivators of honey, and wrote extensively about honeybees, honey rituals, honey myths, and honey-related crimes and punishments.[6] The idea of preserving and sharing a skill through writing was therefore not new to them. A more surprising aspect of Kikkuli's horse manual is that it's written in several languages, slipping in and out of Hurrian, Hittite and the Indic dialect from Mitanni, with some Akkadian, Sumerian and Luwian loanwords thrown into the mix.

Kikkuli calls himself an *assussani*, an Indic word for horse-trainer. Similar words exist in Sanskrit as well as Pali, an Indic dialect used in Buddhist religious texts. In Pali, the word for horse is *assa*; in Sanskrit, it is *ashva*. Through the spread of Hindu and Buddhist culture, both words later entered other Asian languages.[7]

Kikkuli uses Indic words to describe how many laps the horses should run, such as *panza-uartanna*, five rounds, or *šatta-uartanna*, seven rounds. To bless the horses at dawn, he suggests going into the stable, appealing to the Hurrian war goddesses Pirinkar and Šaušga, and exclaiming in Hurrian and Luwian: 'Blessed be the horses!'[8]

At times, Kikkuli combines three languages in the same sentence, as in *triuartanna auzameya tarkumma-anzi-ma kissan* ('three rounds of gallop, one translates this as follows...'). *Triuartanna*, also spelled as *trivartanna*, is an Indic word, meaning three rounds (*tri* is related to the English 'three'; numbers are often quite similar across Indo-European languages). *Auzameya* is Hurrian, and means gallop. A Hittite translation follows, for the benefit of his employers.[9]

Given that Kikkuli attached this Hittite translation, why didn't he just write the whole thing in Hittite in the first place?

One reason might be that he explicitly wanted to convey his credentials and expertise, which were tied to Mitanni and its languages. The Hurrian horse-blessings suggest that there was also a spiritual component. Presumably, Hurrian deities liked to be prayed to in Hurrian.

There may have been another reason. Every time someone mixes languages, they create a new space where all those languages coexist and are brought into some kind of alignment. It's a way of organizing one's world. For Kikkuli, a multilingual migrant in a foreign country, it may have felt quite satisfying to combine the different influences that shaped his life and career, and leave a legacy. From now on, Hittite scribes copying his text would learn all the words he had brought with him, and would gradually make them their own.

Trotting to Thailand

As ancient and rare as Kikkuli's text is, the basic principle of stretching one's languages to talk or write about horses is surprisingly common through history and across cultures.

When a person comes across a new animal, plant, or thing, they have two basic linguistic options. One is to adopt the new thing along with its foreign name. This happened with the word for cumin, which remained intact across so many languages, and it also happened with different words for horse, which migrated from certain languages to others. Often, this type of linguistic migration is part of a broader cultural trend or event.

Just as Kikkuli carried Indic technical terms westwards, from his Mitanni homeland to his Hittite masters, so other migrants, traders, missionaries and pilgrims took Indic words eastwards. From the early first millennium CE, through the spread of Hindu and Buddhist culture, Indic scripts and languages took root in many different parts of South East Asia. Some Sanskrit inscriptions in Java and Cambodia date back to the fifth century.[10] Later, Sri Lankan monks disseminated Buddhist texts in Pali and Sanskrit. Thai, Lao, Burmese and Khmer (in Cambodia) writing are all derived from Indic scripts.[11]

The Thai language borrowed hugely from this Indic treasure, especially when it came to administrative, educational and spiritual matters.[12] Indonesian also soaked up many Indic loans. The word for 'language' is *bhāṣā* in Sanskrit, *phaasǎa* in Thai and *bahasa* in Indonesian.[13] (Bahasa Indonesia, 'Indonesian language', is Indonesia's official language, though many other languages are spoken there.) The word for 'king' is *raachaa* in Thai and *raja* in Indonesian and Malay, from the well-known Pali and Sanskrit *raja*.[14]

Another powerful linguistic influence came from the north, from China. Vietnamese, for example, is strongly shaped by Chinese borrowings.

There are several words for horse in Thai, and they reflect these diverse linguistic and cultural ancestries. One of them is *aachaa*, thought to have descended from the Pali *assa*; another is *àtsawá*, from the Sanskrit *ashva*. According to Titima Suthiwan, a Thai linguist who has investigated a wide range of loanwords in the language, the latter is used in a more formal, lyrical context.[15] A more general Thai word for horse is *máa*. It has a completely separate, northern ancestry, and is thought to derive from the Chinese *mǎ*.[16] The Chinese may in turn have borrowed it from Mongolian, which is tied to a long and famous tradition of Central Asian horsemanship.[17] In Mongolian, a domesticated horse is called *mori* (a wild horse is a *qulan*, one of many fine distinctions in the Mongolian horse lexicon).[18]

Similar borrowings occurred all over the world as people imported horses from other cultures and learned how to tame, train, harness and ride them. The Swahili word for horse, *farasi*, is adapted from the Arabic *faras*, one of many words brought by Arab traders.[19] (The Swahili word for language, *lugha*, is another Arabic loan.)

In many indigenous languages of South America, the word for horse is derived from the Spanish *caballo*, because the Spanish conquerors were the first to introduce horses there. But some communities chose a different approach. Instead of accepting the foreign word for this strange animal, they looked through their existing linguistic inventory and came up with their own, native word for the newcomer. Among linguists, this creative process of word-recycling is known as 'lexical acculturation'.

Big deer, foreign kangaroos

This second method of naming the world involves looking at the new thing, looking around you, and then finding the closest fit among the words you already have. One interesting aspect of the process is that it forces the community to agree on the essence of this new thing, on its defining characteristics.

In the case of horses, their most striking characteristics were that they were very big, but could be tamed. They were therefore often compared either to big, wild animals or to smaller animals that had already been domesticated, such as dogs.

In 1519, messengers told Moctezuma, ruler of the Mexica, that a group of strangers riding on giant deer were making their way to his capital. As the Spanish conquered Central and South America, other communities either named the horse through lexical acculturation, or chose the loanword option. In *Q'eqchi'*, a Mayan language spoken in Guatemala and Belize, the horse is called *kawaay*; in Yaqui, spoken in Mexico, it is *kaba'i*.[20] In Imbabura Quechua, spoken in the northern Andes of Ecuador, it is *kaballu*.[21] In Nivaclé, a language spoken in Paraguay, the word for horse is *kuwayu*. All of these words descend from the Spanish *caballo*. However, some communities went for a different strategy, even within the same language group. In Chorote, a language in Argentina that is related to Nivaclé, the word for horse is *alenta*, meaning 'similar to a tapir'.[22]

In North America, some indigenous communities compared the horse to an animal that was already serving them loyally: the dog. Before the arrival of horses, the Plains communities used dogs to carry or drag provisions, firewood, and tent poles.[23] The Lakota called the horse *sunka waka*, mysterious dog; the Blackfoot called it *ponokaomita*, elk dog.[24] The Navajo word łį́į́' used to mean pet or dog, but was repurposed to mean 'horse'.[25] Aborigines living near Adelaide in South Australia referred to the horse as *pindi nanto*, 'the newcomer's kangaroo'.[26]

The process works in the other direction, too. Cultures that already knew the horse used its name to describe animals they had not seen before. In Afrikaans, a giraffe is a *kameelperd*, a camel-horse. The Greek-derived *hippopotamus* means 'river-horse'. In German, a hippopotamus is a *Nilpferd*, a Nile-horse.

There is a third linguistic option, beyond borrowing a foreign name or recycling a native word: that of inventing a totally new word. In theory, all these communities could have come up with a string of sounds that from then on meant 'horse'. In practice, people don't seem to choose this option very often. Perhaps it's more comforting to pick either a name that carries an echo of foreign expertise, or one that makes the new thing reassuringly familiar. It may look like a monster with stone-hard feet and giant teeth, but it's really just a big, friendly dog.

Honey-eaters and Sorting Hats

Even some animals that we may think of as deeply at home in a region still carry a trace of that head-scratching in their names, an echo from a time when people looked at them and wondered what they were. In Slavic languages, the bear is generally called some variation of *medvĕd*. This is thought to be rooted in a very old compound word meaning 'honey-eater'.[27] The ancient root *med*, meaning honey, may be at the origin of the English mead, a fermented honey drink. In Slovenian, it's *médvęd*, in Russian *medvéd*', in Czech *medvĕd*, in Serbo-Croation *mèdvjed* and *mèdved*, in Bulgarian *medvéd*, in Polish, *niedźwiedź*. In Sorbian, a minority language spoken in eastern Germany that's not to be confused with Serbian, it's *mjedwjédz*.

The naming process can be extended to mythical objects and animals, too.

In the French translation of *A Song of Ice and Fire*, the fantasy novels by George R. R. Martin, the fictional 'Direwolf' creature is rendered as 'loup-garou', or werewolf. Some French fans have been in uproar over this, arguing that a werewolf is nothing like a Direwolf. In European folklore, a werewolf is someone who transforms into a wolf at night. A Direwolf, on the other hand, is more like a big wolf, and never transforms into a human. The French translator retorted that 'loup-garou' was the best option, and pointed out that the story wasn't based on a particular time or frame of reference.[28] In other words, it was made up anyway.

Other translators try to honour the rules of an imagined world, while also adding their own creative flourishes. Jean-François Ménard, the French translator of J. K. Rowling's Harry Potter, is known for crafting expressions that are both witty and meaningful. Thus Hogwarts, the wizards' boarding school, is 'Poudlard' in French, from *poux de lard*, 'bacon-lice'. The Sorting Hat is 'le Choixpeau', a pun on *choix*, choice, and *chapeau*, hat. In an interview with *Le Monde*, Ménard said he had a lifelong interest in magical and hidden worlds, and saw his work as a way to step outside the ordinary: 'Through translation, you enter different worlds and universes.'[29]

Fire and life: spicing up languages

In a recipe for a spicy salad, the food writer Meera Sodha suggests that herbs and chilli can add 'fire and life to your table'.[30] New words for foods and spices can also add fire and life to a language. They can give rise to new proverbs and metaphors, make a story or poem more interesting and vivid, and generally add variety to one's linguistic fare. At the same time, people may feel a little suspicious of a new ingredient, and comparing it to a familiar food can be a way of reducing that anxiety. Across languages, the process of naming such newly introduced foods therefore tends to be similar to that of naming new animals. People either import the foreign name, or they repurpose an existing word for the new ingredient.

In Europe, entire shiploads of unknown fruits, vegetables and spices arrived with Christopher Columbus on his return from his first voyage to America. Ferdinand and Isabella of Spain, who had funded Columbus's journey in the hope of discovering a new spice route to the East, were the first to try his loot. The chilli peppers 'burnt their tongue', but they liked the sweet potatoes and fruit. Later, Ferdinand particularly enjoyed a sweet and juicy fruit with a slightly melon-like flavour, brought to Spain from Guadeloupe.[31]

The Spanish decided that this fruit looked like a giant pine cone, and called it *piña*. The English agreed, and called it pineapple. In Welsh, the fruit is called *pîn-afal* ('pine-apple'). Several other languages borrowed the Spanish word *piña* or the English pineapple, but some communities came up with their own botanical comparisons.

In Yoruba, one of the main languages of Nigeria, the pineapple is called *ope oyinbo*, which translates loosely as 'foreign palm'.[32] It may be a reference to the palm-like tuft on top of the fruit, or the palm-like nest of leaves in which it grows. I came across this lovely Yoruba saying, inspired by a pineapple: *'Ope oyinbo fi didun sewa, oro inu e pe egbeje-'* ('The pineapple is sweet, enjoyable but equally laden with spikes').[33]

Many other languages simply went with *ananas*, based on its name among the Tupi people of Brazil who first cultivated it. Portuguese traders spread this loanword, which entered languages as diverse as Hungarian, Turkish, French, Malay, Hindi and Wolof, spoken in Senegal and the Gambia.[34]

Other imports from the Americas also kept their native names. Some of the most famous are derived from Nahuatl, spoken by the Nahua, the native inhabitants of Mexico along with the Maya and other indigenous groups. Nahuatl is still spoken by around 1.7 million people in Mexico.[35]

The word tomato, *tomate* in Spanish, is derived from the Nahuatl *xitomatl*. It's related to the green-skinned tomatillo, *tomatl* in Nahuatl. It features in a Nahuatl tomato-riddle: *'Zazan tleino, huipiltitich? Tomatl.'* 'What wears a shirt? The green tomato.'[36] The

Spanish (and Portuguese) *tomate* travelled the world as a loanword and generated new proverbs. In German, to have *Tomaten auf den Augen*, 'tomatoes on your eyes', means to fail to notice something obvious.

Some languages came up with their own words instead of adopting a version of the Spanish *tomate*, by comparing this new ingredient to existing ones. In Chinese, there are two words for tomato: 西紅柿 (*xī hóng shì*, literally, red persimmon from the west) and 番茄 (*fān qié*, literally, foreign aubergine).

Chocolate and cocoa (or cacao) are perhaps the most famous Nahuatl loanwords. Cacao, *kakahuatl* in Nahuatl, is in turn a loanword from the Mayan *kakaw*. The Maya borrowed it from the Olmecs, an even older Mexican civilization. Chocolate is a Nahuatl word with somewhat uncertain origins. It may mean something along the lines of 'beaten water'.

'Nzule! Nzule!'

Meanwhile, the chilli, which had burnt the tongues of the Spanish king and queen, continued to bite back. The Ghanaian writer Adela Blay-Brody tells an anecdote involving two kinds of chilli eaten in her community, the Nzema. One is a wild variety called *daza mmale*, 'bird peppers'; the other is a small, round pepper introduced by Portuguese traders.

One day, a group of British sailors arrived in Nzemaland, and were brought to the ruler, Kaku Ackah. He was irritated by the foreigners, 'who were greedy for gold but refused to speak his language'.[37] His cooks served them hot pepper soup, and the strangers burst into sweat, shouted and signed for water, to Kaku Ackah's amusement. Eventually, from overhearing the servants, the British guessed the Nzema word for water, *nzule*. They began shouting, 'Nzule! Nzule!', prompting Kaku Ackah to sneer: 'Look at this! It seems these white men were lying to us. They really can speak our language!'

As Blay-Brody concludes, for a long time the Nzema coast saw no further British visitors. The chilli had not just driven the strangers away, it had prevented them from using their mouths to negotiate and cajole the ruler into giving them gold. All they'd taken back from their expedition was one word of Nzema, *nzule*, water.

Belonging, warmth, and atole

One afternoon, my friend Jake and his sister Laura came over for tea and cake. They grew up in Texas, but their ancestors had immigrated from Mexico. Jake now lives in London, and Laura in Houston. For both, English is their main language, and they speak it to each other. But when I asked them if there were any foods or expressions they thought of in Spanish first, they instantly recalled a whole range of them from their childhood.

One of them was *atole* for oatmeal, or porridge. This piqued my interest, because I'd only ever heard one word for oatmeal in Spanish, *avena*. The puzzle was quickly solved: *atole* is derived from a Nahuatl word, *atolli*.[38] It originally referred to a warm drink made from maize, and was then adapted to porridge more generally.

Laura had asked Jake to buy her oatmeal before she arrived, and he made her some that morning. When she came into the kitchen, he said 'I made you *atole*'. He told me he knew it would give her a warm and happy feeling. Their dad sometimes made it for them, and always said 'I made *atole*' when he did.

The Nahuatl connection did not stop there. Jake's grandmother sometimes warmed tortillas for him on a *comal*, a special tortilla griddle. *Comal* is another Nahuatl loanword, from *comalli*.[39] Sixteenth-century Spanish sources describe people in Mexico cooking tortillas on *comalli* over hot coals. *Comalli* are also mentioned in Nahuatl folk tales and, in clay form, were used long before the conquest.

Atole is not a glamorous word like chocolate and chilli, nor is *comal*. One can't imagine Ferdinand and Isabella of Spain getting excited about porridge and griddles. The strength of these words lies in another quality, one of familiarity and fortitude.

Francisco Javier Clavijero, an eighteenth-century Mexican historian, wrote that the Spanish found *atole* insipid, but that the indigenous communities could not live without it. It helped them bear the strain of farm work. Clavijero added that there were at least eighteen different varieties of this hot maize drink, all prepared and seasoned differently.[40] It's probably been consumed for centuries much in the spirit in which Jake served it to Laura, as a warm soupy bowl or cup of carbohydrates, to comfort and nourish. It doesn't seem a stretch to imagine a Nahua family enjoying it on a cool morning in the hills of central Mexico.

As for *comal*, Jake has a vivid memory of his grandmother warming *tortillas de mais*, corn tortillas, on hers. As he wrote to me after our conversation: 'She'd put a dab of butter and some salt on it after it came off her *comal* … Then she'd roll it up really tight and give it to me.'

In their own quiet way, the words *atole* and *comal* have made a journey just as spectacular as the more famous food and animal names mentioned earlier. They were handed down by Nahuatl-speakers before the conquest; survived the Spanish invasion, and the rise of Spanish as the dominant language of Mexico; made it into modern times; and migrated to the United States, along with Mexican families, where they again resisted being erased by the dominant language, English.

By the time Laura and Jake mentioned *atole* in my kitchen in London, the dish and its name had made its way through many generations and around the world. It was preserved by people who took this word with them wherever they went, like a tiny piece of the place they left behind. Sometimes it's the human love of novelty and variety that makes a word travel far. At other times, it's the opposite instinct: one based on loyalty, belonging, and a memory of home.

The Book Cemetery

One day, I got into the back of my in-laws' car and noticed that Marlène, my mother-in-law, was holding a big stack of documents on her lap. I asked her about them, and she replied casually that they were just some papers she was dropping off at her synagogue, so they could be buried. This was the first time I had heard of the Jewish custom of giving sacred texts and books a burial. Marlène explained that the basic idea was not to throw away anything with the name of God on it. And since all sorts of texts can feature this name – not just prayers and blessings, but also language exercises in classical Hebrew, and so on – the resulting piles of paper can be considerable.

I found it a beautiful and moving practice. Only later did I realize the enormous consequences of this old tradition. Jewish communities have been storing and burying documents in caves and buildings for more than a thousand years, essentially creating giant, multilingual archives somewhat by accident. The Hebrew word for these storage facilities is *genizah*. Some were originally meant as halfway houses where the papers could be stashed until being buried in the ground, but then took on a more permanent role as the crumpled manuscripts and worn scrolls kept piling up.

From the point of view of the worshippers, these papers are essentially just sacred waste. Many of them are not even concerned directly with religious matters, but are letters from ordinary people asking the rabbis for advice on their marriage, or a parenting problem. Through the passage of time, and the strange alchemy of letting things age, these everyday communications ended up acquiring enormous cultural and historical value. They give us a glimpse of day-to-day life in different communities, tell us what people worried about and hoped for, how they educated their children, and how they felt about each other. They also function as accidental language archives, preserving scripts and languages that later fell out of use.

One of the largest and oldest genizahs was discovered in the nineteenth century, in a synagogue in Old Cairo.[1] The Cairo documents range from the ninth to the eighteenth centuries, with the bulk dating to the medieval period, tenth to thirteenth centuries. They include letters by famous Jewish sages, such as Maimonides, and thousands of scribbles of ordinary people.

The Cairo papers are written in Arabic, Hebrew and Aramaic, as well as European languages including Spanish and Greek, documenting a large trading network with a lively international correspondence. The authors freely mixed their scripts and languages. They used Hebrew letters to write Arabic and even Armenian and Greek, as well as Hebrew. It's through letters from this genizah that we know about the girls and women nicknamed 'cumin' and 'little artichoke'.

The ruins of the synagogue can still be seen in Fustat, Old Cairo, but the papers themselves are stored at various libraries, including that of the University of Cambridge. The Jewish community of Cairo donated almost two hundred thousand manuscripts to the university shortly after the genizah was discovered. The monumental task of translating and evaluating them is still continuing, but some of the highlights can be viewed by the public in monthly guided tours.[2] I joined one of these tours to find out more about the polyglot merchants of Old Cairo and their surprising legacy. In the process, I would stumble across another fascinating linguistic phenomenon: multilingual magic.

Scorpions and stick figures

In a small, bright room at the university's library, old text fragments were carefully laid out on long tables. I looked at a strip of squares of text inscribed with Hebrew and Aramaic spells against scorpions, complete with tiny drawings of the arachnids. They dated from the eleventh or twelfth century, and would have been rolled up and worn around the neck in an amulet case. Some had been cut off and sold.[3]

Further along the table was a letter informing Maimonides that his brother had died in a shipwreck. It was stained by the sage's tears. Maimonides himself wrote elsewhere about holding the letter in his hands, day after day, and crying. Here was the physical evidence of his intense grief.

As I moved from one table to the next, I was struck by the mixture of the famous and the ordinary. Many documents related to children. There were exercises by eleventh-century boys and girls learning to write, a stick figure drawn by a bored schoolchild, and letters between parents and teachers. Not all of them were sacred. At one point, the genizah became a general hoard where people dumped their waste paper out of habit.

While the Jewish practice of storing or burying holy texts is widely seen as motivated by respect for the name of God, especially as the Torah forbids destroying anything bearing God's name, it had originally also been driven by a fear of magic.

'Magic' is a rather loose term. It can refer to ancient healing practices that involve actual medical knowledge, such as the use of certain herbs. It can also refer to beliefs based on the power of words alone, such as the spell against scorpions. It may feature a mixture of the two, with spells and incantations uttered to enhance the power of healing brews. Interestingly, these spells are often considered particularly powerful when taken from another language. It's a practice one might call 'multilingual magic', and it exists across time, and across different languages.

Multilingual magic

Multilingual magic involves borrowing words or phrases from a foreign language that is considered spiritually potent, for example because it is seen as particularly old and enigmatic. Hebrew, Aramaic, and Irish, as well as little-known ancient languages such as Oscan from Italy and a Cretan language spoken before the arrival of Greek, have all been used for magical purposes. Sometimes, the language is used along with a medicinal herb bought from that community. At other times, the sound or script alone are considered potent enough.

As Melonie Schmierer-Lee, one of the researchers working on the genizah, guided us through the highlights of the collection, she explained that the original motivation for keeping these papers safe was to prevent other communities from using the Hebrew name of God in magical rituals. Meanwhile, some of the members of the Cairo community couldn't resist dabbling in magic themselves. They bought and sold spells, and some also enhanced their religious scrolls with magical symbols, in order to boost their power.

The Cairo Genizah grew as a by-product of these magical and spiritual practices, until it became an unparalleled depository of medieval Hebrew writing. Ben Outhwaite, the head of the Genizah Research Unit at the University of Cambridge, has described its discovery as 'the most important discovery of modern Jewish scholarship... a seismic event in the history of Jewish letters and in the philology of the Hebrew language'.[4] In a meeting after the tour, he told me that one very important legacy of the genizah is that it shows Hebrew as a living language. There is a common belief that for the two thousand years leading up to the resurgence of modern Hebrew in the nineteenth and twentieth century, the language had been dead, preserved only in liturgy. The Cairo Genizah tells a different story. Hebrew was recited, read and written within the community for worship, but also used in lively letters and everyday paperwork. Jews from different countries spoke it to each other as a convenient shared language.[5]

The day-to-day lives of this multilingual community might have gone unrecorded, had it not been for generations of people who carried their old letters and homework to the synagogue, dropped them through a hole in the wall, and never thought of them again.

Island spells, desert spells

The idea of multilingual magic existed long before the Cairo Genizah. One of the oldest examples is a fourteenth-century BCE Egyptian magical papyrus that contains foreign spells.

Language contact was intense and varied in the eastern Mediterranean during that period, the Late Bronze Age, thanks to flourishing trade. As mentioned before, the rulers of Cyprus, Ugarit, Egypt and the Hittite empire sent each other diplomatic gifts, along with cuneiform letters demanding even better gifts in return. A Cypriot king reminded the pharaoh that he'd recently sent him a generous shipment of copper, and in return asked for an ebony bed with gold details, a gilded chariot, two horses, linen, and some scarves.[6] Exchanges of furniture were so common that a cuneiform vocabulary list compiled by an Egyptian scribe included the words for 'bed' and 'chair'.[7] The tablets were written in Akkadian but influenced by the underlying native languages, and each carried the distinct accent of the sender. One might imagine it like an ancient version of an international team in London or New York, with everyone's English sounding a little different while still being mutually understood.

Medicine and spirituality were an important part of that region-wide swap. The Hittite king asked the pharaoh for a ram, some silver, and 'two large medicinal shrubs'.[8] Some doctors and pharmacists were equipped with quite advanced knowledge and tools. A tablet listing the belongings of a physician in Ugarit mentions lancets, scalpels and forceps.[9] A nomad king at Mari asked for a physician and a diviner of omens to be sent to him quickly, by boat or chariot.[10]

It was not uncommon to mix different cultures in a spiritual context, as a way of ensuring the prosperity and well-being of a city and its people. At Enkomi, the main copper port on Cyprus, a bronze statue of Baal was found, a storm god worshipped in Ugarit on the Syrian coast. It stands on a miniature copper ingot, an homage to the coveted metal that had brought Cyprus sudden wealth.[11] The fragments of a temple to Baal from Ugarit, which are now displayed in the Louvre in Paris, are carved with Egyptian hieroglyphs.

Around 1300 BCE, a ship sank off the Uluburun cape on Turkey's southern coast, laden with luxury goods. Its contents have been carefully dredged up from the seabed. They perfectly match the gifts mentioned in the diplomatic letters, and show how technology, spirituality and languages swirled around the area.

The ship carried ivory and ebony from tropical Africa, copper from Cyprus, tin from ancient Iran or Central Asia, glass beads and pottery from Greece and Crete, aromatic oils, incense, pomegranates, olives, figs and spices such as nigella, coriander and sumac from the Near East; gold pendants with nude reliefs of Near Eastern goddesses; and figurines of Egyptian or Cretan acrobats, with their heads bent so far backwards that they touch the soles of their feet.[12]

A number of different scripts were also on board, such as a gold scarab from Egypt, inscribed with Nefertiti's name in Egyptian hieroglyphs; a wax-filled writing board that once bore an unidentified script; personal seals with abstract symbols; and various amulets carved with magical signs.[13] The crew and merchants on the ship were from different cities in the eastern Mediterranean, judging by their personal belongings, and would have spoken several languages between them.

It's in this context that the mysterious Egyptian papyrus was written, a collection of spells in different languages. It's known as the 'London Medical Papyrus', and is housed in the British Museum.[14] Through its incantations, we can hear a faint echo of languages that may now feel obscure and obsolete to us, but that would have once been part of the soundscape of the eastern Mediterranean, filling not just royal palaces and scribal studios but also inns, ships and harbours, crowded warehouses, and busy markets.

The largest group of spells is in Egyptian, written in hieratic, a kind of Egyptian handwriting. Another collection is in 'the language of those who dwell beyond the desert', probably an Aramaic dialect. And another is in 'the language of Keftiw', as the Egyptians called the island of Crete.

Translating magic

The foreign spells in the London Medical Papyrus pose a fascinating riddle. They appear to have been written down as the healer heard them, and are based on real languages. Evangelos Kyriakidis, who analysed the Cretan portion, suggests that the healer would have done their best to record them accurately: 'A magical spell has to be uttered properly to carry any force; that means it has to be pronounced correctly.'[15]

However, translating the spells is not straightforward. They passed through many mouths before reaching the Egyptians, with everyone repeating them as they heard them. As for 'the language of Keftiw', no one knows what it sounded like in the first place. It was spoken before Greek arrived on Crete. The Cretans wrote this unidentified language down, but the script they used has not been deciphered. It's known to scholars as Linear A, and only offers a fog-shrouded view of the language behind it. Given this unsolved mystery, it's incredible that scholars have managed to make any sense of the Cretan spells at all.

One helpful factor is that Egyptian medical spells tend to follow a formula. Typically, they start with a summary of what the spell is about, followed by a plea to a god to remove the disease and perhaps inflict it on someone else.[16] At times, the healer might slip into the role of a god, and tell the disease to go away. The spell is then wrapped up with some practical instructions for potions and such.

The first Cretan spell starts with an introduction in Egyptian: 'Spell for the Asiatic Disease in the Keftiw language'. A string of Cretan sounds follows, and a concluding instruction in Egyptian: 'This spell is to be said over froth of a fermented drink, urine, and *sd.t.*' (*sd.t.* being Egyptian for a third, unidentified ingredient).[17] The second Cretan spell is for the *sa-mu-na* disease; the concluding instruction in Egyptian is short and basic: 'To be said four times.'[18]

Kyriakidis cautiously parses the Cretan sections for patterns, and tentatively reconstructs the sound of some of its consonants. This may not sound like much, but given how little we know about this Cretan language, it's astonishing that some of it has been preserved in an Egyptian script we can at least read. It also allows us to trace certain connections between the languages of the eastern Mediterranean, for there are hints of a third language in the island spell that may be neither native Cretan, nor Egyptian. In the spell, the mysterious samuna disease is written as *wbq*. This pattern of three consonants is typical of the Semitic language family that dominated the Near and Middle East, and which included Akkadian, Ugaritic, Phoenician and many others. Semitic words are often based on three-consonant roots (such as sh-m-sh, a root found in words for 'sun', such as the Akkadian Šamaš, the Hebrew shemesh, and the Arabic shams). Kyriakidis concludes that the name of the disease in the Cretan passage could be of Semitic origin. This doesn't mean Cretans originally spoke a Semitic language, but they may have been influenced by one, and perhaps borrowed medical terms from it as they traded with Near Eastern cities.

It turns out that a few lines of Egyptian magic can give us some surprisingly concrete evidence of how people in the area lived and communicated. This is even more obvious in the case of the desert spells, which are based on languages we understand far better than those of ancient Crete.

Chasing out demons

The second set of foreign spells, which the Egyptians describe as being from 'beyond the desert', are written in a Semitic language, or a mix of various Semitic languages. Thanks to the similarities across the Semitic family, it's possible to understand the meaning of the spells even without knowing exactly which language they are in. One appears to be an incantation against a strangulation disease, caused by a strangling deity or demon.[19] Another is a spell against worms or snakes. Richard Steiner, who has partially translated these spells, suggests that one is directly addressed to a demon or disease: 'Leave us,' I say, 'leave us.' We have said our incantation. Another may be recited by the patient themselves: Let the strangulation-demons go out, my healer![20]

Steiner also identifies various Middle Eastern deities in the desert spells. One is associated with Phoenicia, a famous coastal trading city where a Semitic dialect was spoken. The magical incantations may have travelled down the coast from Phoenicia, whispered from healer to healer, until they reached Egypt. This would explain the mix of different Semitic influences.

Whatever their precise journey, the foreign spells in the London Medical Papyrus had clearly been carefully memorized, repeated, and transcribed. They must have represented precious medical and magical expertise. Their strangeness was perhaps part of what made them so valuable. Something powerful had been captured beyond the desert, beyond the water, and brought to the healer's hands. An alien sound, fierce enough to drive out demons.

Oscan curses

Ancient Italy was alive with many languages, including Latin and Greek, but also Oscan, Umbrian, Venetic, Etruscan, Ligurian and other regional tongues.[21] While Latin and Greek eventually became dominant, the others resisted for some time. Oscan speakers countered the rise of Latin by making a point of writing in their language.[22] Latin speakers found Oscan useful when it came to certain things – such as issuing a particularly deadly curse.

Curses, written on small sheets of lead, are an important source of information about Oscan. They preserve the language itself, show its contact with Greek and Latin, and even give us an idea of its speakers. According to the Oscan scholar Katherine McDonald, half the names known in South Oscan were found in curses.[23] Oscan was spoken in central and southern Italy, and on the island of Sicily. It had its own alphabet, which ran from right to left, like a mirror version of the more familiar Latin script. The Oscan 'E' looks like this: Ⅎ. And the Oscan 'K' was written thus: Ϗ.[24]

Like the Egyptian incantations, Oscan curse tablets followed a certain pattern. One was a wish format, to be used in wishing someone harm. There was also a prayer format, asking a deity to intervene. One intriguing formula is the harmless-sounding but surprisingly evil comparative mode. This category includes curses such as 'May you become like this corpse' or 'May you become cold like this lead'.[25]

In the world of curses, the Oscan ones stand out in certain ways. Francesca Murano, who has investigated the Oscan tablets in depth, notes that they never directly state the motive for the curse (I somehow found this detail rather unsettling; it reminded me of Josef K., the man in Franz Kafka's *The Trial*, who is arrested without ever finding out why). Some of them combine languages for maximum effect. A bilingual curse in Latin and Oscan lists the names of the victims to be cursed, then goes on to say in a mix of Oscan and Latin: 'May the tongues of them all be rigid'. The idea may have been to prevent them from speaking out against the author of the curse.

The bilingual tablet dates from a period when Oscan was already on the wane, pushed out by Latin. J. N. Adams suggests that using 'a dying language in the sphere of magic' was a way to strengthen the curse, as the obscurity would have been part of its power.[26] Just as the Egyptian papyrus unwittingly saved traces of old Cretan, each Oscan curse allows us to hear the voice of a once-thriving Italian language, long after it has vanished from daily life.

Slaughtering the beast, in Irish

Centuries later, Irish became the foreign language of choice for magical spells. Alderik Blom quotes a scene from a thirteenth-century Icelandic saga, in which a magician summons a storm: 'He went around three times, against the direction of the sun, speaking in Irish.'[27] A medical text from eleventh-century England states that to rid a man or beast of worms, say '*gono mil orgo mil marbu mil*' (Irish, or pseudo-Irish, for 'I slay the beast, I slaughter the beast, I kill the beast').

Today, curses and incantations have faded from common use in many societies. But ancient languages continue to be preserved in spiritual contexts. The world's religions treasure their ancient prayers and blessings, in the original languages. It gives those languages a special status, and connects us to long-dead worshippers.

These links can endure in surprising circumstances. The singer Amy Winehouse loved singing in Hebrew and Aramaic as a child, according to her mother, Janis. 'Ma'oz Tzur', a traditional Jewish song for Hanukkah, was a particular favourite, and Janis Winehouse still has a tape of her daughter singing it.[28]

Freddie Mercury, of Queen, was born to a Parsi family in Zanzibar. His parents had migrated from India, but had ancestral roots in the Zoroastrian community of Persia. Freddie Mercury took pride in his lineage, and once called himself a 'Persian popinjay'. His sister recalled that their home was filled with their parents' daily prayers. These would have been recited in Old Persian and Old Avestan, two languages preserved through Zoroastrian liturgy.

Multilingual ghosts

In some ghost stories, spectres or demons appear and speak in a language no one can understand. Sometimes they utter nonsense sounds, but at other times they speak a real language, typically one that's associated with the past. It's an uncanny use of language that can express complex feelings around memory, loss, and guilt.

I first came across this phenomenon when I spent a year as an exchange student at the National University of Singapore. In the evenings, I'd meet friends at old hawker centres, sitting outside on plastic chairs, eating fried noodles or fish-head curry. A few Singaporean friends who'd done military service (known as National Service) mentioned ghost stories that circulated on the training bases. Almost twenty years have passed since that year in Singapore, but Singaporean National Service ghost stories are still going strong. These days, they are popular on social media, too. The basic narrative is the same as it was back then, and it goes like this:

A new recruit starts his training on a military base surrounded by dense jungle. He is warned that he must not bring pork to the base, because the place was previously inhabited by Malay Muslims who were relocated to make space for the military centre. Their spirits would be offended by the pork. The recruit ignores the warning, brings pork or upsets the spirits in some other way. He is then visited by ghosts, who are either silent, or speak in Malay.

There is one story about a little girl and her grandmother, who loudly count the sleeping recruits. If the girl spots one who is still awake, she tells her grandmother in Malay: 'Grandmother, that brother isn't sleeping yet.'

Online, the Singaporean ghost experience is typically told in Singaporean English, that is, in an English enmeshed with Hokkien (a Chinese dialect) and Malay. Take this 2018 account by a former recruit who claimed to have wandered off base and spotted three ghosts: 'Kinda panic until my *encik* ['sir' in Malay] come check... After book out I *chiong* ['rush' in Hokkien] to nearest temple and ask for amulet.'[29]

On the Indonesian islands of the Riau Archipelago, the cultural poles are reversed. Here, the ghosts tend to be from a Chinese merchant community that used to inhabit these multi-ethnic islands. According to the anthropologist Nicholas Long, 'houses are often considered haunted because they are built on top of a Chinese cemetery.'[30]

This ghostly survival of displaced communities and vanished languages is not unique to South East Asia. Storytellers all over the world have used multilingual ghosts and spirits as narrative devices to show how the past can unsettle the present.

In *Purge*, a novel by Sofi Oksanen, the 'ghosts of Baltic German manor ladies' haunt a house in Estonia, and disturb the Estonians with their 'moist yawns'.[31] In Arundhati Roy's *The God of Small Things*, set in Kerala, the ghost of a colonial-era Englishman occasionally asks passers-by for a cigar, in English. In Tomi Adeyemi's fantasy novel, *Children of Blood and Bone*, Yoruba, a West African language, is presented as a banned magical tongue from the past that is revived as a weapon of resistance. Historically, Yoruba was brought to Brazil, Cuba and other American countries by enslaved West Africans, and survives there in spiritual practices to this day.

Languages preserved through magic and spirituality can form an enduring collective memory. The past speaks to us in a language that refuses to be silenced. Whether they come from beyond the desert or the afterlife, languages have the power to heal, soothe or rattle the soul.

Genizahs, by the way, still exist all over the world to receive discarded holy items. Their proper plural is *genizot*, and at least four drop-off points for them exist in Greater London. New moral dilemmas around this sacred waste now preoccupy the Rabbis, such as whether printed pages and old newspapers containing the name of God need to be buried as carefully as hand-written texts, and whether storing all this paper before burial constitutes a fire hazard. In the meantime, worshippers continue to drop off their homework, hand-outs, letters and worn-out prayer books at storage facilities for burial, accidentally archiving their lives and languages for future generations.

Rosetta Riddles

It's a quiet weekday morning in the British Museum, but the room with the Rosetta Stone is crammed with a large and enthusiastic crowd. People from all over the world are craning their necks to see the multilingual black slab in the display case. The Rosetta Stone is an icon of the history of human languages, thanks to its role in the decipherment of the Egyptian hieroglyphs. You can buy Rosetta mugs, aprons, cushions and lunch boxes at the museum shop. There are Rosetta language courses, and even a Rosetta space probe. The stone is usually depicted the way you see it at the museum, with the top broken off, and a multilingual text scribbled all over it. The text actually includes a tiny self-portrait. It's in the top portion of the inscription, composed of Egyptian hieroglyphs, and shows the stone as it would have looked when it was intact, with a rounded top: ⌓

This little picture of the stone simply means "stele". It's part of a sentence ordering that steles like this one should be put up in temples all over Egypt.

Egyptian hieroglyphs and Sumerian cuneiform were only deciphered within the last couple of centuries. These scripts faded from use around two thousand years ago, and while people continued to be interested in them, they could no longer read them. In the early seventeenth century, an Italian traveller called Pietro della Valle toured the ruins of the Middle East with his multilingual wife and interpreter, Sitti Maani Gioerida, who came from an Armenian family in the town of Mardin on the Turkish-Syrian border.[1] They saw many *lettere strane*, strange or foreign letters, as della Valle called them. Among them were cuneiform signs carved into the sides of ancient monumental buildings, and pressed into bricks. To della Valle, the wedges looked like elongated pyramids, and he speculated that they formed a script. Other scholars and travellers thought that cuneiform might just be decorative. The Egyptian hieroglyphs inspired similar feelings in observers. They yearned to be able to read them, but no one quite knew how to crack the code.

When the hieroglyphs and cuneiform were eventually deciphered in the nineteenth century, a completely new picture of humanity emerged. The span of our recorded history more than doubled. Before then, the oldest Greek and Latin records were as far as we could reach, about two thousand years into the past. Now, we can read cuneiform records dating from before five thousand years ago. It's as if a door that stood slightly ajar had suddenly swung wide open.

Once you have this knowledge, it's hard to imagine life without it. I was looking up *dragoman* in the Grimms' dictionary, which dates from around the middle of the nineteenth century. The Grimms traced the word back to Arabic, and then scratched their heads, and thought it might be related to an Arabic word for 'veiled'. It took me a moment to realize that that was as far as they could go. They couldn't trace the roots to Akkadian, or early Anatolian languages, because none of those had yet been recovered. At the time the dictionary was composed, in the 1850s, Akkadian cuneiform had only just been deciphered. And scholars were only beginning to realize that behind this ancient, strange and still only partly under-stood Akkadian was a shimmer of an even older, totally different language. It would take them several more decades to understand

and reconstruct that older voice. It was Sumerian, humanity's first recorded language.

Decipherment requires an extraordinary understanding of languages, and how they relate to each other. But it also draws on many other skills. An understanding of ancient shepherding and cheese-making can be useful when looking at a tablet from a Middle Eastern palace or temple that received tributes in the form of sheep and dairy products. A knowledge of how people in a given region honoured their gods can help understand the cryptic signs on a clay offering from ancient Cyprus. Finding traces of cocoa beans in an ancient cup helped confirm that the Mayan inscription on it indeed spelled out *kakaw*, cacao. Having records of ancient kings and battles from Greek historians who wrote about the Persians and Egyptians, allowed us to make sense of Old Persian cuneiform and Egyptian hieroglyphs.

Decipherment has to be seen in the context of all these related fields. It requires a knowledge of languages, but also a deep knowledge of people and their environment, paired with a sense of playfulness and openness. It hinges on our ability to relate to each other across time and space, to build a bridge from human mind to human mind.

Signal and noise

The Rosetta Stone dates from 196 BCE and features a priestly decree in support of Ptolemy, a Greek-speaking ruler of ancient Egypt. The inscription on it is divided into three sections. The first is in Egyptian, written in hieroglyphs, a script used in sacred contexts. The second section is in Egyptian demotic, a kind of slanting handwriting used for everyday tasks. The third is in Greek, written in Greek letters, used by the Greek-speaking dynasty that governed Egypt at that time.[2]

As famous as it is, the Rosetta Stone is not the only one of its kind. Similar inscribed stone slabs were put up in other temples, proclaiming the priests' support of Ptolemy in return for tax breaks and other benefits. Several of these stones are now in museums around the world.[3] But the one at the British Museum is special, because it was used in the decipherment of the Egyptian hieroglyphs.

Originally, the Rosetta Stone probably stood in a temple in the Egyptian city of Said. Later, it was moved to Rashid (also known as Rosetta), a harbour town in northern Egypt, and turned into building material for a fort.

In 1799, Napoleon's army invaded Rosetta. More than a hundred researchers and artists accompanied the French soldiers, among them specialists in scripts and languages. When a stone with a trilingual inscription was found in the old fort, they quickly spotted its potential as a key to decipherment.[4]

At the time, European scholars were well aware of the Egyptian hieroglyphs, and had tried but failed to read them. Here, then, was a possible entry point. The stone was stored in the commander's tent, and the Greek portion translated almost immediately. Copies were made by pressing wet paper against the stone and letting it dry. These copies and detailed drawings were dispatched to scholars in Europe, but before the stone could follow, the British defeated Napoleon's troops.

In 1801, British negotiators in Alexandria demanded that the French hand over the stone. The French general had hidden it under some mats in a warehouse. He initially tried to hold on to it. Under an agreement with the British, he was allowed to keep personal belongings; he claimed that the stone was as personal to him as 'the linen of his wardrobe'.[5]

That ruse didn't work. The British took the stone, and in 1802 it arrived in England and was taken to the British Museum, where it is displayed to this day. From the start, it was a crowd magnet.

A nineteenth-century engraving shows a large gathering of orientalists in top hats (and one in a turban) inspecting the inscription.[6]

As I stand in front of the stone, the sound of many languages fills the air, in a pleasing echo of the multilingual exhibit. Next to me, an Italian dad tells his son that the stone dates from a time when '*Gesù era un bambino*', when Jesus was a child. Two French teenagers note that a Frenchman, Jean-François Champollion, managed to '*résoudre les hiéroglyphes*', to solve the enigma of the hieroglyphs. A Korean tour guide tells the story of the stone's decipherment in Korean.

I don't know any Korean, but I can guess the content of the guide's lecture because my ears pick out a personal name, 'Thomas Young'. Young was one of the scholars who cracked the riddle of the Rosetta Stone, using a process similar to what my ears are instinctively doing right now. He and Champollion started by picking out proper names from the unintelligible buzz of the hieroglyphs.

Proper names tend to stay roughly the same across languages. That's why I was able to hear 'Thomas Young' in the Korean guide's explanation. Even today, when journalists around the world write headlines about a US president or a British royal, they will generally retain the original name. In Mandarin, for example, one way of spelling President Obama's name is 奥巴马, Àobāmǎ (there are also some other, similar versions).

The Rosetta Stone had barely entered the British Museum when scholars began to look for proper names in the inscription. They were helped by the fact that the Greek portion repeated the name 'Ptolemy', Ptolemaios in Greek, several times. It stood to reason that this name would also be repeated in the demotic, and the hieroglyphs.

Even more conveniently, the Egyptians had highlighted certain sign groups in the text, by drawing oval frames around them. Scholars speculated that these special signs had been circled because they spelled out the ruler's name, 'Ptolemaios'. Thomas Young, a polymath whose other achievements were in fields as diverse as optics and life insurance, tried to match the individual hieroglyphs to the sounds of that name: p, t, m, l and s. By 1816, he'd come up with several correct matches.[7]

Champollion then deciphered the name of an Egyptian ruler, Ramesses, in another inscription. Using his knowledge of Coptic, a descendant of the ancient Egyptian language, he unravelled more words and signs. By 1822, he'd pieced together the Egyptian alphabet. More work and revisions followed, by Champollion and others, but 1822 is now considered the year the riddle was cracked. As Andrew Robinson writes in his book about the history of decipherment, 'the pharaohs began to speak to us directly through their stone monuments, wall paintings and papyrus manuscripts'.[8]

Young and Champollion were honoured for their work, in death as in life. Young is commemorated by an inscription in Westminster Abbey, London. Champollion's grave in Père Lachaise cemetery in Paris is marked by an obelisk, and fans occasionally leave stalks of the Egyptian papyrus plant there.[9]

Great king, king of kings

What of cuneiform? The wedge-shaped signs were deciphered using quite a similar method. In the 18th century, an explorer called Carsten Niebuhr visited the ruins of Persepolis, built by Persian kings, and made accurate drawings of the cuneiform inscriptions there. Back in Europe, scholars rightly guessed that the inscriptions were in Old Persian, an ancient language that had been reconstructed thanks to its descendant, modern Persian, or Farsi. Scholars already knew the names and titles of Persian kings from Greek and Persian historical sources. This gave them a clue to the content of the royal inscriptions, which were likely to feature the names of the kings who had built the city and commissioned the writing.

The most important of these royal titles, in this context, is *shahanshah*, king of kings. Even for those who don't speak Persian, the repetition in the title is noticeable: shah-an-shah, king-of-kings. This repetition provided the first, vital clue to Georg Grotefend, a nineteenth-century German academic who worked on the Persepolis signs. Grotefend himself didn't know any Persian. He was a specialist in ancient Italian languages, such as Oscan. But a friend had noticed that he was good at riddles, and suggested he might have a go at cuneiform.[10] Grotefend set to work, resorting to dictionaries whenever he needed to look up a Persian word.

Scholars had already noticed that one group of signs was repeated several times in the inscription. Grotefend suspected that this repeated sign group might spell out the Old Persian word for 'king', which would fit a known formula, 'great king, king of kings, son of king…'.[11] The names of the Persian rulers at Persepolis were also known. Using a kind of linguistic jigsaw logic and his trusty dictionaries, Grotefend pieced all of these elements together, and came up with a translation: 'Xerxes, brave King, King of Kings, the Son of Darius the King, the successor of the ruler of the world.'

More material arrived from a trilingual inscription on a rock face in Iran. In the 1830s, Henry Creswicke Rawlinson, a British army officer, climbed up and down the precarious rock face to make wet-paper copies of the signs. The text was essentially a caption for a giant rock carving of Darius, a Persian king, with his foot on a prisoner lying on the ground, as other captives looked on, their hands and necks bound with ropes. One portion was in Old Persian cuneiform, another in Elamite (spoken in ancient Iran), and a third, in Akkadian cuneiform. Just as the Rosetta Stone offered Greek as a key to the Egyptian hieroglyphs, this inscription presented Old Persian as a key to Akkadian, which was unknown until then.

Akkadian's close relation to known languages such as Arabic and Hebrew also helped.

By the 1850s, scholars announced that they could read cuneiform. To test their claim, the Royal Asiatic Society asked four of them to independently translate copies of an Akkadian cuneiform inscription on a stone cylinder in the British Museum. Rawlinson was part of the group, as was Edward Hincks, an Irish clergyman from the village of Killyleagh in County Down, who worked on cuneiform in his spare time. Comparing the four translations, the Society judged that they were close enough, and that cuneiform had indeed been deciphered.[12]

A stranger sound

There was, however, an even greater puzzle waiting to be solved. Hincks, the Irish clergyman, was one of the first to notice it. As he worked on the Akkadian cuneiform signs, he sensed something strange and extremely compelling lurking in their shadow: another, even more ancient language. He came to this conclusion thanks to a simple but very astute observation based on his own Irish heritage. Historically, Irish scribes had gradually adopted a foreign script as their own. They'd initially copied Latin manuscripts for religious purposes, and eventually used the Latin letters to write in Irish. The result was slightly awkward, because the Latin alphabet didn't seamlessly fit the sounds of Irish. In Hincks' eyes, something similar seemed to be happening with Akkadian cuneiform. Here was a language that struggled with its script.[13]

Akkadian words are generally built around a stable core of consonants. This is typical of Semitic languages, including Arabic. Vowels shift and change, but the consonants of a given word tend to stay the same, and convey an underlying meaning. One might think the

Akkadians would therefore have used a script that consisted mainly of consonants. Other Semitic speakers did so. Hebrew, Arabic and Aramaic are written using almost only consonants. The vowels are either lightly indicated by adding dots and dashes above or below the letters, or are left out entirely, and the reader has to add them in their mind. These consonantal scripts fit the logic of Semitic languages very well. The Akkadians, however, used cuneiform, which was made up of syllables. To spell out *šulmani*, peace gifts, you have to write something like *šu-ul-ma-ni*. This actually makes it quite hard to spot the most important consonants, š, l, m, which relate to the meaning of peace and well-being, as in the Hebrew *shalom*. Syllables are just not a very intuitive way of spelling a Semitic, consonant-centred language, because they yoke each stable, unchanging consonant to a flighty, changeable vowel.

Hincks concluded that 'no Semitic people could have invented a system of writing so uncongenial to their language'.[14]

Instead, he thought the Akkadians might have done what the Irish scribes later did. They borrowed an older, existing script, and used it as best they could, to write their own language.

It must have felt thrilling, and maybe even slightly destabilizing, to perceive the shimmer of that older script, and the civilization that invented it. Later, the Akkadian cuneiform tablets themselves revealed the name of that civilization, Sumer, home to the Sumerians. Over the decades that followed Hincks's first intuition, scholars pieced together their ancient, forgotten language. A whole new history emerged, which started with the Sumerians and their invention of writing.

Cakes and Islands

It's late spring, the sun is out, and I'm sitting in a seminar room at the University of Cambridge, trying to carve two ancient symbols into the side of a small clay bull. Projected onto the wall is the model I'm trying to copy, a photo of a 3,000-year-old sacred offering from the island of Cyprus. It is inscribed with two signs:

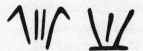

Redrawn by Philip Boyes, after Olivier 2007

The signs are in Cypro-Minoan, a script used on the island from around 1600 to 900 BCE.[1] It's mostly undeciphered, meaning we can't read the texts written in it, also because we don't know which language it records. It survives in a couple of hundred inscriptions. Around the world, only about twenty scholars are studying it. One of them is Philippa Steele, a classicist at the University of Cambridge, who invited me to the seminar. It was a rare chance to see what working with such ancient signs was like, not after they'd been deciphered, but while they still formed an enigmatic code guarding a secret message from the past.

Accounts of decipherment can sometimes sound quite dry and theoretical, but the research at Cambridge was very hands-on.

Philippa Steele and her colleagues had come up with many ways of mimicking the methods of ancient scribes, trying out different styluses and writing materials, inscribing tablets and figurines modelled with clay from a craft shop, and even decorating biscuits and cakes with undeciphered symbols. While the cake-baking was more about the joy of playing with old scripts, the other experiments fulfilled a serious purpose, for one of the difficulties of Cypro-Minoan is that it was written on many different objects. Some symbols look different but were probably meant to be the same. They just came out differently because one was written on a soft, flat tablet, and another on a round clay cow. A third was perhaps scratched into a hard, fired pot by a busy Cypriot olive oil merchant marking his wares before loading them onto a ship. Re-enacting the movements of these original writers can reveal why and how certain signs changed form, even as their meaning stayed the same.

I realized this after the seminar, when I checked the mysterious symbols I'd squished onto my cow against a list of known Cypro-Minoan symbols in Philippa Steele's book, *A Linguistic History of Ancient Cyprus*. None of the ones in the list looked like mine. It appeared that I'd invented two new signs, just by writing Cypro-Minoan badly.

Given how little of this script has been found, it's amazing that we can make any sense of it at all. The fact that we can is largely due to the enduring connections between different cultures and their languages.

Cyprus, a once-sleepy island that had become a major copper exporter almost overnight, did not come up with these signs all by itself. It had looked to its powerful neighbours, borrowed their best ideas, and combined them to invent something of its own. The resulting script may not be as famous as cuneiform, or the Egyptian hieroglyphs. But to the people of Cyprus, it was beautiful and precious enough to be written on a little statue of a sacred bull and offered to the gods. And to us, millennia later, it tells a much bigger story of cultural innovation and exchange, of one small island absorbing languages from all around and fashioning them into something new.

Across the wine-dark sea

Alashiya, as ancient Cyprus was called, was a speck in a region of big and wealthy powers. To the north lay the Hittite-speaking areas of Anatolia, central Turkey. To the east, the vibrant trading cities of the Syrian coast. Sailing south, the Cypriots arrived in Egypt, and moving westwards, they went as far as Crete. All these civilizations experimented with writing. Hittite hieroglyphs, Near Eastern cuneiform, Egyptian hieroglyphs and various Cretan scripts circulated around the eastern Mediterranean. Sometimes they ended up in the same place, as in Ugarit, where two kinds of cuneiform, hieroglyphs and even some Cypro-Minoan tablets were found.

Cyprus could have imported any of those writing systems, and to some extent, it did. The scribes of Alashiya wrote Akkadian clay letters to their diplomatic counterparts abroad, and at least one scribe had come over from Ugarit, and wrote back home to ask for a table and chairs. But at the same time, the Cypriots developed a separate script of their own. It looks somewhat cuneiform-like, in the way certain Cypro-Minoan tablets are covered with dense, small signs. In some tablets, the symbols are pressed into the clay, like in Mesopotamian tablets. Look closely, however, and the signs themselves are rounded rather than wedge-shaped, consisting of curved, drawn lines instead of straight impressions. They are thought to have come to Cyprus not from its eastern Syrian neighbour, but from the opposite direction: from the west, from the island of Crete.[2]

A Cretan civilization known to modern scholars as the Minoans, after the legendary King Minos at Knossos, invented a series of different writing systems from about 2000 BCE. The Minoans were renowned traders, artists and seafarers. They are thought to have copied the art of writing from yet another civilization, perhaps the Hittites or Luwians in Anatolia, or the Egyptians, or a combination of all of them.

Cretan writing began with chubby hieroglyphs. These look quite similar to Hittite and Luwian ones from central Turkey. They include a double axe, a ladder or loom, a wolf or dog, and a simple picture of a fig tree.[3] The Cretans carved these symbols into seal-stones, and later reduced them to simpler signs that were written in lines across a clay page. The fig tree evolved into a sign that looked like this: Ψ.

No one knows exactly which language, or languages, the Cretans spoke when they first started writing. The island had a multilingual reputation, which survived in historical accounts by Greek writers, and in Greek myth, as in Homer's *Odyssey*:

> Out in the wine-dark sea there lies a land called Crete, a rich and lovely sea-girt land, densely peopled, with ninety cities and several different languages. First there are the Achaeans; then the genuine Cretans, proud of their native stock; next the Cydonians; the Dorians, with their three clans; and finally the noble Pelasgians. One of the ninety towns is a great city called Cnossus, and there King Minos rules...[4]

In Greek antiquity, some historians mentioned native Cretan words such as *nikuleon*, 'figs'.[5] In Cretan writing, the fig tree symbol represented a syllable, *ni*, that may originally have been an abbreviation of *nikuleon*. Once Greek arrived on Crete, the islanders re-purposed their signs to spell out Greek words, syllable by syllable.

The fig sign, *ni*, was then used to spell out words that had nothing to do with figs. It appears in words such as *de-mi-ni-a*, 'bedding':
𒌋𒌋 .

Some Cretan symbols were directly copied by another island community, the Cypriots, who perhaps saw them while trading with Crete. The Cypriots developed them into their Cypro-Minoan script, along with other influences. Later, they used them in a simpler set of signs to write Greek. Comparing the Greek texts written with these symbols, it's clear that some kept their shape as well as their sounds as they migrated from one island to another. For example, an elongated cross exists as a sign in all of these different writing systems. It was read as *ro* or *lo*.[6] It appears in the Greek word for field, *agros*, spelled as *a-ko-ro* in the Cretan script: ⳦⳧⳦. The word *agros* later wandered into English words related to fields and farming, such as 'agriculture'.

It's through this web of known and unknown languages that scholars were able to decipher two scripts from Crete and Cyprus, and at least partly make sense of Cypro-Minoan.

Sealstones and amulets

Our image of ancient Crete is greatly shaped by the nineteenth- and early twentieth-century discoveries of Arthur Evans, a British archaeologist. He excavated the ruins of Knossos and named their early inhabitants the Minoans, a nod to King Minos. Some of his views have since been questioned, especially his idea that the Minoans were fundamentally different from their neighbours, and part of a distinctly 'western' cultural heritage.

Evans saw Crete as Europe's cradle of civilization. Ilse Schoep, a specialist in the Bronze Age, argued that his focus on the island was inspired by an ideology that ultimately portrayed Europeans as superior to others. Since literacy was considered a crucial element of cultural progress, Evans was keen to find a uniquely European script. In the process, he downplayed the role of Anatolian and Syrian influences on Minoan writers, and instead cast them as the ancient forefathers of a liberal and sophisticated Greek culture. Thus he described Hittite art as 'cramped and trammelled from the beginning by the Oriental contact. No real life and freedom of expression was ever reached; the art is stiff, conventional becoming more and more Asiatic.' In prehistoric Greece and Crete, on the other hand, he perceived an ability to reshape these foreign elements into an art and script that breathed 'the European spirit of individuality and freedom'.[7]

At Knossos, Evans found dazzling art and pottery inspired by the sea, beautiful frescoes of swimming dolphins, and vases decorated with octopuses. He also dug up various scripts. The oldest of these consisted of pictures carved into small sealstones. Women on Crete were wearing the stones as amulets around their necks, because they believed them to stimulate the supply of breastmilk.[8] They called them *galopetra*, 'milk stones'. Evans bought as many of them as he could find, but noted in his diary that this was not always easy:

Made a final effort to get the galopetra with the two goats out of the woman who owned it. Alevisos (the muleteer) and mine host Giorgios had spent half an hour the evening before arguing with her and the shepherd, her husband, and had particularly urged that I was willing to supply her with another 'milk stone' besides paying them as much as 2 luidi. But in vain. Nor were my efforts in the morning crowned with more success. The woman only pointed to a small bairn and declared that if she parted with the stone it would die for want to nourishment![9]

He found two more scripts on Crete, written on leaf-shaped tablets. They looked flowing and linear to him, so he called them Linear

Script Class A (Linear A) and Linear Script Class B (Linear B).[10] The challenge of deciphering them was very different from the Egyptian hieroglyphs and cuneiform, because of a lack of multilingual texts.

On Cyprus, a descendant of Linear B, known as the Cypriot syllabary, was eventually written next to Phoenician, a known script and language. This made its decipherment relatively quick and easy, through the usual process of finding a repeated word for 'king', as well as personal names and place names.[11]

Early on, Evans and others succeeded in identifying numbers and easily recognizable signs such as 'woman' ⚲ and 'horse' 𐂌 . Ultimately, however, Linear B was deciphered with a novel method based on analysing its internal features. Scholars looked for sign patterns and variations, which they could spot even without understanding the signs themselves.[12] From this, they deduced some grammatical properties.

For example, certain Linear B symbols tended to occur together, in the same sequence. But sometimes the last sign varied, or there was an extra sign at the end. The researchers correctly concluded that these signs formed words with different grammatical endings (in English, a comparable example would be 'Japan', 'Japan's' and 'Japanese').

After Evans's death, the decipherment became an international effort by the American classicists Alice Kober and Emmett Bennett, the British architect Michael Ventris and the British classicist John Chadwick. Kober in particular paved the way with her methodical analysis of the basic structure of Linear B, including the aforementioned grammatical patterns and variations. She did this alongside another monumental transcription project, in which she rendered the course materials at her college in Brooklyn in Braille, the raised font, for the benefit of blind students.[13]

Later, the decipherers matched signs with sounds, which became easier once they realized the texts were in Greek. The broader context also helped. The word for 'total' was correctly guessed because it appeared at the end of a list. The signs for 'boy' and 'girl' were identified because they typically appeared in lists next to the sign for 'woman'. Scholars realized the lists recorded rations handed out to enslaved women and their children.[14]

In 1952, Ventris announced in a BBC radio broadcast that he had deciphered Linear B, helped by his insight that it recorded the Greek language. Today, the effort to fully understand the script and its archaic form of Greek is still ongoing.

It's because of these advances and relationships that we can now look at a tablet in Cypro-Minoan and see a lot more than just a clay slab covered in cryptic signs.

How to read an undeciphered tablet

At the first seminar session, Philippa Steele showed us a picture of the oldest known tablet in Cypro-Minoan. It was found at Enkomi, the copper harbour, and is inscribed with two signs on the side:[15]

Redrawn by Philip Boyes, after Olivier 2007

And with three lines of text on the main surface:

Redrawn by Philip Boyes, after Olivier 2007

Where do you even start? Philippa pointed out that the signs on the side are the same as the ones in the top-right corner. They may have functioned like the title on the spine of a book. When the tablets were stacked or lined up on a shelf, the owner could have glanced along the spines to find the right one. The two symbols on the 'spine' would have acted as a clue to the beginning of the text on the tablet. This suggests that we should start reading the tablet from right to left, starting in the top-right corner.

In the second line, something odd happens. The script changes direction, and runs from left to right. In the third, it changes direction again, and runs from right to left. We know this from looking at the one or two asymmetrical characters in each line. They point in the directions of the writing, like little signposts. This is a common feature of scripts, including the one I am typing right now. Look at E, F and K. They are like little people, pointing their arms to the right, as if to tell you that's the direction you should read in. In scripts that resemble our alphabet, but run in the opposite direction, such as Oscan, the E and K point the other way, to the left. Egyptian hieroglyphs can also be written in either direction, and the pictures of animals and people look to the side the text starts from.

I have to say that when Philippa told me about letters facing in the direction of our writing, it kind of bowled me over. I've been writing in this alphabet for more than thirty years. It never occurred to me that E and F helpfully guide us across the page, towards the right. That's what an encounter with another script or language does, no matter how old: it makes you see your own script, your own language, in a completely new light.

As for the change of direction: while it may seem counterintuitive at first glance, it was not uncommon in the ancient world, and had its advantages. In Greek it's known as *boustrophedon*, meaning something like 'as the ox turns'. In German, it's known as

Schlangenschrift, snake writing. Once you get used to it, it makes for quite smooth reading, because your gaze can just snake down the page, rather than jumping back to one side of the page with every new line.

The signs themselves were a harder nut to crack, because we don't know which language they record. Across the water, in Ugarit, a Cypro-Minoan tablet was found that appeared to be a list of Semitic names. This was deduced from the format of the signs. The central symbols were the same in each line, just like in the characteristic layout of Semitic names, which typically feature a recurring 'son of' in the middle. The way the signs varied also matched certain aspects of Semitic grammar. But on Cyprus itself, the signs were arranged differently, hinting at a different grammatical structure, and a non-Semitic language.[16]

Thanks to the known signs and sounds from Cretan Linear B and the later Cypriot syllabary, we can, however, reconstruct at least to some extent what the text on the Enkomi tablet may have sounded like.

Philippa worked her way through the entire tablet with this method, assigning possible sounds to each sign, based on similarities with these other scripts. It was a lively process, because even just describing and comparing such old, rare symbols requires some imagination. It's less like talking about a modern font, and more like talking about a mystifying work of art, or even a living creature. In Philippa's words, one of the characters had 'sticky out top and bottom bits', another had 'two feet'. Some sounds were far from certain: 'I suspect this is more of a "to" than a "na",' she said at one point. And: 'The Linear A sign looks like a cat's head, with these ears. The Cypro-Minoan sign kind of also has ears.'

Eventually, Philippa read out the whole text as it might have sounded back in ancient Cyprus. Then she concluded cheerfully: 'We have no idea what this means.'

The seminar participants didn't seem to mind. In the world of ancient scripts, giving a full translation of a text is not necessarily the primary goal. One of the most important aspects of Cypro-Minoan, for example, is its role as an east-west innovation, which is apparent even without knowing what the tablets are about. The script challenges Evans's assumption of two fundamentally opposed mindsets, one eastern, the other western. Instead, Cypro-Minoan tells a story of a people who were curious about all the cultures around them, and keen to learn from them. They left enduringly beautiful traces of their writing, not just on the island itself. In Ugarit on the Syrian coast, an exquisite silver bowl was found, inscribed with a few delicate Cypro-Minoan signs. It's displayed at the Louvre, in a side room dedicated to Ugarit, easy to overlook but worth finding for a moment of quiet contemplation and wonder.

Elvish and wet fields

After the first seminar session, we went for drinks at a crowded, lively pub by the Cam, filled with the happy chatter of students and lecturers. I was keen to talk to the rest of the seminar group, and find out what drove them to devote their lives to scripts as old and baffling as Cypro-Minoan.

The seminar was organized by an interdisciplinary research group at Cambridge called CREWS, short for 'Contexts of and Relations between Early Writing Systems'. In the past, scholars tended to focus on deciphering individual scripts. Now, there is a growing effort to understand how different scripts interacted, and what they reveal about cultural contact. Another big change is that anyone can now follow such research thanks to the Internet, which is teeming with experts in ancient scripts sharing their knowledge. On a blog published by the CREWS group, posts about real scripts alternate with explanations of fictional alphabets from *The Lord of the Rings*, *Star Wars* and *Doctor Who* (one telltale characteristic of fictional scripts is that they tend to be very neat and logical; real scripts are messier and less consistent, marked by human errors and shortcuts).[17]

Philippa's own interest in scripts started in childhood. 'I've always loved mythology and history but especially, languages and codes,' she told me later. 'I was very interested in that kind of intellectual challenge.' She joined an archaeology club for children, but the English weather worked against her: 'It was kind of wet fields and not really finding anything.' Instead, languages became her gateway to other worlds: Latin, Greek, Cypro-Minoan, and fictional ones, too. Philippa is not just one of the world's few Cypro-Minoan experts, she's also the former Elvish Officer of the Cambridge Tolkien Society.

At the pub, I was struck by how passionate these researchers were about ancient cultures and languages. As they talked, the long-gone voices of Cyprus, Crete, Ugarit and Anatolia felt more and more alive, calling out to us from the past. I found myself transported to sun-baked harbours where scribes squatted by the doors of warehouses, recording deliveries, dispatching letters, labelling pots, and counting stacked copper slabs for export.

Later, Cassandra Donnelly, a visiting researcher from the University of Texas, told me that early writing was probably a more widespread activity than we might think. Scribes, but also traders and travellers experimented with these scripts.

'We're used to this narrative that writing belongs to elites, or it belongs to people who are employed by elites, so scribes with a little king ruling over them,' she said. 'To my mind, there's a little space to be like, well no, writing is not super complicated, guys, and in fact, there were people who adapted it and did other things beside that.'

She herself had been transfixed by ancient scripts ever since the day she found herself staring at a pearly white letter cut out from construction paper, the Hebrew aleph, at her Jewish nursery in Connecticut. Later, she studied Latin, Greek, Hebrew, Aramaic, Ugaritic, Hittite and Akkadian, and picked up Yiddish when she volunteered at a Jewish old-age home. More recently, she has been learning Marathi, an Indian language spoken by her husband's family. She liked Cypro-Minoan because it was an east-west script, neatly bridging all the languages in her repertoire.

I had the feeling that no language would be too ancient or too obscure to be appreciated here. In fact, as the CREWS blog notes wisely, even if you can't decipher a script, you can always bake it. Philip Boyes, a research associate at the project, explains in a blog post how to make 'Phaistos Discuits', biscuits in the shape of the mysterious Phaistos Disc from Crete. ('Our understanding of this object remains extremely limited. However, it is just the perfect shape to turn into a biscuit!') He also gives a video tutorial on 'Ugaritic Tablet Biscuits', tablet-shaped biscuits inscribed with cuneiform; and instructions for making 'pop-tarblets', pop-tarts made to look like Akkadian diplomatic tablets, inspired by a study session at the British Museum.

I brought this up at the pub, hoping to find out how a group of highly trained scholars had become quite so devoted to cake. People pointed to Anna Judson, an expert on Linear B, as one regular contributor of baked goods. I asked her if baking had given her new insights into ancient scripts. Not really, she said, but it had given her a lot of insight into which scripts were best for piping and icing. Linear B was pretty good, but it sometimes fell off and had to be stuck back on. Phoenician was nice and rounded. She'd baked a cake with Cypro-Minoan on it, and its photo was now in a book about ancient writing systems: 'My only formally published cake.'[18]

It occurred to me that this lovely group of people might be the perfect audience for my only bilingual cuneiform joke. Emboldened by my pint of cider, I told them the joke, the one about the vegetable vendor in Nippur, who talks in Sumerian to the Akkadian-speaking high priest, and he keeps thinking that she's cursing him. *'Where did he go?' 'To the temple!' 'Why are you cursing me?' 'But all I said was, he went to the temple!'* They laughed, and for a moment, this very old story felt completely fresh and new.

On the train back to London, holding my sacred clay bull wrapped in napkins, I felt as if I'd been on the most wonderful adventure. I was already looking forward to the next session, and more drinks at that pub. Perhaps there'd even be cake.

A cuneiform cake

On the morning before the next seminar session, I set about making my first ever script-themed cake. Like the scribes of ancient Cyprus, I had to decide on the material, shape, and of course, the script itself. The shape was dictated by what was available: a round cake tin. As for the material, I decided to keep it simple and make a lemon cake, evoking the fresh and fruity flavours of the eastern Mediterranean.

Finding the right script proved somewhat tricky. Cypro-Minoan would have been an obvious choice, but I couldn't quite face icing a cake in undeciphered symbols, and then presenting those symbols to the small circle of experts who actually knew what they were supposed to look like. After all, I still wasn't entirely sure what Philippa had meant by 'those cat's ears'. No, I would bake a cuneiform cake instead. Hopefully, the Cypro-Minoan experts wouldn't be that familiar with cuneiform anyway, giving me some creative leeway (this particular assumption proved to be totally wrong; some people in the group could read and write not just one, but several cuneiform scripts).

My round cake tin posed another challenge. Cuneiform tablets are traditionally rectangular. Looking for an online image of a round tablet I might copy, I found a beautiful round sky map from ancient Nineveh. It was tempting, but I had a strong feeling that once I'd piped all the intricate symbols onto the cake, they would end up looking nothing like a sky map from Nineveh. Just as I was losing hope, I found the perfect template: a round practice tablet with a scribal exercise.[19] Each line started with the familiar god sign. Even better, if my signs came out lopsided, I could blame it on the original scribe. It would bring to life the exciting rough and tumble of a scribal education. *You call that Sumerian?*

The cake was still warm when I iced it. This turned out to be an unwise move, but I had a train to catch, and better a badly iced cake than no cake. Using the end of a teaspoon as a stylus, I set to work. The warm icing cracked. My god signs looked very unholy. No wonder it was so hard deciphering ancient symbols.

Écrire c'est lutter, to write is to struggle, wrote André Bataille, a scholar of ancient scripts and papyruses. Silvia Ferrara, a Cypro-Minoan scholar, quotes Bataille to remind us that we must always think of the context of writing.[20] The objects that were inscribed, the tools used to inscribe them, the hands that used these tools, all ended up producing writing as we know it.

Bataille's original passage is worth quoting in full, because it paints such a vivid picture of the intense physical process, the slips and shifts and errors, that have shaped all our writing, and all our languages. He starts with the example of a scribe wanting to produce '*un simple baton bien droit*'. That's all he wanted to achieve, this seemingly tiny thing, to make a simple straight mark.

But, oh!, 'the scribe was in a rush, tired or distracted, he was holding his stylus incorrectly, his fingers lacked flexibility, the writing material was poorly positioned on the table or had fibres sticking out, the letter suffered a knock-on effect from its neighbours, the scribe unknowingly preferred arched rather than straight lines etc etc: we are reading /'[21]

Never again will I be able to look at a slanted line / and not see a symbol of foiled human ambition.

The first contact with a script is a kind of heart-to-heart with the original writer. Did you want them to come out this way? Were you just busy, or tired? What's with those feet?

I hoped that the Cambridge scholars would see my cracked cake in this light. *Écrire c'est lutter*, and so is baking. It was a bit crumbly, like an ancient artefact. I wrapped it in foil, and it sat on my lap all the way to Cambridge, emitting a faint scent of lemon.

In the seminar room, my crumbly efforts passed their peer review. I admitted to the flaws of my experiment, especially the warm icing, and suggested potential improvements, such as adding a layer of marzipan. We briefly discussed other potential cuneiform projects: a cylinder seal, for example, made by baking and inscribing a Swiss roll. There was special praise for having baked a round practice tablet – a new development in ancient baking – and for the lemony taste. Between us, we finished the whole cake, and I felt I'd made a small but not entirely insignificant contribution to the field.

That day, we scratched Cypro-Minoan signs into broken flowerpots, mimicking busy traders marking their pots on the go. I learned that writing is traditionally defined as at least two signs in a row, but that scholars are starting to question that definition. Who is to say that a merchant scratching his initial into a pot is not writing? With each of these shifts in current-day thinking, new people step out of the dim light of linguistic history, to be considered not just as cultural bystanders, but as contributors and innovators.

'Here is the donkey'

During my next and last session, I finally got to taste a Cypro-Minoan cake. Anna Judson had brought it. It was a brownie, iced with six Cypro-Minoan signs found on a copper ingot at Enkomi.[22]

Philip Boyes, the CREWS research associate, led the seminar. He talked about the different migrant communities living in Ugarit, such as Hittites and Cypriots. The natives of Ugarit came together in a ritual of atonement and unity, similar to the Jewish day of Yom Kippur. They apologized for any harm they might have done, including any transgressions against minorities. Then they sacrificed a donkey. The whole ceremony is encapsulated in an Ugaritic communal prayer, which lists all the communities, all the wrongdoings, ending with: 'Here is the donkey'.

As a practical exercise, we made up our own alphabet, written in cuneiform signs. As usual, I ran out of space because my signs were too big, making me wonder whether the scribes of the past had better eyesight, or smaller fingers, or both.

I was sad that my time with the Cypro-Minoan crowd was coming to an end. It had been thrilling to play Indiana Jones for a couple of hours a week, and tackle the secrets of the past in Room 1.11. There'd been the pleasure of finding out that you don't have to know Latin or Greek to enjoy the work of classicists. But there'd also been a deeper sense of delight, of reassurance almost. At the time, the newspapers were filled with Brexit headlines, and statements from politicians reminding foreigners like me that we didn't belong here. In that atmosphere, the Cypro-Minoan seminar was a welcome reminder of the cultural lineages that stretch from the east to the west, from the north to the south, and that include Britain too. For as we've seen from Crete and Cyprus, 'insular' doesn't have to be a synonym for isolated. It can also be a synonym for openness.

After the last seminar, on the train back to London, I watched the greyish-blue sky darken, and white fog rise over the meadows. I thought of the people of Ugarit coming together to acknowledge the foreigners in their midst, and about the merry roundabout of ancient scripts. A line from one of Philippa's emails came to mind: 'The history of writing is very much a history of cultural encounters between different groups of people, often ones speaking different languages.'

At home, I placed the new cuneiform tablet on my bookshelf, next to the flowerpot shards and the clay bull. One day, all those books will have crumbled to dust. But the tablet, the pot shard and the bull will still be there. Perhaps scholars will wonder how these three Mediterranean scripts, written by an unusually clumsy hand, came to be in the ruins of a little house in England.

Script-themed Lemon Cake recipe

Beat 200g butter until soft. Add 200g sugar, 3 eggs, 100g self-raising flour, 125g ground almonds and the zest of one lemon. Pour the mixture into a round or rectangular cake tin.

Bake at 180 degrees Celsius for about 35–40 minutes, or until a knife comes out clean. Wait for the cake to cool, then cover with a thick icing made from icing sugar and lemon juice.

Depending on the shape of your cake tin, you can now choose between a range of deciphered, partially deciphered, and undeciphered scripts. You can draw or press these into the icing using the end of a teaspoon, a chopstick, or a knife. Cuneiform signs are pressed into the surface; the Cypro-Minoan characters here are drawn.

If it's rectangular, you may wish to copy the Cypro-Minoan tablet mentioned earlier. If this feels too daunting, you could just copy the ancient *ni* sign, which originally represented a fig tree, and appears in various Cretan scripts as well as Cypro-Minoan:

If your cake tin is round, you could copy a scribal exercise tablet. There is a very clear picture of one on the website of the Metropolitan Museum of Art, New York. It's listed online as 'Cuneiform tablet: student exercise tablet'.[23]

As you punch or draw your signs, consider how the material, the pressure of your hand, the implement you are using, and your own state of mind are affecting the emerging text. If it all ends up looking a bit messy, don't despair: Écrire c'est lutter.

ACROSS THE WATER

Love in South Shields

On a bitterly cold morning in November, I walk across a grassy hilltop in South Shields, a seaside town in northern England. Seagulls circle overhead, piercing the air with their cries. A biting wind sweeps across the open space. From afar, it could be a municipal football pitch, overlooked by red brick terraces. Up close, the grass is dotted with broken columns and chipped foundation stones. They are the remains of Arbeia, a fort at the northern extreme of the Roman empire. Ships arrived at the harbour down the hill. They brought supplies for Arbeia, and for the forts along Hadrian's Wall, which stood just a little further north: olive oil from Spain, wine from France, amber beads from the Baltic coast. People from all over the Roman world arrived on those ships, too, bringing their skills and customs, their crafts and cooking styles, and, of course, their languages.[1]

I've come here to see a very unusual artefact, early evidence of Britain's multilingual history. It's a 2,000-year-old tombstone, put up by Barates, a man from Palmyra in Syria, for Regina, his Celtic wife. The stone was found in the late nineteenth century by workmen digging out foundations for a building. The *Shields Gazette* reported the discovery of the stone with breathless excitement: 'It has carved on it the figure of a woman... With the exception of the face, which is broken off, the carving is in an excellent state of preservation, and of remarkably good workmanship. At the base of the stone is a well-executed inscription...'[2]

Victorian scholars easily read and translated the main inscription on the stone, which was in Latin. Below it was a line in a totally different script. They identified it as an obscure Aramaic dialect, and set about translating it, too. Their research methods were, in many ways, slower and more laborious than today's. To share the inscription among experts at different universities, copies had to be made by pressing wet paper into the letters, then letting it dry. These were dispatched by post, unfolded on large, heavy oak desks, scrutinized and parsed for meaning. As slow as that initial process of sharing the text was, however, the translation itself was remarkably fast. Languages were their Internet. Within two weeks of the find, the scholars produced a full translation of both inscriptions.[3] This is still the translation used today. I find it in a little museum at the entrance to the fort, along with the stone itself.

The museum is officially closed for the winter, but the staff have kindly let me come on a day when they're open for schools. Teachers and children stream in and out of the little space, filling in quiz sheets: *Who is Regina? Is the skeleton in the glass case a man or a woman?*

The tombstone is large and intricately carved. It shows a woman sitting on a wicker chair, with a basket of wool at her feet, and a treasure chest. Below her is a framed inscription in Latin:

D(is) M(anibus) Regina liberta et coniuge
Barates Palmyrenus natione
Catuallauna an(norum) XXX

'To the spirits of the departed (and to) Regina, his freedwoman and wife, a Catuvellaunian by tribe, aged 30, Barates of Palmyra (set this up).'[4]

Crammed into a narrow space right at the bottom of the stone, underneath the straight, upright Latin letters, is a line of curving, flowing text. It looks almost like a footnote. This is Palmyrene, the Aramaic dialect used in Barates' distant home town. It is part of the Semitic family, and shares certain features with Arabic and Hebrew. Some of the letters on the stone, such as the b and the r, are in fact very similar to the ones in the Hebrew alphabet. Like most Semitic languages, Palmyrene is written using only consonants. Read from right to left, the inscription says:

> *RYGN BT HRY BR'T' HBL*
> 'Regina, freedwoman of Barates, alas'

Regina's tribe, the Catuvellauni, lived in and around St Albans. They spoke a Celtic language, which only survives in writing on some coins. In their home in South Shields, Barates and Regina may have mixed Latin, Palmyrene and Celtic, or perhaps they just spoke Latin to each other, with a few convenient loanwords from their native languages. And yet, within that mix, Palmyrene was important enough for Barates to go to the trouble of having it carved into the stone. The script is well executed, by an experienced mason. Why had Barates used Palmyrene, which was not commonly spoken at South Shields? What was a man from Syria, at the other end of the Roman empire, doing here in the first place? Remarkably, we can actually answer those questions, at least in part.

Not just that, but the two inscriptions also offer something else. Using only a few precise words, they give us two different interpretations of the word 'freedom', of what it means to be free.

Tyne and Tigris

The story begins more than two thousand years ago, when Celtic-speaking British peasants inhabited the South Shields area. They lived in roundhouses thatched with heather and bracken, grew wheat and barley, and gathered nuts and berries. When the Roman army arrived, it easily overpowered the native people, and built barracks and enormous stone gates where the old farmsteads had been.

The Romans called their new fort 'Arbeia'. The name may be rooted in the Aramaic word *arbaya*, or *arabaya*, meaning 'Arab'. It was used to refer to parts of the Near and Middle East, as well as to the people who lived there.[5]

As odd as it may seem to call a northern English outpost the 'Arab Fort', there would have been a good reason: an Arab garrison was stationed there. Known as the Numerus Barcariorum Tigrisiensium, it consisted of men recruited by the Roman army along the banks of the Tigris river, in modern-day northern Iraq.

It's mind-boggling to picture the long and arduous journey these men made, and imagine their feelings as they disembarked at the chilly, rainswept harbour. Even more mind-boggling is the fact that many more people made this journey, not just soldiers, but also traders and craftspeople. In the *vicus*, the civilian settlement that sprang up around the fort at South Shields, a multicultural, multilingual community supplied and served the Roman army. They carried out repairs, imported foreign goods, and made jewellery and furniture for the higher-ranked military men and bridles for the horses. It was a lively, active place. Clay tiles have been found on this site bearing the paw prints of a dog and the print of a soldier's hobnailed boot. Metal bits and ornaments from cavalry horses were dug out of the clay, as was jewellery made of shiny black jet, and lots of coins.

Sometime in the second century CE, a Palmyrene man called Barates arrived at South Shields. Palmyra had been occupied by the Romans. It was a caravan city, made rich by passing merchants who paid a fee in return for some protection from bandits and the right to let their camels graze and rest. The Palmyrene merchants did not just sit there and collect taxes, either. Some travelled very widely, by land and sea, as far as north-west India, where they bought even more exotic goods, such as silk from China.[6]

At the time, the caravan trade was booming. Camels had replaced the donkeys of Sumerian and Akkadian times. Traders, accountants and religious leaders scribbled and chatted in Aramaic. Caravanserais sprang up, specialized inns for merchants with extra parking facilities for their camels. Some of them were beautiful and luxurious, with shaded courtyards, baths and their own bread ovens. The vast Roman empire fuelled demand for expensive goods, especially fragrant resins, plants and oils for their religious rituals and beloved bathhouses. This region would come to be associated with fragrances for centuries: Shakespeare's Lady Macbeth laments that all the perfumes of Arabia will not cover the smell of blood on her hands.

Exotic ingredients became so popular with the Romans that in the second century BCE, a Roman playwright called Plautus composed a satirical play featuring made-up spice names. 'Do you use divine seasonings, by which you can prolong the life of men?' one character asks a cook. The cook replies that yes, definitely, those who eat his food will live for two hundred years, thanks to the amazing power of (fictional) seasonings such as cepolindrum, hapalopsis and cataractria.[7]

The trade in such luxury goods brought tremendous wealth to some cities, all of which offered similar package deals: pay us money, refresh your camels, enjoy a meal and a good night's sleep at a caravanserai.[8] Incense was transported through Petra, the capital of the Nabataeans (who also spoke an Aramaic dialect). They eventually produced perfumed oils themselves, and reaped an even bigger slice of the profits.

Palmyra experienced a similar transformation. Once a quiet backwater, it flourished commercially under the Romans, expanded into a short-lived empire of its own under Queen Zenobia, and fell into obscurity again after the Romans razed it in 273 CE. But for a brief period, just three centuries or so, it twirled in the limelight, a glittering, nouveau-riche city with plenty of money to spend.[9]

While Petra spent its money on monumental buildings carved into rock faces, Palmyra developed another speciality. Its inhabitants had a soft spot for beautifully crafted, lovingly detailed tombstones.

Families in the afterlife

Palmyrene tombstones are all about the family. Not only do many of them show extended families, they also celebrate ties that are sometimes overlooked by other cultures, such as relationships between cousins, great-uncles, nephews and nieces. The departed of Palmyra were not shy about showing their affection for one another. On one tombstone, a mother puts her arm around the shoulders of her grown-up son.[10] On another, a nephew rests his hand on the shoulder of his uncle.[11] A wife places her hand on her husband's elbow, a father puts his arm around his daughter, a brother embraces his sister. Small children are held by their mothers, or hover behind the shoulders of older relatives. Some of them reach for their parents or siblings. Sibling ties clearly mattered: one stone was put up by a woman, Shagal, for her sister, Martay.[12]

These portraits were all carved in a similar style, with the deceased men or women dressed in flowing garments, sitting or reclining. The women were shown holding a jewellery box, a basket of wool, or both. The earliest of these stones dates from around 65 CE, and was put up for a woman by her surviving husband, another Barate. The name means 'son of Ate' (*bar* is Palmyrene for 'son'; Ate was a deity).[13]

Palmyrene widowers also marked their grief with slabs of stone.

A man called Shuraiku put up a stone for Martay, his late wife. Sewira mourned his beloved Shallum.[14] Some stones were inscribed in two or more languages: Palmyrene, Greek and Latin, reflecting different layers of foreign occupation, along with the resilient native tongue.

The stone commissioned by Barates, the Palmyrene migrant in South Shields, is often seen as odd and exotic. It's in the Palmyrene style, it marks a mixed marriage, it's a bilingual outcry by a lonely, stranded widower. But in Barates' home town, it was clearly not all that unusual for widowers to express their sadness and loss that way. Nor were bilingual tombstones uncommon. Apart from the ones in Palmyra itself, the curved Palmyrene letters popped up in inscriptions all over the Roman empire, in Hungary, Romania, Algeria, and in Rome itself. What was it about their script that the people of Palmyra found so appealing?

Palmyrenes in Europe

Palmyrene workers and soldiers helped prop up the Roman empire. In Rome, Palmyrene labourers stacked warehouses, and formed an expat community in the neighbourhood of Trastevere. Palmyrene soldiers served with the Romans in Hungary, Algeria and Romania. They carved their cursive script in stone, even in places where hardly anyone could read Palmyrene, often alongside Latin.

This insistence on writing their own language set them apart from other foreigners. Bilingual inscriptions as such were not uncommon in the Roman empire, as we've seen in the case of Oscan. But when a foreign man serving in the Roman army died, he was usually just honoured with a Latin tombstone.

At South Shields, for example, there is a tombstone for Victor, a freed slave from North Africa, put up by Numerianus, a trooper of a cavalry regiment from Asturia, Spain. Numerianus was clearly deeply attached to Victor, and, according to the Latin text, 'most devotedly conducted him to the tomb'.[15] But whatever mother tongues Numerianus and Victor spoke in addition to their army-Latin – ancient Berber and Iberian languages, perhaps – did not make it onto the stone.

By contrast, Palmyrene-inscribed tombstones have been found all over the old Roman empire. They were put up by grieving survivors in Rome, Hungary, Algeria, Romania and, indeed, in South Shields.[16] What was so special about Palmyrene? What did it give those men, that they could not get from a Latin inscription?

We can only speculate, of course, but one element might be emotional. Latin funerary inscriptions are rather dry, stating the deceased's name, rank and age in a formulaic way. Palmyrene inscriptions, on the other hand, are more emotive. They typically end with the word 'HBL', an expression of grief, like 'alas'. Mournful HBLs have survived on various scattered Palmyrene tombs of the Roman empire, like little gestures of comfort. Barates may have wanted to mourn his wife in a language that was familiar and emotionally meaningful for him, while also following the standard Latin convention. So he chose both the script of his old home and that of the Roman empire where he'd made his fortune.

The Classicist J. N. Adams suggests that Barates used 'his native language for himself alone, as it were, at an intimate moment'. It was perhaps also a way of marking his identity: 'In the Latin text he declares himself to be Palmyrenus, and the ethnic pride conveyed by the word is reinforced by the presence of the (...) Palmyrene text.' The Victorians who excavated the stone appeared to feel an affinity with that kind of nostalgic bilingualism, and were familiar with the concept of being dispatched to the furthest reaches of an empire. A passage in a collection of clippings and reports on the Regina Stone compiled by Robert Blair, a Victorian solicitor and antiquarian, reads like a sigh of sympathy for Barates: 'There is something natural in a stranger, far from home, wishing to inscribe on the tomb, that hides from him the object of his fondest affections, some memorial of his boyish days when he was a stranger to sorrow.'

So much for Barates. What about Regina? From the inscription we learn that she was from a southern Celtic tribe, and had been a slave. Possibly, Barates himself bought her, then set her free and married her. In the Latin text, she is a *liberta*, a freedwoman. In the Palmyrene, she is a *BT HRY*. The Victorian scholars who originally translated the words on the stone were not quite sure what this meant. Eventually, they guessed its meaning from the context. 'I suppose that BT HRY is the equivalent of liberta, and translate: – Regina, freedwoman of Bar'ate. Alas!' wrote Professor William Wright, an orientalist at the University of Cambridge in early November 1878.[17] This is an admirable translation, especially given the speed with which it was produced. But it also misses certain nuances of *BT HRY*, this old expression that challenges us to think about what it really means to be free.

Children of freedom

Liberta, in Latin, is the feminine form of 'freed'. The Palmyrene *BT HRY* is a slightly more complex term. *BT*, read as 'bat', is Aramaic for 'daughter'. It's a well-known word in Jewish custom, and, for example, makes an appearance in *bat mitzvah*, the female equivalent of *bar mitzvah* (a coming-of-age ritual, in which children turn into daughters and sons of the commandments, meaning they become responsible for fulfilling certain religious duties).

HRY is a little harder to unravel. It is likely to mean 'freedom', as it shares a root with the Aramaic word for freedom, *herut*.[18] In ancient times, a *bat horin*, literally 'daughter of freedom', was a freed slave. There were two ways for a master to set free an enslaved woman.

One was to say out loud: '*harei at le-atzmekh*' – 'you are hereby your own'. The other was to say: '*harei at bat horin*' – 'you are hereby a free woman.'[19]

That these two phrases were treated as somewhat interchangeable implies that they both expressed the same basic idea. They turned the slave into a free person, someone who was in charge of her own decisions and future.

The Latin *liberta*, on the other hand, has a slightly different meaning. It is the passive, feminine form of *liberare*, to free someone. A *liberta* is not quite a free woman, but a freedwoman. Her new title carries within it the will of her master. It focuses on someone else's action, on someone else's decision to lift the bond. While it may seem like a mere grammatical detail, this difference had big consequences in the real world.

In Jewish tradition, the exodus from Egypt is celebrated with the famous phrase '*Avadim hayinu, ata b'nei horin*', 'Once we were slaves, now we are free people'. *B'nei horin*, also spelled as *b'nei khorin* or *b'nei chorin*, literally means 'children of freedom', just as *bat horin* literally means daughter of freedom. The phrase is recited at the Passover Seder, as part of the retelling of the liberation story. It's seen as an expression of positive freedom, the freedom to do something, to actively go forth, rather than just the negative freedom of losing one's constraint, one's shackles.

The words '*ata b'nei horin*', now we are free, have spread beyond the Jewish community, and have even rung through the White House. Throughout his presidency, President Barack Obama hosted an annual White House Seder along with the traditional blessings and readings, honouring the liberation story as a direct inspiration to the American civil rights movement.[20]

Through Arabic, the HRY-root has entered a range of other languages. In Swahili, *huru* means free, and also refers to a former slave, while *uhuru* means freedom. It's also the first name of Kenya's current president, Uhuru Muigai Kenyatta, whose father fought in Kenya's liberation struggle and became the country's founding president.[21]

From Swahili, this ancient word made yet another surprising leap. It was the title of a bestselling novel in the 1960s, *Uhuru* by Robert Ruark, about Kenya's fight for independence. The American actress Nichelle Nichols was reading this novel when auditioning for a role in *Star Trek*. Gene Roddenberry, the show's creator, was still trying to find a name and backstory for her character, and she loaned him Ruark's book. He told her he liked the meaning and origin of 'Uhuru', and she suggested changing the last letter to 'a', to soften the sound. Roddenberry was delighted, and replied: 'That's it, that's your name.' With that, the Enterprise welcomed Lieutenant Uhura from the United States of Africa on board. In one episode, another character remarks: 'Uhura, whose name means freedom...'[22]

I spent a long time looking at the Latin and Palmyrene letters on the Regina stone, imagining the hand that carved them. I noticed that the fluid spirit of Palmyra had seeped into the austere Latin script: the 'L' letters were gently arched at the bottom, and looked a little Near Eastern. From *BT HRY* to 'now we are free people', to the White House, to *Star Trek*, the Palmyrene footnote at the bottom of the stone connects many different eras and many different lives. But ultimately, it is about two people, Barates and Regina. Was Barates trying to make a point when he chose to remember Regina in two languages, as a freedwoman and a free woman? What did freedom mean to him, and to her?

I took the train back to London later that day, past autumn forests glowing red and orange, leaving behind the windswept remains of the Roman fort.

'Well languaged': The British Art of Language-Learning

In the late sixteenth century, an English traveller described an acquaintance as 'a man well travelled and well languaged'.[1] The first expression, well travelled, is still commonly used today to describe someone who's seen the world. But what happened to the second part, 'well languaged', used for someone who was eloquent in their own language as well as others?

Somehow, the idea of English-speakers as keen linguists seems to have been lost, even though the English language is the product of so many foreign influences. Britain's history is profoundly multilingual, with translation, language contact and language-learning playing an important role in many of its pivotal events. When William the Conqueror compiled the Domesday Book, a survey of the territory he'd just occupied, he hired eleven interpreters to navigate the many languages on the ground.

In recent years, scholars have tackled that multilingual history with energy and enthusiasm, drawing our attention to British innovations and experiments with languages that were previously ignored. They've also firmly reminded us that how we see the past shapes the present.

As the historian Elizabeth Tyler points out, the rise of English to the world's lingua franca has allowed English-speakers not to learn new languages. Foreign language skills in Britain are among the lowest in Europe, and 'the English education system has increasingly turned away from the learning of foreign languages', except in the private sector.[2] (Note that Scotland pursues a much more pro-languages policy.) As a result, paradoxically, 'individual non-immigrant English men and women become more monolingual as the world they live and work in becomes more multilingual'.[3] There are also ideological reasons for this shift. Historians and scholars of English literature were long influenced by nineteenth-century nationalism, and the idea that a country should have only one language.

Tyler and her colleagues offer a more inclusive and generous view of the British Isles as a place where languages have long mingled in fruitful and fascinating ways. This chapter doesn't intend to recount the history of the British Isles through languages, but instead focuses on moments of contact, learning and exchange. We know that different languages arrived here at different times, and that Irish, Welsh, Scottish and English people also took their own languages abroad. What did these linguistic waves feel like for the people who lived through them? How did they experience the arrival of new languages, how did they learn them, and what happened when they took their own languages and scripts out into the world?

Whale-road and bone-house

We can pick up where we left off, with Barates and Regina at South Shields. The native islanders spoke Celtic languages, commonly divided into two subgroups, Gaelic (the ancestor of Irish, Scottish Gaelic and Manx) and British (the ancestor of Welsh, Breton and Cornish). They mingled with people who brought their own languages from afar, as in the case of Barates. Further north, in Scotland, lived the Picts, who spoke a now extinct language called Pictish.

In the dying days of the Roman empire, Germanic tribes such

as the Angles, Saxons and Friesians arrived and settled in England. They are collectively referred to as the Anglo-Saxons, and called their language '*englisc*'.[4] Today that early form of English is known as Anglo-Saxon, or Old English. From the ninth century, Old Norse, a North Germanic language, arrived with the Viking invasions, which had started as hit-and-run raids but led to a more permanent presence. In the eleventh century, William the Conqueror brought Norman French, which became the prestigious language of the royal court and the Anglo-Norman aristocracy, and again transformed the English language.

Whenever I come across Old English documents from before and shortly after the Norman Conquest, I am struck by how intuitively familiar the language feels to me as a German-speaker. I don't mean that they are instantly comprehensible; after all, a thousand years have passed since they were written. But some of the vocabulary, and particularly the sentence structure, stirs a sense of linguistic kinship in me, more so than modern English.

This Germanic influence still shimmers through in countless English words that have German roots. They sometimes pop up in surprising circumstances. Two Scottish friends, Jonathan and Peter, were having lunch at our house and overheard me ask my son for a *Schere*, a pair of scissors. Peter remarked that his granny used the same word for scissors, 'shears'. In England, 'shears' are now used for sheep, and the fancier French-rooted 'scissors' (similar to the modern French *ciseaux*) are used to cut paper. The farm-to-house transformation from rustic German to refined French is common in English. Once animals leave the farm and enter the kitchen, for example, they tend to become French. A cow (from Old English *cū*, similar to the modern German *Kuh*) turns into French-rooted beef (from Old French *boef* or *buef*, similar to the modern French *bœuf*) when it's on the plate. A calf in the field (from Old English *cælf*, similar to the modern German *Kalb*) is served up as veal (similar to modern French *veau*).[5] But it appears that at least in parts of Scotland, the 'shears', perhaps from North Germanic, were allowed to stay in the home.

Germanic languages also left a legacy in English literature: kennings. Kennings are compound words, often metaphorical. Two words are put together to create a third.

Modern German is famously full of compound words, many of which have made it into English as loanwords: *Zeitgeist* (the spirit of the times), *Schadenfreude* (literally, 'damage-joy', taking pleasure in someone else's misfortune), and so on. Others are not that widely known, but perhaps should be: *Verschlimmbessern*, to make something worse by trying to make it better (literally, 'worse-bettering').

Old English was equally rich in compound words or kennings. They appear throughout *Beowulf*, the Old English epic poem composed in the late first millennium CE.[6] It was written in England but features a Scandinavian hero, Beowulf, his adventures in southern Sweden and Denmark, and his pursuit of Grendel, a 'grim demon haunting the marshes, marauding round the heath / and the desolate fens'.[7]

The Irish poet Seamus Heaney, who produced a beautiful translation of *Beowulf* into modern English, compared the process to bringing down 'a megalith with a toy hammer'.[8] Among the 'hand-built, rock-sure' words Heaney had to chip away at were Beowulf's many kennings. *Hronrāde* ('whale-road') refers to the sea. Mortal man is a *bānhūs*, bone-house.[9] Some of the best kennings are reserved for evil in its various forms. There is *brimwylf*, a sea-wolf or water monster (*brim* meaning water), and *grundwyrgen*, a monster rising from the depths.[10] A *gyregiest* is a loathsome stranger. Faced with such creatures, what a relief it must have been for Beowulf to have a *goldwine*, a gold-friend or gold-giving friend, meaning a patron or supporter.

Old English poetry also gives us beautiful metaphors for ships, such as *sæ mearh*, 'sea horse', and *hardviggs*, 'hard horse'.[11] A *mere hrægl*, or sea-dress, is a sail. The word 'seafarer', which comes up many times in *Beowulf* and other poems, is still used in modern English. It's almost identical to its modern Swedish cousin, *sjöfarare*, and the modern German *Seefahrer*, and refers to someone who travels (*fahren*) across the sea.

Old English compounds were not just used in poetry, but also in the law. Some Old English legal terms, like *foresteall*, referring to an attempt to obstruct, have survived into modern times. Others have faded, such as *flymenafyrmth*, a ruler's right to harbour fugitives.[12]

Fighting demons, learning Celtic

How did the Anglo-Saxons feel about the native British languages? Very few reports survive of those encounters. In many areas, the native languages were pushed out by or assimilated into Anglo-Saxon, but at least some Anglo-Saxons learned British.

Guthlac was an Anglo-Saxon hermit who lived from around 674 to 715 CE. He made his home in an old burial mound that had been hollowed out by grave robbers.[13] Sometimes his blissful solitude was disturbed by shrieking demons with horse teeth, and at least once by the sound of British.

According to Felix, the monk who chronicled his life, Guthlac was woken from his nap and went outside to see what the noise was about, when 'he recognized the spoken words of the native British troops climbing the roof; for he in the long-gone annals of former times had been an exile among them, so that he was able to make sense of their chattering speech'.[14]

Other early Christians actively promoted language-learning and exchange, arriving from all over Europe and beyond, and setting up monasteries that doubled as language academies.

In the sixth century, Augustine came to England from Rome, along with a delegation of missionaries and an illuminated gospel to show to the illiterate heathens. He converted Aethelbert, king of Kent, and set up a monastery at Canterbury. The king's wife, Bertha, was Frankish, again showing just how many languages were already spoken in Britain.[15]

Canterbury proved a magnet for more languages. Foreign monks brought manuscripts in Greek and Latin, but also eastern languages such as Syriac. In the seventh century, two well-travelled monks, Theodore of Tarsus from southern Anatolia and Hadrian from North Africa, took over at Canterbury. They oversaw a period of flourishing scholarship that made Canterbury famous across the Christian world.[16] The monks did not just carefully copy and translate manuscripts. They also invented codes and shortcuts, and experimented with different ways of communicating.

Monks at Canterbury, who were banned from speaking outside of religious services, developed a sign language. More than a hundred of these signs are described in an eleventh-century Old English manuscript.[17] They range from the universally understood to the somewhat obscure:

Đonne þu sapan abban wille þonne gnid þu þinne handa to gædere
'When you want soap, then rub your hands together.'

Brecena tacen [ms. tancen] is þæt þu strice mid þinum twam handam up on þin þeah
'The sign for underpants is that you stroke with your two hands up your thigh.'

Gif þu ostran habban wylle þonne clæm þu þinne wynstran hand ðam gemete þe þu ostran on handa hæbbe and do mid sexe oððe mid fingre swylce þu ostran scenan wylle

'If you want an oyster, then close your left hand, as if you had an oyster in your hand, and make with a knife or with your fingers as if you were going to open the oyster.'

Ðonne þu pipor habban wille þonne cwoca þu mid þynum scyte finger ofer oþerne
'When you want pepper, then knock with one index finger on the other.'

Travelling runes

Many monks escaped their cloistered walls and spread their native tongues throughout Europe. In the first millennium, Irish and English missionaries travelled to the continent to convert pagan tribes. They founded monasteries in France, the Low Countries, Germany, Switzerland and Northern Italy. Among them were St Gall, Fulda, Bobbio, Auxerres and Utrecht, monasteries that continued to attract Irish and English monks along with their skills and scholarship.[18]

Multilingual teams of monks collaborated in these monasteries, swapping and copying manuscripts and experimenting with new writing styles. English monks and nuns on the continent created a lasting intellectual legacy. Hygeburg, an eighth-century Anglo-Saxon nun at the German monastery of Heidenheim, wrote two biographies in Latin. The *Oxford Dictionary of National Biography* describes her as the first Englishwoman to have written a full-length literary work.

Scripts circulated as part of this linguistic exchange. The Germanic tribes brought runic writing to England, known as 'futhark' from the first six letters of the Runic alphabet, which are read as f, u, th (written as þ), a, r and k.[19] Old Norse was also written in runes. The runes used to write the initials of Harald Bluetooth, a first-millennium king of Denmark, today form the basis of the logo of Bluetooth wireless technology.

Later, runes and Latin letters appeared side by side in the same text, and different languages were mixed on the page. An example is the th-rune (þ) in the Old English hand sign list mentioned earlier, and the Latin-derived word *pipor* (pepper) in the same list. A ring from the ninth century, found in Lancashire, features an inscription in runes and Latin letters: '*Ædred mec ah Eanred mec agrof*', 'Aedred owns me; Eanred engraved me'.[20]

A whalebone casket from the early eighth century, found in France, is engraved all over with runes and a Latin-based script developed on the British Isles. The carvings feature scenes from Roman, Jewish, Christian and Germanic myths, and the text is in Old English and Latin.[21]

In Ireland, monks used the Latin alphabet to copy sacred texts. They developed a second script, known as 'insular minuscule', for more casual, day-to-day letters and lists.[22] Irish monks introduced insular minuscule to England, and it spread to the continent.

In the late eighth century, an English monk, Alcuin of York, helped continental Europeans develop their own standard script, known as Carolingian minuscule. It was adopted widely in the monasteries of Europe and made it possible for knowledge to be shared more easily.[23]

Royal family ties formed a web of languages. In 1080, a Flemish monk wrote somewhat mournfully that 'the daughters of kings and princes... marry into foreign nations and far-away kingdoms. They are destined to learn barbarous customs and strange languages'.[24]

English kings married Flemish and Frankish princesses, who brought their mother tongues with them. As Elizabeth Tyler writes in her study of foreign women at English courts, 'virtually all royal women in eleventh-century England were multilingual'.[25]

Foreign-born kings also brought their languages to England. The

Danish king Canute employed a circle of Old Norse poets. Bruce O'Brien argues that during the late first and early second millennia, 'the English were always translating'.[26] English, Welsh, Scandinavian languages, Scots and Norman were spoken at royal courts, and mingled with the clergy's Latin, Greek, Hebrew, Aramaic and Arabic.

The troubles of Brother Aethelweard

As multilingual as Britain was both before and after the Norman Conquest of 1066, some people viewed foreign languages with alarm.

In the 1070s, Canterbury was haunted by a terrifying case of linguistic possession. A young English monk called Aethelweard had been living quietly at the monastery when one day, as he attended mass, he was 'fully possessed by a demon'.[27] He was dragged out of the church, tied down, prayed over by monks and the archbishop himself, but nothing helped. When they tried to put him to bed, he screamed blasphemies at his fellow monks.

Then, in a culmination of horrors, Aethelweard, who knew no language other than his own, started speaking French. As the narrator recalls:

> Some of those who were standing nearby and extending their hands to prevent the flight of the enemy remarked among themselves in the French tongue that he was running about like a little cat, but the possessed man, who was totally ignorant of that language, smiled and replied fluently using diminutive forms in the same tongue, 'Not like a kitten, but like a puppy'.[28]

The monks appealed to St Dunstan, who eventually chased the demon out, along with his disturbing fluency in French. Aethelweard sighed in relief: 'The enemy, who was tormenting me, has departed'. His brother monks were profoundly shaken by the event. They saw it as a punishment for having strayed from the path and indulged in the love of gold, silver, musical instruments and expensive clothes, as well as 'horses, dogs and hawks with which they frequently promenaded about'.[29] After Aethelweard's French incident, they gave away their hawks and gold, and returned to a simpler and more devout way of life. They didn't miss their past luxuries, but 'looked back upon those things as if they were excrement'.

William's struggles with English

William the Conqueror gave up on language-learning for a common reason: he felt too old and too busy. According to Orderic Vitalis, a Shropshire monk who wrote a history of the conquest, William was initially keen to learn English, 'so that he could understand the pleas of the conquered people without an interpreter, and benevolently pronounce fair judgements for each one as justice required'.[30] However, 'advancing age prevented him from acquiring such learning, and the distractions of his many duties forced him to give his attention to other things'. This was unfortunate, because it led to a linguistic disaster.

On Christmas Day 1066, English and Norman aristocrats and clergymen gathered at Westminster Abbey for William's coronation, surrounded by a cordon of Norman guards and knights. The English Archbishop Ealdred placed the royal crown on William's head, then asked the English if they would accept him as their king. Geoffrey, the French-speaking bishop of Coutances, asked the Normans the same, in French. In the words of Orderic, 'all of them gladly shouted out with one voice if not in one language that they would'.

The guards, however, were spooked by the 'harsh accents' of English, and thought the native crowd was rising against the occupiers. In the ensuing commotion, the guards set fire to some buildings, which led to general mayhem and looting. Joy turned into terror as 'men and women of every rank and condition rushed out of the church in frantic haste. Only the bishops and a few clergy and monks remained, terrified, in the sanctuary, and with difficulty completed the consecration of the king, who was trembling from head to foot.'[31]

Orderic concluded that 'the English, after hearing of the perpetration of such misdeeds, never again trusted the Normans who seemed to have betrayed them, but nursed their anger and bided their time to take revenge.'[32]

William was not entirely put off languages. In 1085, he commissioned the Domesday survey, a comprehensive overview of the conquered country, its people, and their land holdings. Since William's officials spoke Norman, but the natives spoke English, Cornish, Welsh, Old Norse and various other languages, eleven interpreters were hired to help with the task. The findings were recorded in Latin.[33]

Stephen Baxter, who has analysed the languages of the Domesday book, notes that while the multilingual process may sound confusing and laborious, it had its advantages. The French learned not just details of daily life, but also specific legal terms that only existed in English at the time. It gave them a better grasp of the place they were ruling.[34]

Even as the Anglo-Saxons and then the French gradually edged out the native Celtic languages, there were a few who resisted. In the mid-thirteenth century, the Welsh poet Dafydd Benfras wrote a poem that proudly declares his allegiance to the original voice of Gwynedd, a county in Wales:

Ni wybum erioed medru Saesneg,
Ni wn ymadrawdd o ffrawdd Frrangeg;
Pan geisiais-i esill Enilleg,
Cam oedd, neud ydoedd Wyndodeg!

'I never knew how to speak English
I do not know a word of passionate French;
When I attempted to utter Enilleg (a language, possibly Old Norse),
It was crooked; it was the language of Gwynedd!'[35]

Coffee houses and English puddings

In the centuries that followed, merchants, sailors, spies, diplomats and refugees took over from monks and nuns as language importers and exporters.

John Gallagher paints a vibrant picture of this period in his book, *Learning Languages in Early Modern England*. In the sixteenth to eighteenth centuries, English was a niche language spoken by few outside the island. Anyone venturing abroad had to acquire foreign languages to make themselves understood. English merchants bought textbooks to learn how to haggle over 'Flanders bonelace', 'Romane serges' and 'Hollands linnen' in Flemish.[36] Travellers didn't just prepare for business deals, either. *The Spanish Schoolmaster* by William Stepney, a textbook published in 1591, includes the Spanish for 'he hath gotten her with child at the first copulation with her' and 'she is a proper woman but she hath great buttocks'.[37]

Once on the road, English travellers shared tips for picking up languages. One method was to visit foreign churches and listen to the sermons there, or chat with nuns, because they never tired of talking. When they returned home to England, some travellers continued speaking foreign languages with their English friends, for the sheer enjoyment of it.[38]

In London, a lively community of language-learners congregated in private homes and public spaces. Immigrants eked out a living teaching French and Italian in the coffee houses of Covent Garden and around St Paul's, an area teeming with printers, booksellers and stockbrokers.

In 1707, an Italian gentlewoman advertised classes 'at Mrs Guedon's in St Andrew's Street, by the Seven Dyals, and the Sign of the Barbers Pole'.[39] In 1711, a French gentleman offered free public classes at the Blue-Coat coffee house near the Royal Exchange, apparently as a promotion for paid private tuition. One Italian teacher alternated between coffee houses near the Royal Exchange and Charing Cross, serving the commercial and literary communities. Bathsua Makin, a seventeenth-century polyglot proficient in Latin, French, Greek, Hebrew, Italian and Spanish, proposed a language academy where anyone could learn to be multilingual like her. A seventeenth-century writer suggested that London functioned as England's third university along with Oxford and Cambridge, because one could study a wealth of subjects and languages there, including Syriac, Arabic, Turkish and Polish. Servants and landladies, the 'invisible educators' of language-learning, passed on their language skills in their interactions with visitors and tourists.

The language exchange went both ways, as newcomers learned how to talk their way through London. French visitors learned to politely reject English food, using this model dialogue from *Nouvelle Méthode Pour Apprendre l'Anglois*, published in 1685:

—What dish is that, madam?

—This is an english pudding. Will you be pleased to tast on't?

—By all means, madam. Truly 'tis not unpleasant. But I fear it is heavy on the stomach.

—Sir, I confess this is a Dish that do's not so presently agree with French Palates. But the generality of them do in time grow in love with it.[40]

My favourite story from Gallagher's book is about Fynes Moryson, an English traveller in Italy, who meets a man who claims to be German. When Moryson tries to speak to him in German, the man quickly says he was actually raised in France, and speaks French. But when Moryson switches to French, it turns out he doesn't speak that, either. Not wanting to torment his new acquaintance, Moryson changes back to Italian, and eventually realizes that the man is an Englishman, like himself. They are both travelling in disguise, as English Protestants on the continent often did. After an initial moment of panic at being found out, the German-French-Englishman is relieved to meet someone from back home, and the two end up sharing a room at the inn.[41]

Some of these well travelled and well languaged people transformed British history. William Caxton, who brought the first printing press to England, spent much of his adult life in the Low Countries, having moved there as a young merchant. Back in London, he set up a printing shop with a Flemish partner, the fittingly named Wynkyn de Worde. Caxton also translated French books into English, but worried that because he was from Kent, his English was 'brode and rude' (broad and rude). He also feared that it might have deteriorated further after thirty years in the Low Countries.[42]

Caxton noted, however, that even the English themselves didn't always understand each other. Once, he observed a northern merchant asking a woman in London for 'egges', eggs (borrowed from Old Norse). The southern woman had no idea what he meant, and thought perhaps he was speaking in French. Another person had to intervene and explain that the merchant meant 'eyren', which was another, Germanic-derived English word for eggs. Caxton pointed out that this posed a dilemma for someone translating a text into English. Which word should they pick: egges or eyren? 'Certainly it is hard to please every man', he concluded.[43]

In Shakespeare's *Henry V*, an entire scene unfolds in (somewhat mangled) French. Henry courts the francophone Katherine, who tries to learn English from her maid, Alice. '*Comment appelez-vous la main en anglais?*' she asks Alice ('How do you say "hand" in English?'). '*La main? Elle est appelée "de hand"*,' Alice replies. A bawdy, comical dialogue unfolds, which hinges on certain English words sounding rude to Katherine's French ears ('foot' is pronounced as '*foutre*', to fuck, and so on).

Later, Henry declares: 'O fair Katherine, if you will love me soundly with your French heart, I will be glad to hear you confess it brokenly with your English tongue.'[44]

In the centuries since then, English has absorbed even more influences, soaking up words and expressions from languages as geographically distant as Hindi, Nahuatl and Swahili. Colonial-era imports such as veranda, shawl and 'pyjammas', defined in an Anglo-Indian dictionary as 'a pair of loose drawers or trousers, tied round the waist', have made it into many other languages.[45]

English has also found new power bases abroad. Today, American English is the most popular form of written English outside the UK, even in European countries that are geographically close to Britain (a more British linguistic influence persists in former colonies such as India, South Africa, Australia and New Zealand).[46] The future of the language may well lie in Asia or Africa, judging by the large, young populations of English speakers in countries such as India and Nigeria, and their enormous impact on music, film and literature.

Global Trade, Global Languages

As the reach of traders and sailors expanded, languages came into contact across vast distances and were irreversibly changed as a result.

In the East, the spice trade had long spun a complex linguistic web. By the fourth century CE, China was importing cardamom from Cambodia and Vietnam, cloves and nutmeg from Indonesia, and a spice called 'long pepper', or *pippali*, from India.[1] Over time, China's trading network expanded, and seafarers found ways to stay healthy over long voyages. In the fourteenth century, Chinese sailors planted herbs and spices such as ginger from South East Asia in wooden troughs on their ships, to prevent scurvy.[2]

During the first millennium, Persian and Arab seafarers brought many enduringly popular spices into circulation, such as cinnamon from Sri Lanka. In the process, they also spread inventions and loanwords related to travelling, navigation and seafaring. The Persians may in fact have taught the art of seafaring to the Arabs. As John Keay notes in *The Spice Route*, Arabic contains many Persian loanwords for nautical terms, such as *bandar* for port, and *shah-bandar* for harbour-master.[3]

A trilingual inscription on a stone slab found at the port of Galle in Sri Lanka survives as a monument to eastern commerce and language exchange. It dates from around 1400, and was carved in China and brought to Sri Lanka as a diplomatic gift. It's inscribed in Chinese, Tamil and Persian, each written in their respective scripts.

In all three texts, China presents offerings of gold, silver, silk, sandalwood and oil, but the recipient differs in each language. In Chinese, the offering is dedicated to Lord Buddha. In Tamil, it's for a local deity identified with Lord Vishnu. The Persian inscription has been damaged, but a remnant mentions 'the light of Islam'.[4]

Through famous European spice ports, such as Venice, flavours from hot countries entered colder climates.

Around 1000 CE, an English document stated that ships arriving in London at Christmas or Easter must pay tax in pepper. By the thirteenth century, a Persian writer observed a startling cosmopolitanism emerging in a city on the Rhine, probably Mainz. 'It is astonishing that although this place is in the Far West, there are spices there which are to be found only in the Far East,' he noted, adding that pepper, ginger, cloves and other spices all appeared there 'in enormous quantities'.[5]

Indonesian spices such as cloves and mace even appear in a fourteenth-century guide to Cuman, a Turkic language, written by German and Italian missionaries in Crimea. The text lists the names of various spices in Latin, Persian and Cuman, such as galangal, a root related to turmeric and ginger, which appears in Cuman as *choligiā*. Alexander West, a philologist specializing in old Indonesian texts, suggests the spices would have travelled by ship to Cairo, and then to Crimea.[6]

Many of the spices bought and sold on such journeys are still in common use, such as pepper and cinnamon. Others have vanished from kitchens and pharmacies, along with their names. Who still uses scammony, quinanth, sinoper, turbith and tabasheer? They appear in an almost three-hundred-strong list of goods and spices by Pegolotti, the fourteenth-century Florentine author of a guide to global markets and trade routes.[7]

*

Black mushrooms and lemongrass

As merchants put down roots far from home, hybrid languages emerged.

The Peranakan communities of Malaysia, Singapore and Indonesia descended from Hokkien-speaking Chinese merchants who settled in South East Asia, brought their dialects and culture with them, and picked up local ways. Many married Malay and Indonesian women.

These mixed families invented a distinct cuisine that combines South East Asian ingredients such as coconut, kaffir lime, galangal and lemongrass with Chinese ones, including black mushrooms, noodles and various soya-bean products.[8] Their architecture, clothes and vibrantly coloured pottery fuse Chinese and South East Asian influences.

Similarly, the Peranakan dialect combines Malay, Hokkien, and loanwords from the Portuguese merchants who also traded in South East Asia ('Peranakan' means 'locally born' in Malay).[9] The dialect is also known as Baba Malay and was originally referred to as 'bazaar Malay', a simplified kind of Malay used for business deals.[10] Over time, Baba Malay evolved into a creative, expressive form of communication that was more than just a sum of its source languages.[11]

The Peranakan communities are a very obvious example of how cuisines and languages circulate via trade and come together to form something new. This process doesn't even have to involve precious and unusual spices. In East Asia and South East Asia, three fairly simple ingredients travelled through different cultures and languages, transformed them in the process, and were also transformed by them. They are soy, rice and fish. Not only did they inspire food traditions as diverse as Chinese, Vietnamese, Japanese and Korean cuisine, they also took on different symbolic meanings and generated different metaphors in each culture that adopted them.

They show the long-lasting impact of trade and exchange, to the point where borrowed ingredients and words are not even thought of as foreign any more, but have become an essential and seemingly age-old part of a language and culture.

The Languages of Soy, Rice and Fish

One of my favourite novels, *Strange Weather in Tokyo* by the Japanese writer Hiromi Kawakami, tells the story of two unlikely lovers. Tsukiko is a woman in her thirties, who feels lonely and adrift. One night, she visits an *izakaya*, a traditional Japanese bar, and bumps into her old teacher, Sensei (meaning 'teacher'). They become friends, and very slowly, over cups of sake and many tofu-based snacks, they fall in love.

The simple story beautifully conveys the passage of time. Tsukiko and Sensei go mushroom picking in the forest with friends from the bar, and make miso soup with fresh mushrooms over a camping burner. As the weather turns colder, they eat *yudofu*, hot tofu served with a dipping sauce of sake, soy sauce and dried fish flakes. When Sensei eventually invites Tsukiko over for dinner, he serves yudofu with cod and wintery chrysanthemum greens. Tsukiko notes that when she makes yudofu, tofu is the only ingredient. Later, she recalls thinking 'that this was how people who didn't know each other developed a familiarity'. By the end, she makes yudofu that way too, with cod and chrysanthemum greens.

Such acute sensitivity to the seasons is a recurring motif in Japanese literature, in Japanese art and cooking, and in the Japanese language. The passing seasons are tied to subtle yet powerful emotions, such as *natsukashii*, a kind of nostalgia, or *mono no aware*, a sense that things are impermanent. What's noticeable in Kawakami's novel is that the endlessly varied and metaphorically charged dishes are all based on the same basic ingredients: fermented soy (tofu, soy sauce, miso), rice (rice and sake, rice wine) and fish (as fish flakes, cod, and other fresh fish). Discreet seasonal accents are added, for example by the cold-weather chrysanthemums.

As their feelings for each other deepen, Tsukiko and Sensei are taken through the year by a succession of dishes that are ultimately variations on a constant theme of soy, rice and fish. This is no accident. Fermented soy, which arrived in Japan from China, plays a central role in its culinary history. Another important cultural lineage emerged out of ceremonies around rice and tea. A third cultural strand could be called 'fish culture', and is tied to Japan's island identity, its long coastlines abundant with seafood, fish and seaweed. These ingredients inspired an intricate culinary culture, and they also profoundly influenced the Japanese language.

The fish paste range

Fish, rice, and different kinds of fermented soya-bean products are the building blocks of Japanese food. The anthropologist Erino Ozeki calls this the 'standard taste' of Japanese cuisine, a kind of sensory baseline created by the deeply savoury combination of dried fish, seaweed and fermented soy produce.[1]

Miso soup, *miso shiru* in Japanese, is a classic example of this. It consists of *dashi*, a broth of kombu (kelp) and dried fish flakes, into which miso, a fermented soya-bean paste, is stirred. Together, these ingredients create the savoury taste known as umami. In Japanese cuisine, dashi is also used to stew vegetables, and added to marinades and dipping sauces along with soy sauce, sake, and so on. Vegan versions of dashi use kelp and dried vegetables to achieve the umami effect.[2] In all these different combinations, the ingredients come together to produce a taste sensation that is greater than their individual flavours. However, they also each have a long and fascinating individual lineage.

Naomichi Ishige, an anthropologist who spent decades researching the food cultures of Japan and its neighbours, defines a region he calls the 'fish paste range'.[3] It includes parts of southern China, Vietnam, Cambodia, Thailand, Laos, Burma, West Malaysia, Japan and south-west Korea, among others.

Fermented fish pastes and fish sauces emerged in these countries as part of rice paddy farming. Fish would swim into flooded rice fields during the rainy season and be trapped by the farmers as the waters receded. This seasonal bounty was then preserved to last until the next season, by adding salt and making it into a fish paste. In countries with long coastlines, fish came from both rice paddies and the sea. It should be noted that west of this fish paste region, in Bangladesh, an extremely vibrant fish culture is reflected in the Bengali language, which has many words for different fish varieties. The writer Ishita Saha lists a delightful and astonishingly varied 'A to Z of Bengali Fish' on her food blog.[4]

The linguist Dan Jurafsky ties these ancient fish cultures to the development of different language groups. The people who first experimented with fermented fish lived in South East Asia and southern China, and spoke Mon-Khmer (which evolved into Vietnamese and Cambodian), Tai-Kadai (which became Thai and Laotian) and Hmong-Mien (which became modern Hmong). According to Jurafsky, traces of these ancient languages survive in some southern Chinese dialects, and in the names of rivers and mountains.[5]

It may appear surprising to mention Japan, a country that famously closed itself off to the world for 200 years, in the context of trade and exchange. But Japan was very much part of this shared fish culture, and later imported other foods and techniques, such as tofu, from China (and indeed borrowed the Chinese writing system).

In Japan, the earliest records of fermented fish paste survive in the form of wooden labels that were attached to goods paid as tax. They date from around 700 CE, and one of them refers to salt-fermented fish.[6] *Shiokara*, a paste made from marine animals such as squid, still exists as a snack in Japan. There were also other methods for preserving fish. *Narezushi* is fish fermented with salt and rice. Instead of dissolving into a paste, it retains its texture and takes on a faintly sour taste as lactic acid forms.

From the fifteenth century, more lightly fermented versions of *narezushi* appeared, which became known as *sushi*. Today, sushi refers to slices of raw fish served on vinegared rice. As Ishige says, a hint of the original fermented taste lives on in this slight sourness.[7] Some types of sushi also still feature preserved fish, such as *shime saba*, cured mackerel. *Nigiri-zushi* refers to a slice of fish on vinegared rice; *sashimi*, to slices of raw fish dipped in soy sauce and wasabi; and *maki*, to seaweed rolled around rice with fish or vegetables in the middle.

The modern style of serving sushi harks back to the nineteenth century, when Tokyo was known as 'Edo'. It's here that sushi meets a particular style of living, and talking. The 'Edokko', 'child of Edo', as the residents of Tokyo were known, had a reputation for being boisterous, loud, and dynamic. This spirit was best captured by the go-getting merchants, craftsmen, entertainers and workers in the city's bustling commercial district, the *shitamachi*, or downtown area. Food vendors wandered the streets with wooden containers on their shoulders, loudly advertising their wares. Snack bars served sushi or noodles. The hectic, high-energy atmosphere of the *shitamachi* is captured in many vibrant woodblock prints from that era.

In other parts of Japan, diners were used to softer, gentler tones. But the vibrant, enthusiastic Edokko style of serving sushi caught on, and is associated with sushi to this day. Naomichi Ishige highlights how modern sushi chefs still honour that Edokko heritage every time they shout a loud welcome when a new customer comes in. They wear workmen's coats, and worker-style twisted towels around their heads.[8] He describes it as 'one of the last occupations that still maintains the proud manliness of the Edo workman'.[9] Sushi-shop slang is part of this performance. Sushi chefs use specific words for common ingredients, for example referring to soy sauce, shoyu in Japanese, as *murasaki* (literally, 'purple').

Despite this boisterous atmosphere, sushi restaurants still have certain ways of doing things, and this includes how the food is eaten. To name just one simple but surprisingly tricky custom, when one eats a piece of fish on rice, one is supposed to turn it before dipping it, so that the fish touches the soy sauce, but the rice doesn't. I learned this when living in Japan, but can't say I mastered it. Ishige says it's perfectly acceptable to avoid this problem by using your fingers. I've heard this advice, too, but haven't had the courage to try it out in public.

Fish was not just served on its own, but also combined with other ingredients to create an underlying, satisfying taste. From the eighth century, Japanese records mention an early form of dashi, made by boiling dried fish to produce a liquid seasoning. Kombu is also first mentioned around that time, as a nutritious supplement for the vegetarian diets of Buddhist monks.[10] Rather than masking other elements of the meal, especially vegetables, dashi draws out and accentuates their flavours. That's because kombu is rich in natural glutamates, which enhance flavours.

Rice has already been mentioned as deeply intertwined with this fish culture, as a fermentation device, and in the form of rice paddies where fish can breed. It is also revered in its own right, as a symbol of food as such. In Chinese, *chi fan* means 'to eat rice', but also 'to eat' in a more general sense. Similarly, in Japanese, *gohan* means 'rice', but also 'meal'. In Korean, *bap* means 'rice', and also 'food' or 'meal' (of any kind).

Soy originated in China. The most famous soy product is probably tofu, *dòu fu* in Chinese. The nutritious and adaptable blocks of fermented soy can be added to soups, stews, stir-fries, or even eaten cold. Tofu was especially popular with Buddhist monks looking for a protein-rich alternative to meat, and spread widely throughout the region. In English, tofu is sometimes referred to as bean curd, but in most countries around China, people just borrowed the Chinese name. Japanese, Korean, Vietnamese, Nepalese, Tibetan, Burmese, Mongolian, Khmer and Thai all use the word tofu, adapted to their native sounds.

A monk sips morning tea

In Japan, fish, soy and rice are embedded in a culture that values a certain aesthetic. This includes, for example, an appreciation of imperfect, impermanent beauty. A keen sense of the passage of time, reflected by changes in the landscape and in the lives of plants and animals, is part of this sensibility.

According to Ishige, this aesthetic evolved together with the tea ceremony, which evolved from lively tea parties in the fourteenth and fifteenth centuries to a calmer and more refined style. This newer ceremony valued reflection, spirituality and simplicity, and an awareness of natural beauty, conveyed by carefully chosen and arranged flowers, scrolls, pottery and laquerware. A haiku by the seventeenth-century poet Matsuo Bashō captures the spirit:[11]

A monk sips morning tea,
it's quiet,
the chrysanthemum's flowering.

As in *Strange Weather in Tokyo*, the chrysanthemum doubles as a metaphor for late autumn and winter. Such season words, called *kigo* in Japanese, are an essential part of the haiku tradition. They evoke a specific time and place, but also a feeling of transience. Chrysanthemum, *kiku* in Japanese, is always associated with the cold season. *Hana*, blossom (in the context of haiku, cherry blossom), conjures up spring.[12]

Of course, there is always a danger of tipping into cliché when talking about the nuances of Japanese culture, of painting a fantasy world where everyone recites haiku under the falling cherry blossoms, while eating their seasonally appropriate meal from a lacquer box. It helps to remember that this love of detail and nuance can also be deployed for comical effect, to entertain, and to enjoy the lighter side of life. Here's another chrysanthemum haiku by Bashō, which appears to be gently poking fun at the whole idea of standardized seasonal words:[13]

> When the winter chrysanthemums go,
> there's nothing to write about
> but radishes.

The Japanese way of living with the seasons can be very addictive. I was talking about this to Ann Tashi Slater, an American author and long-time Tokyo resident. We both felt that being exposed to this sort of seasonal awareness had changed us, and sensitized us to certain things. Once a language gives you a word for something, you can't help but notice it more in your own environment. Ann has explored that process in an essay for *Catapult*, an online literary magazine. She wrote it during *tsuyu*, the summer rainy season:

> Tsuyu' means 'plum rain,' because now is when plums ripen on the branch. Before I came to Japan, I thought rain was just rain. I've since learned there's shito-shito ame, a light, quiet rain—not to be

confused with shobo-shobo, also a light, quiet rain, but in a slightly negative sense. Zaa-zaa is a torrential downpour, potsu-potsu is scattered drops when it's starting to rain, and bota-bota is heavy drops as rain begins to fall.[14]

Such finely graded lists have a revered history in Japanese literature. Their most famous appearance is in *The Pillow Book*, written by a courtly lady called Sei Shōnagon about a thousand years ago. Each of her list entries snatches a moment, a feeling or observation, just before it vanishes. Here are 'things that make one's heart beat faster':

Sparrows feeding their young. To pass a place where babies are playing. To sleep in a room where some fine incense has been burnt. To notice that one's elegant Chinese mirror has become a little cloudy. To see a gentleman stop his carriage before one's gate and instruct his attendants to announce his arrival.

Japanese word lists aren't just the preserve of the lyrical and beautiful. Ishige, for example, mentions a tongue-in-cheek list of words that describe chopstick-related blunders. There's *nigiri-bashi*, 'clutched chopsticks': grabbing both chopsticks together, as if wielding a knife. *Sashi-bashi*, 'piercing chopsticks': stabbing food with your chopstick to pick it up. *Kaki-bashi*, 'raking chopsticks': bringing the bowl to your mouth and using the chopsticks to rake in food. *Kami-bashi*, 'chewed chopsticks': biting your chopsticks. *Yose-bashi*, 'dragging chopsticks': using your chopsticks to drag a bowl towards you. *Mayoi-bashi*, 'hesitating chopsticks': hovering over shared dishes with your chopstick as you decide what to eat. And *namida-bashi*, 'crying chopsticks', which Ishige defines as 'allowing soup to drip like tears from the tips of chopsticks'.

This list should probably be treated with some caution, as enjoyable wordplay, rather than the chopstick equivalent of the Code of

Hammurabi. Some of the infractions described, such as stabbing your food, really are frowned upon, not only in Japan but also in other cultures that use chopsticks. On the other hand, I haven't ever actually seen any adult chew their chopsticks or wield them like a knife.

There are Japanese words that capture a certain experience or feeling so perfectly, so poignantly, that you can't let go of them.

More than a decade ago, I learned three expressions from Elizabeth Andoh, a food writer and expert on Japanese food. Elizabeth is American, but has lived in Japan almost all her life. We were preparing a spring-themed picnic, featuring preserved cherry blossoms. While explaining different seasonal ingredients, she mentioned that you could use them in three ways: slightly before their actual season, as a kind of sensory anticipation; at their peak; or slightly after the season, as a lingering farewell. In Japanese, these three moments are captured by the words *hashiri* 走り, literally 'running towards', *shun* 旬 as the 'peak of season', and *nagori* 名残り, 'lingering'.

In *Kansha*, a cookbook inspired by Japan's vegan and vegetarian traditions, Elizabeth Andoh describes how she gradually became more attuned to the seasons. She'd grown up in a big city, and was not used to living by nature's rhythms. Then a Japanese friend introduced her to *hashiri*, *shun* and *nagori*. They transformed her experience of food and nature.

'Hashiri are those eagerly awaited foods you finally find at market: the early spring peas… or autumn's first wild mushrooms,' she explains in *Kansha*. She defines *shun* as 'that magic moment when a food is at its peak of flavor', such as cobs of corn bought from a roadside grill on a hot summer's day, or juicy leeks in winter. Finally, *nagori* is 'culinary regret'. As the weather warms, the street vendors of roasted sweet potatoes pack up their stalls. You might fight the trend, and buy aubergines in late autumn, 'knowing they can't be as tasty as the ones stewed with young ginger during the summer rains'.[15]

It's hard to explain why some concepts stay in your heart. I heard many different expressions while living in Japan, and worked my way through many vocabulary lists, with varying success. But this idea of anticipating a seasonal taste, enjoying it at its best, then stretching out the farewell by enjoying it just one last time, is one that really took root in my imagination. At one point I could no longer remember the words themselves. But the concepts behind them remained so vivid in my memory that I ended up emailing Elizabeth to ask her to remind me of the words.

I encounter *hashiri*, *shun* and *nagori* in many different situations. I may remark to my husband that it's getting cold, and he'll rub his hands and reply that marmalade season can't be far away. This will set off a marmalade craving, and I'll scour the shops for Seville oranges. I'll scoop up a bagful as soon as they arrive, and make a batch that brightens up the winter. However many jars I fill, they'll inevitably be finished by early spring. There may still be some Seville oranges on sale, tempting me. The crocuses are already out, the citrus season is over, it's time to move on... but perhaps I should just make one more batch, enjoy that bittersweet taste one more time, before leaving it behind for another year.

In those moments I think of Japan, and feel a certain kinship and gratitude to the person who shared my predicament, who understood my futile urge to grasp a season and make it last a tiny bit longer, and who put that feeling into words.

*

The taste of resistance

In Vietnam, the culinary history of fish, rice and soy is layered with that of foreign invasions and occupations. The earliest and most enduring foreign influence came from China, which occupied northern Vietnam for much of the first millennium.

Just as Thai borrowed hugely from Indic languages such as Pali and Sanskrit, Vietnamese was significantly shaped by Chinese words and ideas. Even the name Vietnam, which translates as 'Viet of the South', displays this influence. From the third century BCE, the Chinese referred to various tribes living south of the Yangzi river as 'Yue' 越, meaning beyond (in Vietnamese, the word is pronounced as 'Viet').[16] 'Nam' is adapted from the Chinese word for south, *nan* 南.[17] Various Chinese rulers and officials named the emerging entity south of the river as Yue Nan or Nan Yue. Later, they also used the name 'An Nam', meaning something like 'the pacified south' or 'the settled land of the south'.[18] (This is written as 安南 in Chinese, *an* 安 meaning peace; *nan* 南 meaning south.)

For much of their history, the Vietnamese wrote in Chinese characters, both in the classical Chinese script and in a modified Vietnamese version. From the seventeenth century CE, European missionaries spread the Latin alphabet, which was later promoted by French colonizers at the expense of Chinese. Still, the Chinese-Vietnamese fusion persisted in the culture and language. *The Song of Kieu*, a great Vietnamese literary classic from the early nineteenth century, retells the plot of an older Chinese novel with a Vietnamese heroine.[19]

The Chinese introduced many new ingredients to northern Vietnam. Among them were tofu, tea, sesame seeds, wheat noodles and wonton dumplings. They also brought culinary techniques and customs, such as eating with chopsticks. Southern Vietnam, on the other hand, was shaped by ideas and languages arriving from

India and Cambodia, such as Sanskrit and Pali, the languages of Hindu and Buddhist scripture.[20] Arab, Persian and Malay traders also imported exotic flavours and foodways. Southern Vietnamese cuisine reflects this distinct influence, with dishes such as curries based on coconut milk, spiced with cinnamon, anise, clove, ginger, turmeric and ground coriander. Later, in the nineteenth century, French colonization added yet another culinary and linguistic layer.

All these foreign influences, especially Chinese and French, are reflected in the Vietnamese language around food.

The oldest Vietnamese ingredients, including rice and fish, tend to be wrapped in native vocabulary. The Vietnamese words for husked, uncooked rice (*gao*) and rice seedlings (*lúa*), and for fish and fish-related tools and activities, such as fish (*cá*), fishing line (*dây câu*) and fish trap (*bẫy cá*), are probably all native.[21]

Other common ingredients that have been used for centuries still go by names that were loaned from the Chinese. Among them are the words for bean or soya bean (*đậu* in Vietnamese, from the Chinese *dòu*, as in *dòufu*, tofu), pepper (*tiêu*, from the Chinese *jiāo*), sugar (*duòng*, from the Chinese *táng*) and honey or nectar (*mật*, from Chinese *mì*).[22]

In his history of food in Vietnam, Vu Hong Lien notes that wheat-based dishes such as wonton dumplings and stuffed buns are still seen as Chinese food in Vietnam. Sesame oil is also still reserved for Chinese dishes, which are highly prized, but considered distinct from Vietnamese cuisine.[23] Toasted sesame seeds sprinkled on plain boiled rice, on the other hand, became a more integral part of the Vietnamese diet as a staple food for vegetarian monks and nuns in Vietnamese temples.[24]

During the French colonial occupation, Vietnamese people embraced French novelties such as pâté, mayonnaise and baguettes, and combined them with their own ingredients. They adopted French foods such as butter and bread, which in Vietnamese became *bo* (from the French *beurre*; *bo* can also mean beef, from *bœuf*) and *banh* (from *pain*).[25] New vegetables entered Vietnamese kitchens under their modified French names: *cà rôt* (*carotte*, carrot), *cà tô mát* (*tomate*, tomato), *súp lo* (*chou-fleur*, cauliflower).[26] Some were referred to by Chinese-French hybrid names, such as *đậu poa*, pea, based on the Chinese-based word for bean, and the French *petits pois*.[27]

This mixed heritage continues in the domain of popular drinks. The word for tea, *chè*, is derived from the Chinese *chá*, while the word for coffee, *cà phê*, is adapted from the French *café*. The Vietnamese word for wine, *vang*, is based on the French *vin*.[28]

The Vietnamese created native names for many European vegetables by comparing them to known ingredients. This was typically done by adding *tây*, meaning Western or French, to a similar-looking Vietnamese vegetable. Thus the Vietnamese word for potato is *khoai tây*, 'Western taro', khoai being a kind of taro root. My personal favourite is the Vietnamese word for asparagus, *mang tây*. It means 'Western bamboo shoot'.[29]

All these culinary and linguistic strands came together in the Vietnamese struggle for independence. Certain staple foods sustained the Vietnamese resistance, both in nutritional terms and as an expression of resourcefulness and identity.

During the anti-colonial war against the French, Vietnamese fighters developed a guerrilla method of cooking rice, to avoid detection. It involved setting up a stove in a covered hole in the ground, from which long, damp tunnels led the smoke away and cooled it.[30] Vietnamese communists used this system again during the war against the Americans.[31]

Sesame, brought in by Chinese occupiers many centuries before, became another food of resistance. It was added as a nourishing supplement to the communist fighters' rice rations. They used their knowledge of the land to find wild vegetables, such as bamboo shoots.

Meanwhile, the southern Vietnamese troops fighting alongside the Americans faced various dietary difficulties. Their rations consisted of the familiar rice, *nuoc mam* fish sauce and salt, along with tinned meat or fish. Many Vietnamese fighters found the tinned meat unappetizing, skipping it even if it meant a less nourishing diet.[32] The supplies were often disrupted by logistical problems. Buying fresh fruit and vegetables in villages was seen as risky, as civilian informers might see them and tell the guerrilla. (Indeed, Ut Tich, a famous communist fighter, once spotted enemy soldiers as she went to market to buy food for her six children; she told her guerrilla unit, and they successfully ambushed the enemy.[33])

The Americans felt similarly suspicious of Vietnamese food. Not only were Vietnamese and American diets profoundly different, but the language barrier meant the two sides couldn't explain unfamiliar ingredients to each other.

As Michael Morris, a Vietnam war veteran, recalled in a *New York Times* opinion piece: 'One day when I was on patrol, a little girl stopped me and indicated, by sign language, that she needed my help (she spoke no English, and I understood almost no Vietnamese).' The girl gestured towards a mysterious box filled with wet dough, which turned out to be a rice noodle press. Morris helped her make the noodles, but 'had no urge to sample this or any of the other food prepared by the Vietnamese'. He preferred American fare: tinned spaghetti, meatballs and chicken noodle soup. He still shuddered at the memory of the ubiquitous nuoc mam fish sauce, fermenting in open pans on the rooftops of rice paddy farmers: 'Think of the smell of rotten fish, but several orders of magnitude more concentrated and foul.'[34]

In the late 1960s, a US officer decided fish sauce would surely spoil in the heat, and replaced it with soy sauce. Vu Hong Lien described the decision as calamitous, a disaster for the morale of the South Vietnamese troops: 'The canned food made in the USA was alien enough for many south Vietnamese soldiers, but the replacement of the much-loved, traditional nuoc mam with soy sauce was the last straw.'[35]

Vietnam absorbed all these foreign influences, reworked them into native versions, and eventually exported their multi-layered cuisine to the world. *Banh/pain* has boomeranged back to Paris in the form of Banh Mi, a Vietnamese sandwich. *Bo/bœuf* is a classic ingredient in Bo Bun, a popular warm noodle salad served in Vietnamese restaurants in France. It consists of rice noodles, herbs, vegetables and beef or tofu (in Vietnam, this dish is called 'Bun Bo Nam Bo', 'Noodles with beef from the south', a name that combines the French-derived *bo*, beef, and the Chinese-based *nam*, south). Nuoc mam fish sauce is now sold in the US and many other parts of the world, enlivening Vietnamese dishes as well as all sorts of trendy fusion food.

Because of the looping, twisting ways in which food and languages travel, Vietnamese soups and salads can often be found alongside Japanese sushi on the menus of 'pan-Asian' restaurants. Connoisseurs tend to recoil at the pan-Asian concept, at the thought of mashing up such highly distinct cuisines. But in a way, you could say it returns us to the roots, to a rice paddy flooded with fish, the source of so many stories.

Major languages and language groups in Mexico and the Caribbean in the early 1500s

Gulf of Mexico

M E X I C O

N A H U A T L

TOTONACAN

Tenochtitlan

Coatzacoalcos

Putunchan

MIXTEC

MIXE-ZOQUEAN

M A Y A

PACIFIC OCEAN

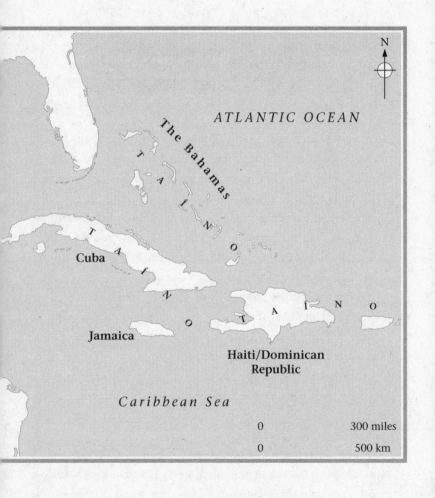

'La Lengua': Interpreters in the Colonial Age

In August 1492, Christopher Columbus set sail from Spain, hoping to find a westwards trading route to Asia. With him were two interpreters, fluent in various European and Middle Eastern languages. Columbus himself, who was originally from Genoa in Italy, also spoke several European languages. Even within Spain, a multitude of languages coexisted, many of them still in use, such as Castilian (Castellano, now treated as standard Spanish), Catalan and Basque, as well as a number of smaller regional languages.[1]

On this particular voyage, those language skills turned out to be useless. Hundreds of languages were spoken on and around the continent that Columbus eventually reached, and not one of them was related to the Indo-European family.

All invaders face a basic linguistic challenge. To capture a new territory, they may only need weapons and ruthlessness. But to capture the inhabitants' accumulated cultural intelligence, they need to understand their language.

From the moment Columbus and his crew first sighted land, at Guanahani in the Bahamas, finding a way into that native wisdom was one of their central missions. They were aware that the people they met did not just have precious raw materials. They also had knowledge. They knew which other communities lived in the area, their habits, and the languages they spoke. They knew safe travelling routes, and the sources of fresh water along the way, and how to process raw ingredients into palatable food.

Gathering, editing and translating this expertise became a central goal for the Spanish, long after Columbus had died and others followed in his wake.

As early as 1503, the Spanish royal court encouraged the Spanish invaders to marry indigenous women, 'so that they may communicate with and teach one another'.[2] Later, the children of mixed couples used their bilingualism as writers and translators. Spanish-Quechua bilinguals wrote histories of the conquest of the Inca empire in Peru, and translated a range of European literature into Quechua. Their Mexican equivalents did the same with Nahuatl.[3]

Eventually, this effort became enormously complex and sophisticated, involving teams of translators versed in several scripts and languages, scribes, editors, and of course, printers, who distributed the resulting texts in Europe.

One particularly influential figure in that process was Bernardino de Sahagún, a Franciscan friar from Spain who learned Nahuatl, one of the main languages of central Mexico. In the late sixteenth century, Sahagún set about collecting proverbs, stories and general musings from Nahua elders. He sent out teams of researchers, who asked the elders to write down their contribution in Nahuatl scripts. Bilingual students then transcribed this into the alphabet. From there, Sahagún translated it all into Spanish.

The result was a sprawling compilation known in English as *General History of the Things of New Spain*. It includes a loose collection of proverbs and metaphors that may have been intended as teaching materials for missionaries learning Nahuatl, based on direct quotes from the elders. Thelma Sullivan, a Nahuatl expert, describes these informal jottings as 'word pictures' that illustrate the life of the Nahuas, as well as their thoughts and feelings.[4]

The work of these later generations of translators and interpreters built on the dictionaries and bilingual texts compiled by earlier ones. But how did the very first Spanish explorers bridge the language gap? How did they do this for languages that had never been in contact before, and were not even linked by a third language?

Linguistic hostages

One quick and brutal strategy was to kidnap people and force them to act as guides and interpreters.

A couple of months after they left Spain, Columbus's crew spotted Guanahani, an island in the Bahamas, inhabited by the Lucayans, or Lucayos in Spanish. A group of unarmed Lucayans appeared on the beach. Columbus went ashore with some of his men, planted a flag in the ground, and declared that they'd taken possession of the island.[5] He noticed that these friendly, unarmed people had a gift for languages: 'I have observed that they soon repeat anything that is said to them... I will bring half a dozen of them back to their Majesties, so that they can learn to speak.'[6] To speak, in this context, obviously meant to speak Spanish. Their own language was Taino, of which different variants were spoken throughout the Caribbean.

Columbus had seven Lucayan men 'brought aboard so that they may learn our language'. The men initially communicated through signs. They also told the Spanish the names of the places around them, including more than a hundred island names.[7]

As Columbus sailed from island to island, he met more indigenous inhabitants, exchanged gifts with them, and noticed that they wore gold bracelets. He asked them where the gold was and showed them some pieces of gold he'd brought along, to make sure they understood the question.[8] The Lucayans continued to explain the area to him through signs, and guided him towards fresh-water sources.[9]

The ships reached Cuba and Haiti, inhabited by more Taino speakers. En route, the Spanish abducted a group of a dozen men, women and children. As they were about to sail away, they were followed by a man whose kidnapped wife and children were on board. He begged to be taken along rather than lose his family, and they promptly took him, too.[10]

From now on, the new encounters featured interpreters: the imprisoned people on board the ships, who quickly picked up some Spanish. As more people appeared on more islands, speaking 'in the proud language common to all the peoples in these regions',[11] they communicated by signs, and also through a few words translated by the kidnapped interpreters. Already, the beginnings of a sophisticated dialogue were starting to emerge, with meaningful gestures, illustrative objects such as lumps of gold, a few words and place names, and some early, basic translations.

Some of the crew stayed on Haiti; the rest returned to Spain, along with a group of captive island interpreters. They were displayed to Isabella and Ferdinand of Spain, along with chilli peppers and sweet potatoes. More voyages followed, with larger fleets, landing on Guadeloupe, Antigua and, eventually, Venezuela, Honduras and Panama. European settlements, or colonies, were established in the wake of the explorers.

For the Taino, the Spanish arrival was disastrous. Almost all of them were eventually killed by European diseases such as smallpox and even the common cold, to which they had no immunity. By about 1600, only a century after Columbus spotted their land, the Taino community had been mostly wiped out. The Taino did not write their language down. The only way to study their culture and belief system is through the artefacts they left, such as human-shaped ceremonial stools, called *duho*.[12] Taino loanwords also continue to be used in many modern languages, including the words barbecue, hurricane, canoe, hammock and tobacco.[13]

A second strategy was to train a Spanish crew member in a local language. Cristóbal Rodríguez, a sailor who accompanied Columbus on his later trips, was the first European to learn a language from the Americas. He acquired Taino on Haiti, by living with native speakers. According to Bartolomé de Las Casas, a sixteenth-century Spanish colonist and historian, Rodríguez was 'nicknamed "la lengua" ("the tongue") because he was the first to know the language of the Indians from this island, and he was a sailor who had spent several years working among the Indians, without talking to any Christians, to learn it'.[14]

Later, conquerors such as Hernán Cortés found shipwrecked Spanish sailors who had been captured by indigenous communities and mastered their languages while living among them.

Doña Marina, chief interpreter

Since many different languages were spoken in and around the Americas, the kidnapping strategy was repeated over and over by Columbus and his successors, such as Hernán Cortés. People were either just bundled onto the ships or handed over by chieftains as part of peace deals.

In one of these peace deals, a chieftain on the coast of Mexico gave twenty women to Cortés and his men. One of them was baptized Marina by the Spanish. Pronounced with her native accent, this became 'Malina'. Later, after her fortunes had changed dramatically, her people turned this into an honorific form: 'Malintzin'. In one of the linguistic boomerang effects that are so common in human history, 'Malintzin' was then heard by Spanish-speakers as 'Malinche'.

Malinche, as she is known to this day, is possibly the most famous interpreter of the conquest era. She helped the Spanish prise open the many, many indigenous languages of Mexico. Her voice mediated between the two most powerful men in her world: Hernán Cortés, who had come to conquer her land, and Moctezuma, the god-like ruler of the feared and mighty Mexica.

Cortés called her 'la lengua', the tongue, the interpreter. And she did have a magical tongue, one that could produce four or five languages. Not just that, but she understood how these languages related to each other, how they could be translated, which additional interpreters were needed to fill the gaps, and how they could be recruited in slightly more diplomatic and skilful ways than kidnapping. She rose to become what the Sumerians would have called *ugula eme-bala*, a chief interpreter.

In Mexican Spanish, Malinche's name is synonymous with selling out, betraying your people and heritage, cosying up to powerful foreigners. However, she's also been defended as someone who just did her best with what she had. After all, many indigenous people translated for the Spanish. In the conquest of Peru, an indigenous man known as Felipillo learned Spanish from the conquerors, and interpreted between them and Atahuallpa, the Inca ruler.[15] Without such mediators, the two sides would have struggled to communicate at all. As one Inca leader told the Spanish: 'it is quite impossible for me to understand your weird language'.[16] (Felipillo's status in Peruvian culture is also conflicted, with some accusing him of treason, and others arguing that he ultimately sided with his people.[17])

In the 1960s and 70s, some Mexican American feminists adopted Malinche as an icon. They dedicated bilingual poems to her, defiantly declaring '*Yo soy la Malinche*', I am Malinche.[18] Loved or loathed, she's been recognized as a crucial figure in the conquest, inspiring countless books, essays and films. And yet the skill that catapulted her into her unlikely role is often strangely ignored: her multilingualism.

Her ability to interpret between languages, which is a second skill in itself, has also often been taken for granted.

A closer look raises many questions. What do we know about the languages Malinche spoke, and how she learned them? What does something that's quickly typed out on a keyboard – 'she interpreted between Cortés and the Mexica' – look like in real life? And how did it feel to navigate such a diverse soundscape, where a single misunderstood word or phrase could lead to death and destruction?

Relatively few details are known from Malinche's life, and there is no direct record of her thoughts. However, we know quite a lot about the languages that shaped her. Among them are different varieties of Nahuatl and Maya, two language families that are deeply intertwined with the culture and history of Mexico before the conquest.

Through these languages, and their broader history, we can at least partly reconstruct how an anonymous girl from a riverside hamlet near the Gulf of Mexico came to be the voice of the Spanish conquerors.

Malinche's Languages

Some time around 1500 CE, a girl was born in a place called Coatzacoalcos, amid a patchwork of cornfields, near a river that led to the Gulf of Mexico. We know little about her early life. Her birth name was never recorded, and many different stories were spun around her origins. We do, however, know which languages were spoken in the different areas where Malinche lived, and which ones she ended up using. We also know the foods, habits and world views that shaped and were shaped by these languages, and which give us at least an indirect insight into Malinche's life and heritage.

Malinche's birthplace was in the land of the Nahuas, different groups who all spoke a form of Nahuatl.[1] Camilla Townsend, who reconstructed her life in her book *Malintzin's Choices*, described it as a neat and ordered landscape, reflecting the Nahua idea that nothing stood alone: 'Four walls enfolded the hearth, and four rooms looked in on the courtyard, just as the sky was divided in four directions. Her own family's cornfields lay between other families' cornfields, and all those cornfields blanketed together, with all their many separate names, made up the lands of the kingdom.'[2]

Nahuatl is the southernmost member of the Uto-Aztecan family, which comprises languages still spoken in indigenous communities as far north as modern Oregon. The Nahua themselves recounted in their histories that they'd originally come from north-west.[3]

Despite their ordered world view, their existence was far from peaceful. Nahua groups such as the Mexica, later known as the Aztecs, subjugated other communities and demanded tributes from them. They ensured each group had a 'Nahuatlato', an interpreter who spoke Nahuatl.[4] These linguistic links would later help the Spanish gain entry into the web of Mexican languages.

Malinche learned several of these languages as a child. In Coatzacoalcos, the lower-ranked families spoke a language called 'Popoluca'. The name is a Nahuatl word for the sound of a boiling thick liquid, such as maize porridge, and is also metaphorically used by the Nahua to mean 'babbling'. Popoluca speakers call their own language Nuntajiyi, 'true speech'. It belongs to the Mixe-Zoquean family, and its speakers had originally arrived from further south.

To the east of Malinche's home lived the Maya, who spoke completely different languages. All of these language families are still active, with about 1.7 million Nahuatl speakers in Mexico, 850,000 Maya speakers (adding to a strong Maya community in Guatemala), and a smaller group of Popoluca speakers, numbering some tens of thousands.[5]

Malinche herself may have been the daughter of a Nahua nobleman and one of his concubines, and is thought to have grown up speaking Popoluca as well as Nahuatl. Her daily life would have revolved around the domestic chores dictated by her environment: fetching water, pounding maize, and making tortillas, called tlaxcalli in Nahuatl.

Tortillas and hummingbirds

Just as the family's life revolved around these basic foods and routines, so did the Nahuatl language. There are many Nahuatl proverbs and riddles featuring plants, animals and different foods. A whole range of human experiences and emotions were expressed through tortilla sayings and tortilla metaphors.[6]

Here is a Nahuatl tortilla riddle: 'What travels along the foothills, making tortillas with its hands? A butterfly.' (Because the butterfly patted its wings together, as if flattening a tortilla.) Another Nahuatl saying warned people not to be childish, like 'a young woman who still carries around her dolls and makes mud tortillas'.[7] A Nahuatl-speaker might complain about his share of a tortilla by saying: 'What you have given me is so small, can a hummingbird see it?', referring to the hummingbird's tiny sips of nectar.[8] A bereaved person might be urged to at least have some tortilla: 'Do not grieve so, do not turn away from the straw base of the jug and the folded tortilla. Take a little, take something. Do not neglect yourself, as your grief may turn into sickness.'[9]

Townsend quotes a Nahuatl song in which a dying baby tells his mother to bury him by the hearth, and weep for him every time she makes a tortilla; but if people ask her why she weeps, she's to tell them: 'Because the firewood is green, and makes me weep with so much smoke.'[10]

An ordered life, then, consisting of the calm routines of tortilla-making and hearth-kindling, and keeping one's emotions in check, except in some very private moments. This calm was often threatened by conflict.

The most powerful of the Nahua groups were the Mexica. Their stronghold was Tenochtitlan, a magnificent city inland of Coatzacoalcos. Mexica merchants came to the coast to buy colourful feathers for their clothes and headdresses, and shells and mother-of-pearl to make into offerings for their gods.[11] In wartime, the Mexicas also procured bloodier tributes: human prisoners of war, who were taken to the top of stone pyramids and sacrificed by having their hearts sliced out of their bodies. There was also the risk of being captured and enslaved.

This was what happened to Malinche, in circumstances that are not entirely clear. She was between the age of eight and twelve when slave traders took her by canoe down the river to the sea, and then east along the coast, to Maya territory. Townsend suggests that her community may have given her to the Mexica as a peace offering to avert war, and Mexica merchants then sold her further east.[12]

The traders took her to a port where enslaved people were sold for cacao beans or textiles, and where different groups came to trade. Malinche was bought by a group of Chontal Maya, who took her to their town of Putunchan on the coast of Tabasco. The Maya are famous for their cultural achievements, and Malinche would have witnessed the luxurious lifestyle of the elite. Wealthy Maya men and women wore intricately crafted gold jewellery. Maya artists and writers carved hieroglyphs into stone, wrote books on bark paper, and created complex calendars with astronomical observations and predictions.[13]

In Putunchan, Malinche learned Chontal Maya as well as a very different variety, Yucatec Maya. She was still only in her teens, but now spoke four languages: Nahuatl, Popoluca, Chontal Maya and Yucatec Maya. And she was learning to understand the cultural differences and similarities between the people who spoke these languages.

Mayan, Nahuatl and Mixe-Zoque were different language groups, but they had been in contact for a long time. Certain foods and practices had wandered from one community to another, spreading loanwords and creating a common cultural repertoire. The most famous of these loanwords is probably cacao, the seeds of the fruit of the cacao tree.

Chocolate cultures

The Olmecs, the earliest recorded civilization in Mesoamerica, already processed and consumed cacao seeds. Cacao residues dating from as early as 1500 BCE were found in jars, bowls and bottles in former Olmec cities.[14] The Olmecs spoke a Mixe-Zoque language, in the same family as Popoluca. They did not write down their word for cacao, but it survived as an Olmec loanword in Mayan, where it was spelled as *kakawa* in Mayan hieroglyphs. Some of these hieroglyphs appear on Mayan bowls with cacao residues, providing material evidence for the linguistic link. The Mayans roasted and ground the cacao beans, mixed them with water and the red achiote flower, and poured the resulting drink into a cup from a height, to create a frothy top. Cacao became a popular drink among the elites all over the region. Nahuatl-speakers adopted it from the Mayans, along with its name, which became *cacaoatl* in Nahuatl.

Each culture integrated cacao into their own rituals and language. After the Spanish conquest, a Nahuatl elder would fondly remember it as *yollotl, extli*, heart and blood. As he recalled: 'These words were said of cacaoatl because in the past it was precious and rare. The common people and the poor did not drink it. For this reason it was said: Heart and blood, worthy of veneration.' Heart and blood refers to the human sacrifices, special occasions when cacao was drunk. It was thought to be intoxicating, and consumed only in small amounts, by rulers, powerful commanders, and great warriors. Some sweetened it with honey, or used naturally mild varieties, while others enjoyed the pure, bitter taste.[15]

The Nahuatl also used the word *chokolatl* to refer to cacao and other hot drinks or broths. In one Nahuatl language, for example, *chokolatl* is a broth made of pork tripe.[16] The word is thought to be derived from *choko*, which may mean something like to beat, or stir; and *a*, meaning water.

Cacao culture, then, gave rise to all sorts of interesting linguistic innovations. It would inspire many more over the centuries that followed, as cacao and chocolate spread around the world, as both loanwords and prized foods.

Malinche would have known the name for cacao in four languages, but, as a slave to the Chontal Maya, probably never had a taste of it at the time.

In 1518, Spanish ships arrived at the coast. On board were several Maya boys and men kidnapped by the Spanish. They told the Chontal that the Spanish were offering gifts, and were looking for food and gold.[17] There were some skirmishes, the Spanish procured the goods they wanted, and eventually withdrew. Some months later, they came back. This time they had a Spanish man with them, Jerónimo de Aguilar, who spoke Yucatec Maya. He was a young shipwreck survivor who'd lived with the Yucatec Maya for eight years, effectively spending his entire twenties with them. He appeared to have developed an affinity with them, for he dressed like them as well as speaking their language.

The Chontal Maya told the Spanish to turn around and leave, and when that wasn't effective, attacked them with arrows.[18] But the Spanish had steel weapons and horses, and their more lethal weapons prevailed. The defeated Chontal Maya offered a tribute: jewellery, carved statues, lizards, four ducks, two sandals with golden soles, cloaks, and twenty young women, for the Spanish to use as they wished. 'Cortés received this present with much joy,' reported Bernal Díaz del Castillo, one of Cortés' men, who later wrote about the conquest.[19]

Malinche was one of these women. Along with the others, she was baptized and given a Spanish name: Marina. In her own accent, she pronounced it Malina. She might have slipped into obscurity, a young woman traded from one man to another, had it not been for her language skills. The multilingual landscape of Malinche's world baffled the Spanish conquerors and gave her the key to help them.

*

'These ones have the gold!'

The two languages that facilitated Malinche's first successes were Nahuatl and Yucatec Mayan. We know this from the Spanish chronicles.

A Mexican TV series from 2018, *Malinche*, recreates a crucial scene beautifully in all the original languages, letting it unfold like a linguistic thriller. Initially, Jerónimo de Aguilar, the shipwreck survivor and former captive of the Maya, acts as Cortés' mouth and ears. He helps him talk to the various Maya groups. But then two messengers approach the Spanish, with gifts of gold. Cortés doesn't understand a word they say. Neither does Aguilar. In the TV series, he explains to Cortés that there are dozens of languages spoken here, and he only knows Mayan. Cortés explodes that he doesn't care about the other languages: *'Estos, estos, estos tienen el oro!'* – 'These ones, these ones, these ones have the gold!'

It's here that Malinche steps into the game. The encounter with the mysterious messengers really happened. Cortés was irritated and frustrated at Aguilar's inability to talk to them. He couldn't even find out who these men were, who sent them, and most importantly, where they got their gold. Then Malinche made it known to Aguilar, in Yucatec Mayan, that she understood the men's language. They were Mexica, and spoke Nahuatl.

One can imagine how this would have instantly transformed Malinche in Cortés' eyes. This girl, given to his men along with food and feathers, knew the language of gold. From then on, he and his men called her Doña Marina. In his memoir, Bernal Díaz del Castillo calls her a *'tan excelente mujer y buena lengua'*,[20] such an excellent woman and good interpreter. At some point, the indigenous people even addressed Cortés as 'Malinche'. Díaz del Castillo speculates that this was because she accompanied him everywhere, and spoke for him.[21] Several times he notes that she was good at negotiating with people, and charmed them with her friendly and winning tone.[22]

Initially, Malinche, Cortés and Aguilar formed a translation chain. Cortés said something to Aguilar in Spanish. Aguilar said it to Malinche in Mayan. Malinche said it to the Mexica in Nahuatl. And back again, from Nahuatl via Mayan to Spanish, to Cortés. Of course, this considerably lengthened and complicated every interaction. Later, Malinche learned Spanish herself, and directly translated for Cortés.

In August 1519, Moctezuma was told by his messengers that a group of strangers riding on giant deer were on their way to his capital, Tenochtitlan. With them was 'a woman from this land, who speaks our Nahuatl tongue. She is called La Malinche, and she is from Teticpac. They found her there on the coast.'

Vanilla voices

Malinche did not just interpret, she also actively sought out and recruited interpreters in languages she did not speak herself. When Cortés and his men were approached by Totonacs, for example, none of Malinche's languages helped. Totonacan is yet another language spoken along the Gulf of Mexico. The Totonacs were the Mexicas' official vanilla suppliers. They'd been cultivating vanilla for a long time and had developed a method for processing the pods to maximize their fragrance. Totonac vanilla was eventually sidelined in favour of cheaper vanilla from Madagascar, but is still highly prized (the name vanilla is thought to be derived from the Spanish *vaina*, meaning scabbard, sheath or pod).[23]

The Mexica liked to add vanilla to their treasured chocolate drink. Nahuatl has its own word for vanilla, *tlilxochitl*, a compound meaning 'black flower'. It wasn't quite a voluntary trade, however.

The Mexica sent tax collectors, who were treated with fear and reverence and served cacao in great quantities, as Bernal Díaz recalled. The Totonac were also expected to hand over people for the Mexica's sacrifices.[24]

The Totonac were quite willing to strike an alliance with Cortés against the Mexica. But they had no shared language to communicate that willingness. Then Malinche found Totonacs who could speak Nahuatl, presumably because of their dealings with the Mexica. Another translation chain was formed, from Spanish to Mayan via Aguilar, to Nahuatl via Malinche, to Totonacan via a Nahuatl-speaking vanilla grower. Through this chain, Cortés found out that the Totonac were tired of having to pay taxes to the Mexica and ready to join forces against them.[25]

The Spanish marched on Moctezuma's capital, burning villages and killing warriors and civilians. Through Malinche and Aguilar, they interrogated captives and negotiated with rulers. In Nahua paintings of the conquest, made on bark paper, Malinche appears next to Cortés, more like a co-ruler than a servant.[26] As they neared Tenochtitlan, they passed increasingly beautiful and dreamlike cities, with lime-glazed stone buildings and pyramids that sparkled in the sun, lush gardens and ornamental ponds, markets offering gold and silver jewellery, colourful parrots, hawks and owls, barbers and pharmacies, all connected by lakes, avenues and canals where people in canoes glided past.[27] Finally, on a wide avenue that led to Tenochtitlan, they were received by nearly a thousand dignitaries, and then by Moctezuma himself.

It is hard to imagine any other circumstances under which Moctezuma would even have heard of Malinche, let alone met her, let alone spoken to her. She'd been an enslaved child, making tortillas for a minor Maya chieftain. In ordinary times, her only view of the great pyramid at Tenochtitlan would have been as a prisoner of war, being readied for human sacrifice.

This was not even the peak of Malinche's power. She would go on to meet Moctezuma several times, translate between him and Cortés, and indeed outlive the ruler of the Mexica. She had a son with Cortés, who was later declared legitimate and taken to Spain; then she married one of Cortés' men, and had a daughter with him. She travelled back to her birth place, and, according to Bernal Díaz del Castillo, met her people and reconciled with them. By the time she died – of a European disease, like so many of her people – she had not only made it through the tumultuous, violent years of the Spanish conquest, but manoeuvred herself into a position where powerful men continued to rely on her. And she did all this while maintaining her cultural identity: she protected herself with a Spanish helmet and armour when necessary, but proudly wore indigenous dress all her life.

I try to picture her, on that avenue in Moctezuma's capital. The Spanish give us their own version of the encounter. Moctezuma walked toward Cortés, supported by two noblemen. Cortés got off his horse and walked towards Moctezuma.[28] As Díaz del Castillo remembered: 'Then Cortés, though the *lengua* doña Marina, told him that his heart was now glad to see this great prince.'[29] Moctezuma responded with similar pleasantries, through Malinche.

It must have been a very strange feeling for this woman from a little coastal town, who had been handed from one man to the next all her life, to suddenly stand between these two powerful men and know that, for this moment at least, until her fortunes changed again, they both depended on her. Without her, they would be completely lost on that avenue, helplessly flailing about in each other's unintelligible sounds.

Translator, Traitor?

The Rosetta Stone has become the ultimate symbol of translation, the human ability to juxtapose languages and transfer meaning from one to the other. Why hasn't the same happened with Malinche? Why aren't there Malinche language schools, Malinche exchange programmes and Malinche space missions?

Somehow, multilingual people aren't treated with the same generosity as multilingual objects. The Rosetta Stone allowed two colonizing forces, France and Britain, to prise open the secrets of ancient Egypt. Malinche did the same for Spain, and the languages of Mexico. And yet one is an object of veneration, while the other has been treated as a symbol of cultural treason. Malinche shares this fate with many other interpreters in history, who found themselves trapped between two sides.

'The concept of the interpreter as traitor is as old as the profession itself,' argues Rachel Mairs in her study of translation and betrayal in Greek and Roman times. She puts this down to the idea of serving two sides, but also to a threat posed by bilingualism itself: 'There is always the potential for a bilingual person to mislead monoglots. Moving between factions, privy to sensitive information, and frequently called upon to pass on unwelcome news, the interpreter is a natural target.'[1]

Mairs gives the example of a Greek interpreter working for the Persians in the fifth century BCE. They sent him to the Athenians, to ask them to surrender. The Athenians were outraged by his service to the enemy. They were particularly aghast that 'he dared to use the Greek language in the command of Barbarians', and promptly executed him.[2]

Other Greek- and Roman-era interpreters were killed not for their language use as such, but for serving the enemy. Mairs compares their mistreatment to the twenty-first-century ordeal of Iraqi interpreters working for British forces in Basra. After the British withdrew, they became targets of brutal and deadly attacks by other Iraqis, who accused them of treason.[3]

Irish interpreters working for the English in sixteenth-century Ireland, known as *truchmen*, found themselves in a similar predicament. As Patricia Palmer notes in her study of the politics of translation during that era, 'the political and military developments that brought New English and native Irish into a closer and increasingly violent proximity also brought two languages into confrontation.'[4] The promotion of English and suppression of Irish became part of the conquest, but in the meantime, the language gap needed to be bridged somehow. Palmer points out that historians often gloss over or ignore this gap, which would have existed in almost every sixteenth-century English-Irish interaction. Misunderstandings and mistakes would have been frequent, with solutions ranging from employing skilled interpreters to resorting to simple signs and gestures. Some communicated through Latin, or used Latin-speaking monks as translators. Bilinguals also stepped in, including descendants of previous English settlers. They were, however, seen as inherently unreliable, as the 'English with the Irish hearts'.[5]

The English were rather quick to accuse their translators of scheming, lying and spying. 'Blessed, fittingly perhaps, with names like Lye and Tattle, interpreters were mistrusted figures,' according to Palmer. 'To cross between languages was, in a way, to slip across enemy lines.' The 'lack of a trusty interpreter' was a typical complaint among the English.[6]

A multilingual matriarch

In the colonial era, European powers kidnapped, trained and recruited interpreters all over the world, using similar methods to Columbus and Cortés.

Krotoa was a girl born in 1642 into a community of Khoe (also known as Khoi, or Khoi-San) traders on the Cape Peninsula of South Africa.[7] When she was twelve years old, her uncle gave her to a Dutch commander called Jan van Riebeeck. Krotoa had a talent for languages; according to one observer, she spoke 'fluent English, Dutch, French and Portuguese', in addition to South African languages. Riebeeck wrote that she spoke Dutch 'almost as well as a Dutch girl'.[8]

Her own language, Khoekhoe, was also very influential. It features characteristic click sounds. It's thought that other South African languages with clicks, such as Zulu, Ndebele and Xhosa, borrowed them from Khoekhoe. They imported them along with Khoekhoe loanwords, and also slotted them into existing words.[9] Spelled in line with the Khoekhoe conventions, Krotoa's name is rendered as !Goa, and would have started with such a click sound.

Under Riebeeck's authority, Krotoa was baptized and given a Dutch name, Eva, and soon served as his interpreter. The Dutch came to rely on her as an informant and adviser, but were unsure of her loyalties. They noted with some concern that whenever she visited her old home, she slipped back into her traditional dress of animal skins. At the same time, some of her people accused her of having become Dutch.

Krotoa ended up giving the Dutch useful and imaginative advice.

At one point, she persuaded them to woo a chief by sending him cinnamon, cloves, nutmeg, mace, pepper, sugar, a few good violinists, and a Dutch clown. Over time, however, the Dutch came to distrust her. They suspected her, correctly, of also giving information to her own people. The end of her life was marked by disease and alcoholism, which was possibly rooted in abuse during her younger years. She was imprisoned several times by the Dutch for rowdy drunken behaviour and died at the age of only thirty-two.[10]

Even more than in the case of Malinche, Krotoa's reputation has been rehabilitated. Her people now celebrate her as a 'matriarch of resistance', who passed them important strategic intelligence and turned the tables on the Dutch.[11]

The Khoekhoe language has also played a wider restorative role. Sara Baartman was a Khoe woman exhibited at European curiosity shows. After her death in 1815, her body continued to be displayed in French museums. After the end of apartheid, South Africa demanded that her remains be returned, but France refused. The South African poet Diana Ferrus wrote a moving poem for Baartman, 'I've come to take you home':[12]

> I have come to take you home, home!
> Remember the veld,
> the lush green grass beneath the big oak trees?
> The air is cool there and the sun does not burn...

In 2001, Nicolas About, a French senator, submitted a bill authorizing the restitution of Baartman's remains to South Africa. About argued that she should be returned to her people so that they could bury her, restore her dignity, and let her rest in peace. In an unprecedented move, the bill included a poem: Ferrus's tribute to Baartman. He cited it as evidence of the continuing emotional impact that Baartman's treatment as a trophy inflicted on South

Africans. The argument was followed by the poem itself, translated into French:

> Je suis venue pour te ramener à la maison—
> La maison... te souviens-tu du veld?
> De l'herbe verte et gorgée de sève, sous les grands chênes
> Là-bas, l'air est doux et le soleil ne brûle pas... [13]

Baartman's remains were returned, and she was given a traditional burial. The poem was later translated into Khoekhoe, and displayed in an exhibition. Denver Toroxa Breda, a Khoekhoe language activist, saw it there and welled up, imagining how utterly lonely Baartman must have felt.

'For four years she could not speak the Khoekhoe language to anyone, she had to make sense of this violent and foreign world in a language that was not hers,' he writes in a review of the exhibition. 'And so to see this poem I've Come to Take You Home also meant that we have brought Sarah's mother tongue home.'[14]

'A slight knowledge of the barbarian language'

In the nineteenth-century United States, Chinese interpreters mediated between Chinese immigrants and American officials. Again, both sides harboured suspicions of each other. The Americans suspected the interpreters of undermining their work and siding with their fellow immigrants. Meanwhile, Chinese intellectuals sneered at translators as 'frivolous rascals' whose skill consisted of 'nothing more than a slight knowledge of the barbarian language and occasional recognition of barbarian characters'.[15]

In all these confrontations, languages take on a deeper symbolism. They may play a conciliatory and restorative role, as in Baartman's return, accompanied by a poem that moved from English to French, and eventually, Khoekhoe. Conversely, they may represent a dangerously flexible identity, with a risk of disloyalty.

Today, a surge of linguistic nationalism seems to be gripping parts of England, with people being told to speak English, or being attacked for speaking other languages, or even for speaking English with a foreign accent. It's as if in times of crisis, multilingualism in itself becomes problematic and threatening, an unstable cultural mix that needs to be purified. Of course, as we've seen, there is no such thing as a pure or stable language, or even an unchanging monolingualism. All languages change, always. They like to wander, they have a restless soul. Languages are border-crossers and shape-shifters, and there isn't much humans can do to stop that.

Nahuatl, by the way, has a word for such an innate sense of restlessness: *icxiyoyomocaliztli*. In the words of Alonso de Molina, the author of a Nahuatl dictionary published in 1571, it's the equivalent of the Spanish *andariego*, meaning an urge to travel.[16] In German, we also have a word for this urge. We call it *Wanderlust*, literally, a desire to wander.

LONGING AND BELONGING

The Children Who Invented a Language

About a hundred years ago, on a peninsula off the eastern coast of Papua New Guinea, a group of children gathered in the darkness of their dormitory. They'd been taken from their mothers and brought to a children's home run by German missionaries. Their new home was called Vunapope, 'The Pope's land'. Here their lives followed a strict routine of prayers, meals, lessons and hard work in the garden of the missionary station. Their mother tongues were banned; only German was allowed.

The children adapted to the routine and, outwardly at least, to the German language. But at night, when the nuns were out of earshot, they whispered in the familiar voices of home. They took German expressions learned in the classroom and merged them with familiar speech patterns. During the day, they had to obey the missionaries' language and follow its rules. Among themselves, they could change its sounds and structure as they saw fit.

Gradually, the wordplay and secret jokes evolved into a new language, one spoken only by the homesick children. When they grew up, they continued using it. It was passed on for generations, and survives in a small community of speakers to this day. The children themselves had different names for this language. Some called it 'Falsche Deutsch', wrong German, or 'Kaputtene Deutsch', broken German. But gradually, it became known by a prouder name: Unserdeutsch.[1] Our German.

Creating Creole

All over the colonial world, oppressed communities took the languages of the occupiers and fashioned them into something new. The resulting hybrids are known as Creole languages. In the past, they were often derided as inferior or comically distorted versions of the European originals. But Creole languages are as expressive, sophisticated, dynamic and multi-layered as any others, and researchers have increasingly studied them in their own right.

Unserdeutsch is an unusual Creole language, in that it was invented by children. Many children come up with secret codes. But the Unserdeutsch speakers held on to their language, refined it, and taught it to their descendants, who in turn taught it to theirs. It was intertwined with a specific identity, one shaped by different cultures, and by a regional tradition of using secret languages for spiritual purposes. Unserdeutsch spanned the conflicts and contradictions of these children's lives, the painful experiences and feelings of loss and alienation, and somehow turned it all into a coherent, expressive whole.

It was only in the 1970s that a linguist, Craig Volker, came across an Unserdeutsch speaker by accident, and began researching the language. Today, Unserdeutsch is fading, pushed out by English and weakened by the dispersal of the original community. For the past few years, another linguist, Péter Maitz, has led a project to document it before it vanishes, along with the story of the children who invented it.

*

The Babel Islands

In the 1880s, German trading companies in the Pacific persuaded Germany to take over a number of islands as a source of migrant labour for their plantations. The Germans arrived late to the colonial enterprise in the Pacific, as they did in Africa. By the time they set up their colonies, European languages such as English and Spanish had been spread widely in the region for centuries by missionaries, plantation owners, sailors, traders and clerks. Indentured Chinese labourers brought several dialects. These languages joined an enormously multilingual native repertoire. Hundreds of indigenous languages were spoken in the area, most by small communities of fewer than five hundred speakers.[2] In addition, there were secret languages and codes used for rituals, to communicate with spirits and animals, or to share confidential information.

German missionaries and colonial administrators often referred to the region as 'Babel' and seemed perplexed by this extreme multilingualism.[3]

In these kinds of situations, where many different groups come into contact and need to communicate, two common solutions emerge.

One is to choose an existing language as the lingua franca, that is, a shared means of communication. As we've seen, Akkadian emerged as such a lingua franca in Bronze Age diplomatic letters, allowing the rulers of Ugarit and Mitanni to ask the Egyptian pharaoh for gold without the need for translators. Today, English functions as a lingua franca in much of the world. Picture a Slovenian tourist meeting a Japanese tourist in a hot spring in Iceland. They are likely to use English with each other, even though neither speaks it as their first language, nor is it the language of the place.

Another, related solution is to create a pidgin language, that is, a simplified language based on existing ones, in which to talk to outsiders. Within the community, the native language may still be preferred, with the pidgin variety only used for practical dealings with others.

A third option is to learn the other groups' languages, but that can be difficult once the diversity becomes overwhelming.

Before the colonial era, Pacific Islanders used all those strategies. They learned the languages of nearby communities, and also developed their own pidgins and commonly understood sign languages.[4]

As colonialism brought about the forced mass movement of plantation workers, those local strategies died out. Instead, pidgin English, a simplified English, took over. It was probably initially developed by workers on Samoan plantations to speak to each other, and their overseers.[5] Indentured Chinese labourers helped spread it from island to island.[6] Guides and interpreters used it to communicate with new arrivals from non-English-speaking countries. Thus, a German colonial expedition to an island called New Hanover, in the Bismarck Archipelago, reported in 1900:

'We reached New Hanover in the morning of the following day and we dropped anchor in a wide bay on the south coast. A little river called Saula by the natives flows into it. As soon as we had gone ashore, we were drenched by a violent shower of rain. In spite of this, we continued our way into the interior under the guidance of a Pidgin English speaking Samoan.'[7]

'Pidgin' refers to an evolving language that is still at a spontaneous, experimental stage. Once pidgin becomes standardized and established, through a process called 'Creolization', it is known as Creole. This means the language has acquired its own set of rules and conventions, and is spoken from birth by a generation of people. (Confusingly, some languages are called pidgin, but are actually in the Creole category.)

Creolization can also refer to the broader phenomenon of a new culture emerging out of colonial oppression. As Françoise Vergès writes: 'Creolization occurred under a situation of severe constraints, under the yoke of slavery, colonialism and racism, in situations of deep inequalities, of forced circumstances and of survival strategies.'[8]

Such innovation took place across many regions and involved different European languages, such as French, English, Dutch, German, Spanish and Portuguese. Creole languages emerged in places as diverse as Martinique in the Caribbean (French-based Creole), Java (Javindo, a Dutch-based Creole), and Cape Verde off northwest Africa (Portuguese-based Creole). Creolization challenged the colonial rulers, who tended to discourage different groups from mixing.

In the Pacific, the pidgin English devised by plantation workers evolved into Tok Pisin, a Creole language. Today, Tok Pisin is one of the official languages of Papua New Guinea. One reason for its enduring use is that Papua New Guinea and the islands near it are so incredibly multilingual.

Islanders used Tok Pisin with each other, as well as with the colonial administrators, Chinese labourers and shopkeepers, and different merchants, missionaries and travellers. It became a lingua franca across a very diverse region. Not that everyone embraced it. Some, such as the Tolai people who lived on the Gazelle Peninsula, used Tok Pisin only reluctantly, seeing it as an uncivilized language.[9] They preferred their mother tongue, Kuanua.

It was on the Gazelle Peninsula, part of the island of New Britain, that the Germans established their administrative capital. They initially accepted Tok Pisin as the lingua franca. Many other languages were spoken on the peninsula, including Kuanua; Tagalog, brought by Filipino sailors; Malay; several Chinese dialects; and various European languages, including English and Swedish.[10]

*

The children's home

In 1897, the Vunapope Catholic Mission on the Gazelle Peninsula opened a boarding school for the mixed-heritage children of European men and local women.[11] The name Vunapope is itself a cultural hybrid, consisting of 'Vuna', the Kuanua word for place or land, and 'Pope'.[12]

The boarding school was motivated by two goals. One was to spread Christianity through the island communities, by starting with the children. In 1932, Father Arnold Janssen, who was in charge of the Vunapope school for twenty years, wrote that the idea was to inculcate the children, who'd then spread the faith, like sourdough. The missionaries also saw European culture as generally superior. Janssen suggested taking mixed-heritage children from their mothers as soon as they were weaned, to ensure that they absorbed the missionaries' European ways and the German language.[13]

The children who arrived at the mission spoke Tok Pisin, shaped by the languages of their different islands. The fathers' origins varied widely. Janssen mentions Filipinos, Indians, Germans, Swedes, Norwegians, Finns, Danes, Englishmen, Australians, Spaniards and Pacific Islanders. Descendants of the Vunapope schoolchildren also recall Japanese, Chinese and Indonesian ancestors.[14] Some children lived with both parents, and would have been exposed to all the languages in the family. Others were raised only by their mothers, in extended families.

Until the early 1900s, the children still kept in close touch with their mothers, and travelled back home for festivals and ceremonies. The German missionaries saw the mothers as warm and loving, which to their minds was a defect rather than a strength. They feared that the children were being spoiled, and were too immersed in their island cultures. Their visits home were increasingly curtailed. Eventually, the children were mostly cut off from their mothers, and their home languages.[15] The goal was, after all, to raise children entirely shaped by European traditions and beliefs.

At school, the children were forced to learn standard German, and speak it at all times. Any use of Tok Pisin was punished.[16] At the same time, they were constantly reminded that they were not fully German. In this harsh environment, removed from their loved ones and the sounds of home, the children came up with an ingenious survival mechanism: their own language.

The language game

Craig Volker, the Unserdeutsch researcher, was told by older speakers that the language started as something of a game. It was a way to release stress after a long day of speaking standard German, under the constant threat of punishments.

In their dormitories, the older students would tell the younger students stories. Sometimes, they used picture books from the school library, and added a running commentary of German words, slotted into Tok Pisin sentences. It was an in-joke, a way of lightening the mood and acknowledging their shared experience. After all, they all knew Tok Pisin, they were all being forced to learn German, and they were all yearning for home.[17]

One Unserdeutsch speaker described the language as being inspired by laughter and 'Quatsch', nonsense. Another said it was invented specifically in the girls' dormitories. Older girls were put in charge of the younger children at the school. They made up the language, and taught it to the children in their care.[18]

As the trips home became rarer, and the children grew more isolated, these spontaneous experiments turned into a more standardized form of communication. The children no longer spoke it only in the dormitories, for entertainment. They also used it in other situations, as long as there were no German nuns nearby. Even if someone overheard them, they would have probably thought they were obeying the rules and speaking German, just a bit clumsily. The subversive Tok Pisin was well hidden underneath all those German words.

There are two established ways for new languages to appear. One is evolutionary, that is, gradually, over a long time, through tiny shifts and modifications. The other is known as 'catastrophic': sudden, like a bang, in one big eruption. 'Catastrophic' is a technical term in linguistics.[19] But in this case, the birth of the language was also catastrophic in quite a different sense. It was a mental, emotional, cultural catastrophe. Children were snatched from their families, raised in an institution, beaten and humiliated, generation after generation.

Out of this rupture, they created something new. But the violent origin story remains alive in the language. Reading about the grammar and vocabulary of Unserdeutsch, it is noticeable how many sample sentences recorded from native speakers feature memories of beatings, punishments, and degradation. And yet it is also a funny and humorous language, a children's language, playful and cheeky. This mixture is one of the many things that makes it unique.

Unserdeutsch formed a useful common language for this multilingual group, though that was not its only function. After all, the children learned to speak, write and read in standard German, as taught by the nuns, and could have just used that to communicate among themselves. As its name suggests, Unserdeutsch, 'our German', fulfilled another role: it was their language, made up of their influences, their experiences, their origins, their familiar sounds.

Moving between languages, adjusting to different contexts, is part of the Unserdeutsch tradition. The children only ever spoke it among themselves, and once they were adults, to their children.

They used other languages with the outside world. It remained *their* German, a unifying language that helped them survive the racism they faced in daily life.

Something else made Unserdeutsch special, and precious. It was a secret language, in a region where secret languages carried a special significance, and were used for sacred and ritualistic purposes. Usually, young children would not yet have been initiated into them. But at least one of the children at Vunapope did know such a secret language: shark-calling, the gift of talking to sharks.

The girl who spoke to sharks

Elsa Petterson was born in 1911 on the island of Tabar, one of many small islands clustered around the larger island of New Ireland.[20] Her father was the Swedish owner of a coconut plantation on Tabar. Her mother was the daughter of a chieftain. I first came across her story through a German radio programme by the journalist Rebekka Endler, who interviewed her daughter, Maria Chan.[21]

Elsa was a spirited and adventurous girl, who loved climbing up coconut trees and exploring the island. One day, in a very unusual move, she was initiated into an art that was normally only taught to the men on Tabar. It involved singing or calling out to sea, in a language understood, and indeed enjoyed, by sharks.

Shark-calling is a ritual known from various villages on and around New Ireland. On these islands alone, some twenty languages are spoken.[22] Within that lively soundscape, the islanders developed a complex system of fishing-related beliefs and customs, accompanied by songs and codes.

The musicologist Gerald Florian Messner describes different kinds of shark-related rituals in the area. In one rite of passage, a young man is thrown into the water, and symbolically reborn as a shark hunter.[23] When the hunters are out at sea, they sing songs in Kara, an island language, to attract the sharks. Here is one:

Tupalum tapunen sa – aga tupalum tapugdn sa
Ri lo pugun vuluni mat mat ri lo pugun vuluni mat beua-I
'Dolphin wake up yes dolphin wake up
They often wake up the dead, they often wake up the dead, the reef shark.'[24]

Another goes:

'Albatros flies around / Albatros comes down to sit on / the back of the shark.'[25]

After these songs the shark-caller recites a spell four times:

metaq tare-i veua tare-i
'My eye sees, shark sees.'

The shark appears, drawn in by the songs and chants, and is caught with a rope, pulled onto the canoe, and killed.

On the island of Tabar where Elsa and her family lived, sharks were revered as protective, totemic animals. Messner reports that a man from Tabar told him about an ancient tradition of catching baby sharks and raising them in stone basins on a beach. They were fed with pork and chicken, given a name, and later released during a special ceremony. When called by their humans, they were supposed to come to their aid, or hurt their enemy.[26]

According to her daughter, Elsa managed to persuade the elders on Tabar to teach her this art. They admitted her to their ceremonial hut, a sacred place at the heart of every village.

'For some odd reason my mother was the only woman that was

allowed into the one in Tabar,' Elsa's daughter, Maria Chan, recalled in the radio interview. 'And she told me they had skulls hanging in there, bones. She was always very proud of it now, that she was the only woman that was allowed to go in.'[27]

Elsa never used her skill to hunt and kill sharks. Instead, she bonded with them, following the Tabar tradition. Her daughter drew a clear distinction between other islanders' ways: 'There is shark-calling in New Ireland, where they put the shells together and the sharks come, but Mom doesn't do that. She just talks.'

It was a happy childhood. Elsa told her daughter that she had a very good life on Tabar, filled with adventure. This came to an end when Elsa's mother died, and her Swedish father felt unable to look after the children. Elsa and her younger sister were sent to the mission in Vunapope, where they arrived in the early 1920s.

Their new life was strictly regimented: church, breakfast, school, hard work in the garden, dinner, evening prayers, bed. As for shark-calling: that was banned. The nuns told her it was idolatry, praying to false gods. Elsa stopped using her skill. It would be fifty years before she spoke to sharks again.

It was only after dark, when everyone was supposed to be asleep, that a different, more comforting sound emerged. A mishmash of new sounds and more familiar rhythms, expressions and jokes. Just as Elsa had been initiated into shark-calling, so she was now let into this secret language. It was a rite of passage, allowing her to become part of the group.

A secret code

By the time Elsa arrived, change had come to Vunapope. Australia had seized the islands from Germany during the First World War, and English was now the official colonial language. But that didn't change the use of Unserdeutsch, which by then had been in use for years and become entrenched in the children's lives. In class, they spoke English and German. Privately, away from the nuns, Unserdeutsch was their voice.

This was a structure echoed all over the islands. Elders spoke in code to each other to keep their conversations hidden from women, children, and outsiders. Hunters changed or encrypted their speech so that animals and evil spirits couldn't understand them.[28] Secrecy was a flexible concept; you could always invite more speakers. In the highlands of Papua New Guinea, speakers of three different, ordinary languages used the same secret language.[29]

Craig Volker found remarkable parallels between such secret languages in the Pacific, and Unserdeutsch. For example, islanders typically changed the words or grammar of an existing language to make it unintelligible. Unserdeutsch works in quite a similar fashion. Grammatically, it borrows some features from German, and others from Tok Pisin. The words are mostly German, but some are from Tok Pisin, and ultimately from other, underlying languages. This makes the language opaque to outsiders, and gives it a unique sound and logic.

For example, Unserdeutsch replaces the German *der, die, das* ('the', in the masculine, feminine and neutral form), with a simpler: 'de'. Thus *die Frau*, the woman, becomes 'de Frau'.[30] Other constructions actually become more gendered. In German, *mein Liebling*, my darling, is always in the masculine form, even when referring to a woman. Unserdeutsch corrects this inconsistency, and uses an invented, feminine form for women: 'meine Liebling'.

Like Tok Pisin, Unserdeutsch differentiates between an inclusive 'we' (all of us, including you), and an exclusive one (all of us, but not you). In Unserdeutsch, the German word *uns*, us, is used for the inclusive form: '*Uns zwei am sprechen so schön*', 'The two of us are talking so beautifully (together)'.[31] In contrast, the Unserdeutsch *wir*, we, is exclusive: '*Dann wir hat Mittagessen*', 'Then we (but not you) had lunch'.

The Unserdeutsch plural is formed by adding *alle*, 'all', to a noun, just as in Tok Pisin. *Alle knabe* means 'boys' (*Knabe* being an old German word for boy). However, unlike Tok Pisin, Unserdeutsch has a passive form: '*In diese sorte zeit viele dings war nich gesprehen von*', 'At that time, many things were not spoken about.'

Salzwasser, hambak, maski

In terms of its vocabulary, Unserdeutsch is heavily based on German, with additions from Tok Pisin and other languages. Some of the German words are somewhat archaic, which gives Unserdeutsch a lyrical, literary note. *Knabe*, Unserdeutsch for boy, is such a word. In standard German, it has been replaced by the more modern *Junge*.

'Herrgemahl', from the standard German 'Herr Gemahl', is Unserdeutsch for 'husband'.[32] In modern standard German, the word for husband is *Ehemann*, which literally means something like 'married man'. In conversation, people often just refer to their male spouse as *Mann*, man. 'Herr Gemahl', on the other hand, translates as something like 'sir spouse'. It has a much more formal and refined quality.

Other expressions are word-for-word translations from Tok Pisin. In Tok Pisin, *liklik haus* means toilet. Literally, it translates as 'little house'. Unserdeutsch speakers turned this into 'kleine Haus', 'little house'. As in: '*de tür war weg von de kleine haus*', 'the toilet door was missing'.[33]

'Salzwasser' is Unserdeutsch for 'ocean', from Tok Pisin *solwara* ('ocean'), from the English 'saltwater'.[34]

Some words are introduced directly from Tok Pisin, such as

hambak, meaning to fool around: '*Wenn du hambak un alle schwester sehen du…*' ('When you fool around and the sisters see you…') *Maski*, from Tok Pisin, means although, or nevertheless: '*Alle schwester war gut zu mir, maski, i hab imme de stock gekrich.*' – 'Although the sisters were good to me, I always got the stick.' Other words are rooted in indigenous languages. The Unserdeutsch word for chicken, *kakaruk*, is borrowed from the Kuanua language of the Tolai.[35]

English-derived words from Tok Pisin, such as *orait* (all right), are liberally used to mark the start of a phrase or emphasize a point. Numbers are usually given in English. In later generations, this English influence became stronger, and new loanwords were slotted in, as when a speaker told a researcher: '*Du hat ge-mention ihre mutter*', 'You mentioned her mother'.

Volker argues that Unserdeutsch wasn't just invented with similar methods to traditional secret languages from the region, it also fulfilled a similar purpose. It allowed the children to initiate newcomers into their little society, and exclude hostile or prying ears. At the same time, it created what he calls a 'psychological distance' between the children and the missionaries. Outwardly, they were following the rules. Inwardly, they treasured their difference, their uniqueness, their sense of self. Speaking Unserdeutsch was a subtle form of resistance.

'That's how they all became family, because they only had each other,' Yvonne Lundin, a third-generation Unserdeutsch speaker, told Endler. 'They all were… I guess abandoned.'

An Unserdeutsch heritage

Elsa grew up, and married another Vunapope survivor. He had been taken there as a child, just like her. All he remembered of his mother was that she was called Nakai, that she had long, beautiful hair, and that he missed her.

The marriage was by the missionaries' design. They matched the graduates of the children's home with each other. Through these arranged marriages, Unserdeutsch was handed on to the next generation. The Vunapope children had always used it with each other and naturally continued to do so when they reached adulthood and set up homes of their own. Not just that, but they continued to work for the missionary station, and sent their own children to school there.

The Unserdeutsch speakers kept other German traditions, too. They cooked *Rouladen* and *Sauerbraten* – heavy German meat dishes – in the tropical heat. They ate pickled herring, '*Rollmops*', and *Leberwurst*.[36] A German seafaring song called '*Seemann, deine Heimat ist das Meer*', 'Sailor, your home is the ocean', became the community's unofficial anthem. It goes:

> *Seemann, lass das Träumen*
> *Denk nicht an zu Haus*
> *Seemann, Wind und Wellen*
> *Rufen dich hinaus...*

> 'Sailor, stop that dreaming
> Don't think of home
> Sailor, wind and waves
> Are calling you away...'

For generations, the Unserdeutsch community played this song at funerals.

'It just brings everyone to tears because it's such a yearning song. I think a yearning song of the ocean... I guess it's also a song of belonging. It's a song that binds us,' Yvonne Lundin told Endler.

While Unserdeutsch was rarely written, at least one couple did so to publicly mark their private grief. Like Barates, the Syrian immigrant to Roman Britain who'd inscribed a tombstone for his late wife in Palmyrene, they put up a stone for their deceased daughter in English and Unserdeutsch. It stands in the Missionary Cemetery at Vunapope:

Cherished,

Magdalena Nainai Lundin,

born 1936 – 1947 died

Aufwiedersehn meine Liebling.

That last line is in Unserdeutsch. It means, 'Farewell, my darling'. The endearment, *meine Liebling,* is in the feminine case, a construction that does not exist in standard German. But it exists in Unserdeutsch, the language these parents spoke to their child.[37]

Unserdeutsch today

In 1975, when Papua New Guinea became independent, the vast majority of Unserdeutsch speakers emigrated to Australia. They continued speaking Unserdeutsch. They continued singing 'Seemann' whenever they buried one of their own. Little by little, English took over.

Today, there are some one hundred, mostly elderly speakers of Unserdeutsch, most of them in Australia. Those who live close to each other speak it at picnics, funerals and weddings. But many are isolated, with no one to talk to in this language of their memories. One of the handful of Unserdeutsch speakers still living in Papua New Guinea told researchers he spoke it to his flowers every morning, since they were the only ones who understood him.[38]

Unserdeutsch might have vanished unnoticed by the wider world, had it not been for a chance encounter. In the 1970s, Craig Volker was teaching German at a school in Australia when he noticed a surprisingly proficient student. She spoke fluent German, but with a peculiar accent. She turned out to be Yvonne Lundin, the third-generation Unserdeutsch speaker.

These days, many Unserdeutsch speakers express pride in their heritage, and want to at least preserve its legacy for their descendants.[39] Recordings, photos and a wealth of other Unserdeutsch material has been published online by the Institute of Germanic Languages and Literatures at the University of Bern.[40]

There are endangered languages that have been around for thousands of years, which were suppressed but are now being revived. Unserdeutsch isn't like that. It is, in some ways, a fleeting language. It was invented in a catastrophe, an emotional and cultural emergency. It helped tie together the community of speakers, and declined when they were dispersed.

To me as a German speaker, Unserdeutsch sounds familiar in an uncanny way, like a face you recognize from somewhere, but cannot quite place. It is German, but not German. There is one recording of it that I find particularly moving. It's one of the early recordings from the 1970s.[41] Theo Hartig, an Unserdeutsch speaker, tells the story of a German fairy tale, Rumpelstiltskin.

A king kidnaps a poor miller's beautiful daughter and tells her she must spin straw to gold overnight. As she sits in her lonely cell, a little man appears, offering to help in return for a favour: 'What will you give me if I spin all this straw for you?' In Unserdeutsch: '*Was du wid geben mich, wenn ich spinnen alle diese Stroh fi dich?*'

Eventually, the little man urges her to give him her firstborn, once the king marries her: '*Wo du bist nachher de Königin, du musst geben mich der erste Kind.*' ('Later, when you are Queen, you must give me your first child.')[42]

In Unserdeutsch, both lines include a slight rhyme: *mich/dich*,

Königin/Kind. That's only possible because the structure is more like English, with the noun at the end, than like German, which puts the verb last. There is a songlike, chanting quality to Unserdeutsch, which lends itself to storytelling.

After several roomfuls of straw are spun to gold, the king marries the miller's daughter. She gives birth to a child, and the little man comes to claim the baby. She begs him in tears to let them be: '*I geben di mein ganze reichtum solange wenn du ni holen mein kind weg von ich*' – 'I give you all my wealth if you don't take away my child.'

He retorts that he doesn't want riches; he wants a living thing. But if she guesses his name, he will release her from the promise. She sends out messengers to find out all the names in the land. One by one she tries them out on him. None of them break the spell. Finally, one of the messengers comes back and tells her that he observed a curious little sprite dancing around the fire, singing: 'Today I bake, tomorrow I brew, and the next day, I take the queen's child. No one knows, no one knows, that my name is Rumpelstiltskin.' The queen confronts the little man, and calls him by his name. Furious, he rips himself in two.

It seems to me, whenever I listen to this recording, that there can be no better language than Unserdeutsch to tell this particular German fairy tale, about a mother in despair, offering up her child – and then, at the last minute, managing to keep it.

As for shark-calling: after the nuns banned Elsa's gift as idolatrous and diabolical, she did not use it for decades. She married, had children, lived her life in Unserdeutsch, made Sauerbraten, sang 'Seemann'. Then one day, in the 1970s, she heard that her son was in distress out at sea. His ship had sunk. It was not clear if there were any survivors. She hurried to the beach, and there she called to the sharks one more time, asking them to protect her son.

He was found a few days later, clinging to a piece of wood from the shipwreck, dehydrated, but alive. With him was a woman with her two children, also alive. They'd been drifting for days. He told his family that throughout those days, a large shark had been circling them, and kept the other sharks at bay.[43]

'He said he's never seen a shark that big,' recalls Maria Chan, Elsa's daughter. 'And he still talks about it to today.'

Cinderella and the
Innkeeper's Daughter

Once upon a time, there was an innkeeper in the old German town of Kassel. His inn was on top of a steep hill, so steep that visitors had to crack their whips to drive their horses up the last stretch. The explosive sound of the whips, *knall* in German, gave the inn its name: Knallhütte, 'bang-hut'. Every night, straw was spread out over the floor of the Knallhütte, and the weary, dusty guests bedded down for the night. Some of them had brought jokes, riddles and stories from far away, and told them over a nightcap.

The innkeeper's daughter, Dorothea, poured beer for the guests and listened to travellers' stories, for which she had an amazing memory. She knew two languages, German and French. Her ancestors were French Protestants who'd come to Germany as refugees. All her life, she would remain close to the French community and worship in a French church.

One day, long after she'd left the inn and had raised a family of her own, she met two brothers, Jacob and Wilhelm Grimm. They were acquaintances of her French priest, and were looking for people who knew fairy tales. Dorothea Viehmann, as she was called by then, became their most prolific and valued contributor. Once a week, she travelled into town from her cottage in the village of Niederzwehren outside Kassel to sell vegetables. When she was done, she went to the Grimms' flat. They served her wine and coffee, accompanied by a silver spoon, and she told them fairy tales, some forty in total, more than any of their other narrators. Her protagonists were often hard-working, resilient women like herself, the Cinderellas of this world. Which was in fact one of the stories she gave the Grimms: Cinderella, or as she's known in German, Aschenputtel.

As much as Dorothea Viehmann's stories became associated with a mythically German landscape of dark forests and castles, they actually reflected a much more fluid, culturally mixed, border-crossing legacy. Indeed, several of the Grimms' main contributors came from a similarly multilingual background. Their experiences of upheaval, migration and displacement shaped the fairy tales enjoyed by people all over the world today.

Some were of French ancestry, like Dorothea Viehmann, and their bilingualism influenced the stories they told. They mixed German and French, often quite unconsciously. It's the reason that in the Grimms' original version of Little Red Riding Hood, she carries a *'Bouteille mit Wein'*, a 'bouteille of wine'. Others recreated French fairy tales they knew from childhood, such as Sleeping Beauty, in a German setting. There was also a retired soldier, who gave the Grimms violent military revenge dramas inspired by a life spent on the battlefields of Europe. In the stories they told, this colourful group of narrators seem to have found a sense of safety and stability, one perhaps craved by the Grimm brothers themselves. The resulting oeuvre is neither French nor German. It's a product of many countries and many different languages, filtered through each narrator's unique experience and creative interpretation.

The story hunt

Wilhelm and Jacob were born in the late eighteenth century in the German town of Hanau. Their three siblings, Ferdinand, Ludwig and

Lotte, later helped them collect stories. But only Jacob and Wilhelm would become world-famous as '*die Brüder Grimm*', the Grimm brothers, which was what they called themselves. Perhaps they liked the way it echoed the anonymous sibling units at the centre of so many fairy tales: the seven brothers, the three sisters, and so on.

Their father died when they were still children. A restless period ensued as they moved between different towns. It was when they studied law in the medieval university town of Marburg that their lifelong project of story-gathering began to take shape. They lived in a crooked little house on a steep hill that led up to a castle, amid a maze of cobblestone streets with quirky names such as 'Barfüßerstraße' (Barefoot Street) and 'Speckkuchengasse' ('Bacon Cake Alley'). As Jacob Grimm later remembered, he would leave his home every day and make his way through the twisting alleys of the old town, to a nest-like house perched midway up a flight of steps. This was the home of Friedrich Carl von Savigny, his law professor and mentor, who infected the brothers with his love of history and literature.[1] They became part of a circle of writers and editors, and eventually decided to gather and publish a collection of fairy tales.

Fairy tales typically feature a nameless protagonist in a nameless country, referred to only by their status or profession: the king's youngest daughter, the cunning little tailor, the swineherd, the miller, the cook.

The story begins with them in their normal habitat, doing ordinary things. Little Red Riding Hood's mother gives her a basket with a bottle of wine and food for her grandmother. Sleeping Beauty is spinning wool. Hansel and Gretel are skipping into the woods, looking forward to a nice walk with their father and stepmother. Aschenputtel is cleaning the oven, fetching water, scrubbing the floor, and wondering if this will ever end. Then something unforeseeable happens. 'Good morning, Little Red Riding Hood,' says the wolf.[2] Sleeping Beauty pricks her finger on the poisoned spindle and falls into a deep sleep. Hansel and Gretel's parents take them into the darkest part of the forest and abandon them there. Aschenputtel goes to the ball.

A quest unfolds, often combined with a riddle or test. Strange creatures emerge from fields and woods to help or hinder the protagonist. Dwarves, witches, sorcerers and speaking animals appear as themselves, or in the guise of other creatures. The characters are unfazed by this incursion of the supernatural. When Little Red Riding Hood bumps into a talking wolf who wishes her a *'guten Morgen'*, she simply replies: 'Thank you very much, wolf.'

Inversion, disguise and revelation are part of the game. The toad turns into a prince. The princess disguises herself as a maid. The wolf dresses up as the grandmother, the evil maid dresses up as a princess. Dirt turns into gold, gold into dirt. Brutal motifs recur in different stories, as do magical objects. Birds appear out of nowhere to drop a millstone on the villain. In one version of Cinderella/Aschenputtel, birds peck out the evil sisters' eyes.

Numbers are important. A hero or heroine is given the keys to three, seven, or thirteen doors, all of which they are allowed to open, except that last one, which is forbidden, but of course they can't help but open it anyway. They stumble into a room filled with the severed heads of those who previously breached the taboo.

Ovens can be good or bad. The witch threatens to roast Hansel in an oven, but is then pushed into it herself. Sometimes they're sanctuaries. A prince hides in an oven, a doctor hides in an oven.

The Grimms would end up devoting their lives to these simple and yet so compelling stories. In 1805 they moved to the town of Kassel, into a flat at Marktgasse Nr. 17 in the old town, close to the Sonnenapotheke, a pharmacy. There, they began to ask people to tell them fairy tales, which they then wrote down. Many gave them little more than bullet points, which the Grimms fleshed out. Friends and neighbours, including the pharmacist and his family, became their first contributors. Among this early cohort were Marie Hassenpflug and her sisters, Jeanette and Amalie, from a family of French refugees.

Refugees and Sleeping Beauty

Marie Hassenpflug and her sisters were eager narrators. They gave the Grimms more than thirty stories, shaped by a Franco-German heritage that had its own share of drama and upheaval.

Their ancestors were Huguenots, French Protestants who'd fled religious persecution in their home country. Tens of thousands of Huguenots sought refuge all over Europe, and beyond. Many went to Britain, where they introduced the word refugee, from *réfugié*. Some made it as far as South Africa, where they founded vineyards.

The Huguenots were renowned artisans, and several Protestant European rulers were keen to offer them sanctuary and benefit from their skills. Kassel was in such a Protestant area, which lured Huguenots with tax breaks but also, crucially, the promise that they could practise their faith in their own language, French.

Typically, groups of Huguenots left under the leadership of a pastor, settled in or near Kassel, built a French church, and recreated life as they'd known it. Huguenot villages sprang up where only French was spoken. Because of this structure, the French language was often preserved over several generations.

Dorothea Viehmann's great-grandfather, Isaak Pierson, had been one of the first of these refugees, following his pastor to Kassel. The Hassenpflugs' great-grandfather had come to Germany in 1730, from a town in the French Alps. He'd been a Protestant preacher there, and escaped in the middle of the night after a friend warned him that he was about to be arrested.[3]

The Hassenpflug children still grew up in a French bubble. Their mother had been raised by the great-grandmother, which squeezed the generations closer together, forming an even more watertight Francophone unit.[4] Their brother, Ludwig Hassenpflug, recalled the great-grandmother as 'a Frenchwoman through and through', who only socialized with other French refugees, and banned the German language in her home.[5]

Marie and her sisters were raised in French, attended a French school, and worshipped in a French church. They felt ambivalent about this, as if they didn't belong to either France or Germany. As Amalie Hassenpflug later wrote: 'It's our family's fate never to be at home anywhere.'[6]

Perhaps surprisingly, French became their link to the Grimms. They met them through the family of their French pastor. In 1808, they started attending the brothers' tea parties, and flourished there.

Marie Hassenpflug told them the story of Sleeping Beauty, 'Dornröschen' ('thorn-rose') in German. She'd heard the story as a child, possibly from a French book. In French, it's called 'La Belle au Bois Dormant'. It was published in a seventeenth-century collection by Charles Perrault, a French writer.

In Marie's version, adapted by the Grimms, the queen is taking a bath when a frog suddenly crawls out of the water. He tells her she's going to have a daughter before the end of the year. When the girl is born, the king and queen invite twelve wise women to a grand dinner, excluding a thirteenth, because they only have twelve golden plates.

Towards the end of the feast, the rebuffed wise woman crashes into the palace and utters a curse: on her fifteenth birthday, the girl will pierce her finger on a spindle and die. Another wise woman reduces the curse to a hundred-year sleep.[7]

Years later, the prophecy is fulfilled; the teenage princess touches the spindle and falls asleep. The Grimms added an elaborate, ghostly flourish to this scene. In their version, the king and queen, the dogs and horses, the flies on the walls and the fire in the hearth, all drift off into a magical sleep. The cook, who is about to slap the kitchen boy, finds his hand frozen in mid-action.

A hundred years later, a prince climbs into the castle and finds an eerie scene. All around him are sleeping people and animals. Even the pigeons on the roof have tucked their heads under their wings. Inside, the flies are sleeping on the walls. In the kitchen he finds the frozen cook, his hand raised. The maid sits immobile in front of her half-plucked chicken. Upstairs, next to the throne, lie the sleeping king and queen. 'Everything was so quiet that he could hear his own breath.' Finally, he reaches the tower and opens the door to the little chamber where the princess sleeps. He kisses her, and the spell is broken. The fire flares up again and continues cooking the meal, the roast crackles in the oven, the cook slaps the kitchen boy, who cries out in protest. The maid finishes plucking her chicken. There is pure relief in these lines, a return to a comical register after the mass-suicide-like description of the slumbering royal court.

Compare this to Marie Hassenpflug's own brief ending: 'When he came into the castle, he kissed the sleeping princess and every-thing awakened from the sleep.' That's it.[8]

The Grimms censored Marie Hassenpflug's version slightly. In her story, the prince gets into the princess's bed.[9] In the Grimms' version, this is reduced to a chaste kiss.

A bouteille of wine

Jeanette Hassenpflug, Marie's younger sister, gave the Grimms the story of Little Red Riding Hood, in a particularly charming bilingual retelling. In her version, the girl's supposedly rustic and rural mother suddenly slips into surprisingly refined French:

Da sagte einmal seine Mutter zu ihm: komm, Rothkäppchen, da hast du ein Stück Kuchen und ein Bouteille mit Wein, die bring der Großmutter hinaus, sie ist krank und schwach, da wird sie sich daran laben.[10]

'One day, her mother told her: Come, Little Red Riding Hood, here is a piece of cake and a bouteille with wine, take it to your grandmother, she is ill and weak, she'll enjoy it.'

In later versions, the Grimms replaced the bilingual 'Bouteille mit Wein' with the fully German 'eine Flasche Wein.'[11] By then, they were keen to present their project as authentically Germanic, though in their commentaries they always acknowledged many different influences.

Once the Grimms had depleted the repertoire of friends and acquaintances, they tried to find more sources, initially without much luck. The earthy folk whose oral culture the Grimms were hoping to tap were either too busy or just not interested.[12] But then, just as things were looking a bit hopeless, the Grimms found Wachtmeister Krause, a retired soldier.

The soldier

Like Dorothea Viehmann and the Hassenpflug sisters, Wachtmeister (Sergeant) Krause had some French ancestry. His stories, however, were influenced not so much by French children's books as by thirty years of trudging around European military campaigns. He was old now, and lived in poverty and neglect.

Krause gave the Grimms about a dozen stories, and was paid with a cast-off pair of trousers for each contribution. Later, he stayed in touch with them, and occasionally wrote letters humbly asking for another pair of trousers, if the brothers happened to have any spare.

The retired sergeant liked to tell stories about down-and-out veterans, and animals booted out after years of faithful service:

A farmer had a loyal dog who was old and had lost his grip. So the farmer told his wife: 'I want to shoot old Sultan dead, he's of no use to us any more.'[13]

The Grimm scholar Heinz Rölleke, who has excavated many of these contributors' biographies, describes Krause's oeuvre as '*schlage-tot-Geschichten*',[14] that is, 'beat-to-death stories', or revenge fantasies. In a typical Krause narrative, a small-time soldier kills and destroys everyone in his way until he becomes king. He is then betrayed by the people around him and ends up killing them all. 'And then he is king forever and that's the happy end. They are wishful fantasies of an impoverished soldier,' Rölleke writes.[15]

There is a more playful side to the old sergeant's stories. One of his characters is given a military backpack, which he only needs to slap and a corporal and six soldiers armed with rifles step out. Slap it further, and another 150 men come marching out, and then a whole cavalry. Another character is given a hat that you only need to turn, and a battery of cannons start firing.[16]

Were Krause's visits to the Grimms a form of talking therapy, an attempt to overcome post-traumatic stress? Who knows. The stories themselves have a comforting element to them, despite the brutality. Sultan the guard dog survives in the end. He teams up with a wolf, who pretends to steal the farmer's baby. Sultan foils the staged kidnapping, saves the day, and is granted a new lease of life.

If you strip away the military embellishments, Krause's stories are really Cinderella tales. A hard-working person is humiliated and abused by those who benefit from their labour. And yet, against the odds, they triumph.

The first group of storytellers, including Krause and the Hassenpflugs, yielded enough material for the Grimms to publish a collection in 1812. The following year, in the summer of 1813, the brothers wrote to their brother Ferdinand to tell him of an excellent discovery. Charles François Ramus, the French pastor in Kassel, had told them about a proper source, the kind of contributor they'd been looking for all this time: an older woman with a wealth of stories. They had found Dorothea Viehmann.

No witches

Just as the Hassenpflug girls liked to tell stories about young women like themselves, and Krause liked to tell stories about ex-soldiers like himself, so Dorothea Viehmann had a strong penchant for protagonists forged by hardship and deprivation, just like herself.

By the time she met the Grimms, she was widowed and sharing a cramped cottage with her daughter and six grandchildren. She knew the French pastor because she still worshipped at his church, and supplied him and his family with vegetables.

The brothers were ecstatic about their new contributor. 'We now have a magnificent source,'[17] Wilhelm Grimm wrote to his brother Ferdinand, adding that she was 'incredibly knowledgeable and a very good storyteller'.[18] They transcribed her words for three, four hours at a time, fuelled by coffee and wine. She seemed to enjoy the job, too, and apparently told the French pastor how honoured she felt, and that she was given 'a little silver spoon with her coffee, as fancy as anyone'.[19]

Dorothea Viehmann's repertoire is very distinctive. Her princesses aren't sleeping beauties in enchanted castles, but tough women who fight their way back to a good life after being betrayed by those close to them. Strikingly, her fairy tales never feature witches. Even when she told a version of a story that usually included a witch, she changed it to make it witch-free. A family rumour had it that people in her village were accusing her of being a witch, which was why she wasn't keen to promote that particular stock character. It's also possible that she'd simply had enough of seeing older, independent women like herself maligned.

Above all, she had a tender spot for people tossed about by life, as in her most famous fairy tale. Here is the opening passage of Cinderella or Aschenputtel, in Dorothea Viehmann's version:

> The wife of a wealthy man became sick, and as she felt the end draw near, she called her little daughter to her bed and said: 'Dear child, stay devout and good, so God will always be with you, and I will look down on you from heaven, and be all around you.' With that, she closed her eyes, and departed.[20]

The girl's father remarries, and her life is ruled by misery: 'From morning to evening she had to do heavy chores, rise before dawn, carry water, light the fire, cook and clean.' At night, she sleeps in the ash of the hearth. On top of that, her haughty stepsisters mock her. They say she looks filthy, and call her Aschenputtel, from *Asche*, ash.[21]

One day her stepsisters go to a ball at the palace. With the help of a pair of friendly white doves, Aschenputtel manages to trick her stepmother into letting her go, too. She visits her mother's grave under a hazel tree, and receives a gold and silver dress and embroidered silver slippers. At the ball, she dances with the prince all night, but flees before he can find out who she is. The same thing happens the next evening. The third time, the wishing tree gives her a pair of golden slippers. The prince paints the palace steps with sticky tar, catching one of her slippers as she runs off at the end of the night.

He goes from house to house with it, looking for the foot that fits the shoe, and eventually finds Aschenputtel. There's a big wedding, and the doves pick out the evil stepsisters' eyes.

Dorothea Viehmann could have ended it there. Instead, she added:

> After Aschenputtel lived happily with the king for a year, he goes on a journey and leaves her all the keys, with the order not to open a certain chamber. But as soon as he is gone, a treacherous nurse tells her to unlock the forbidden chamber, wherein she finds a well filled with blood. She is thrown into this, while still weak from the birth of her little son, by the evil nurse, who then lies down in her bed to replace her; but the guards hear the desperate cries, rescue the rightful queen, and punish the wrong one.[22]

This is a very Dorothea Viehmann ending. In another of her stories, about a princess and a horse called Fallada, the evil-doer is punished by being shut in a barrel studded with nails and dragged through the main street. She liked to sprinkle in gory details, and to remix the different stories she had heard all her life, starting with those travellers' tales at the inn.

Cinderella, Aschenputtel, Ashiepattle

In the UK, Aschenputtel is generally known as Cinderella, from the French Cendrillon (*cendre* meaning ash). There is another British name for her, however, mentioned in Jamieson's Scottish Dictionary: 'Ashypet, Ashiepattle, a neglected child, employed in the lowest kitchenwork.'[23] This one is more Germanic-rooted. Cinderella and Aschenputtel/Ashiepattle are slightly different characters. Cinderella has a fairy godmother, for example. Aschenputtel only has her mother's grave, and the helpful birds. Other languages offer even more varieties, including some in which Cinderella is a boy. The Grimms recorded a Norwegian variant in which a kitchen porter sleeps in the ashes, and ends up marrying the king's daughter. They also mentioned German versions in which the ash-smeared protaganist is a mistreated servant or a boy bullied by his brothers.[24]

'It was an age-old custom for the unfortunate one to sit in the ashes,' the Grimms concluded, noting that even Odysseus 'sat down on the hearth among the ashes' to prove his humility. Nor is the basic narrative exclusive to Europe. In his study of Hindu food-images, A. K. Ramanujan points out that 'in the Kannada folktale of Hanci, a Cinderella-type story, the young woman is identified with and by a special kind of rice she makes, not by a slipper'.[25]

'A magnificent source'

The Grimms proudly displayed a portrait of Dorothea Viehmann on one of their covers, and praised her in a foreword as someone who 'kept the old legends firmly in her memory and said herself that not everyone had this gift'. They described how she would repeat her stories calmly so they could transcribe them, never altering them in the repetition, and correcting 'any mistakes as soon as she noticed them, mid-speech'.[26] While they gave full credit to her as a narrator, they did not mention the mixed cultural background that had given rise to her stories. It was only much later that scholars such as Rölleke uncovered the international collaboration underlying these supposedly authentically German folk tales.

On a Sunday in September 1814, the Grimms went to the village where Dorothea Viehmann lived. They recorded her last contribution, a story about the devil and his grandmother. The grandmother is kind and wise, and tries to fix her diabolical grandson's mischief. A silver spoon makes an appearance, too.

★

One can imagine an alternative ending for Aschenputtel, in which she doesn't marry the prince. Instead, she uses her gold slippers to buy a little cottage with a garden, where she grows herbs and vegetables. It's a modest life, but she likes it that way. Every now and then she walks through fields and forests to the big town, where she visits two young brothers. They are always hungry for stories. In their nice, warm living room, she talks and talks as she stirs her coffee with her silver spoon. She tells them stories that came across the border with her ancestors, and stories she heard from dusty travellers as a child, and stories that she simply made up, which are entirely her own.

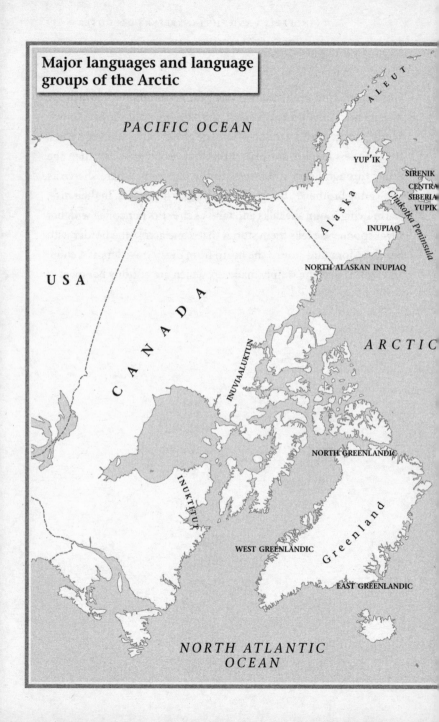

Major languages and language groups of the Arctic

PACIFIC OCEAN

YUP'IK

SIRENIK

CENTRA

SIBERIA

YUPIK

Chukotka Peninsula

INUPIAQ

ALEUT

Alaska

NORTH ALASKAN INUPIAQ

USA

CANADA

ARCTIC

INUVIALUKTUN

NORTH GREENLANDIC

INUKTITUT

Greenland

WEST GREENLANDIC

EAST GREENLANDIC

NORTH ATLANTIC OCEAN

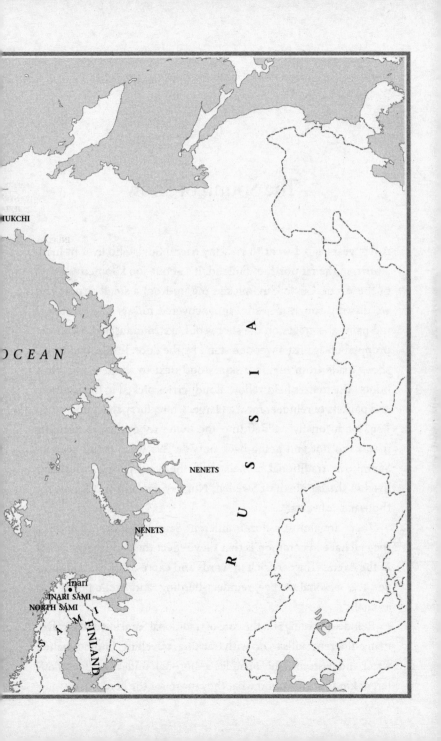

The Sound of Snow

A few years ago, I went to visit my friend Suvi, who lives in Inari, a town in the far north of Finland. It's about 300 kilometres north of the Arctic Circle. Suvi picked me up from a small airport and we drove through majestic, snow-covered forests to a cluster of red-painted cottages on the shores of Lake Muddusjävri. Skis were propped up against a wooden stand by the door. Inside, traditional shoes made from reindeer skin stood next to slippers and snow boots. The freezer held yellow cloudberries picked in the summer, and packets of reindeer meat. A large, white, furry sheepdog called Jieŋâ occasionally padded into the living room, before deciding it was too hot and going back outside. We were at the heart of Sápmi, the traditional homeland of the Sámi people, who have lived in the far north of Sweden, Norway, Finland and Russia for thousands of years.

There are almost a dozen different Sámi languages. One thing they all have in common is that they reflect the daily reality of life in the Arctic. They are rich in words and expressions around snow and ice, seasonal change, reindeer-herding, and Arctic plants and animals.[1]

Reindeer-herding is at the core of traditional Sámi life, and involves many different skills to do with tracking, travelling, finding shelter, water and pastures. This includes a thorough understanding of different kinds of snow, and what they mean for the herd.

In North Sámi, which is spoken by about twenty thousand people in northern Sweden, Finland and Norway, *vahca* refers to freshly fallen snow that can soften the underlying, harder layer and help reindeer dig for the nourishing lichen underneath. *Seaŋáš* refers to the granulated snow that forms at the bottom of several layers, usually from January to April. Reindeer can easily dig through *seaŋáš* to find food.[2]

Čearga is snow that has been stirred up and blown around by strong, cold winds. This broken, frozen, icy snow is so hard that neither the reindeer nor their herders can dig through it. It can be up to one metre deep. *Čearga* also makes it hard to track the reindeer.

Geardni is snow that melts and refreezes as an ice crust. It's not as packed as *čearga*, but also makes it harder for the reindeer to graze.

Čiegar is a winter pasture covered in old snow that's been dug up and trampled by reindeer. *Fieski* is a winter pasture where reindeer have dug up the snow only recently. *Suovdnji* is a hole dug in the snow by a reindeer looking for lichen.[3]

All these terms are still commonly used among North Sámi-speaking reindeer herders.

While North Sámi is still quite widely spoken, other Sámi languages are much rarer. Inari Sámi, the ancestral voice of the area where Suvi lives, is spoken only by about four hundred and fifty people. Among them are Suvi and her children.

In some ways, teaching children an endangered heritage language should be no different from any other kind of multilingual parenting. The same reasons apply: giving your children a sense of identity and belonging, connecting them to their family's history and traditions, making it easier for them to learn more languages later on, and, of course, allowing them to enjoy the unique beauty of the language itself.

And yet, as I would discover during and after my visit, there is something special about bilingual parenting in a language at risk.

It's not just about transmitting a language. It's about trying to infuse an entire way of life with new energy and strength.

Arctic beauty

The Sámi family, and the Eskimo-Aleut family of Siberia, the Aleutian Islands, Alaska and Greenland, represent our northernmost languages. They stretch across a part of our planet that some would think uninhabitable, a harsh landscape of intense cold. Against the odds, people have thrived there, and have created things of beauty. Their languages capture an extraordinary history of resilience and resourcefulness. They contain knowledge that is crucial to surviving in this extreme environment.

Suvi is originally from southern Finland, and moved to Inari in her twenties. She first learned North Sámi, and later Inari Sámi. When I recently spoke to her on a video call, she said one of the things she loved about the language was the way it connected her to the forests and lakes around her. Inari Sámi place names, for example, convey a wealth of information accumulated by previous generations.

'The original place names carry so much meaning,' Suvi said. 'Every stone, every marsh, every hill – these place names tell stories. Whether it's wise to go there, what people used to do there. Suddenly, it's not a wilderness any more. This myth of "wilderness" collapses. Every place has been marked with an enormous amount of knowledge, because people have been here a very long time.'

When the place names are translated into Finnish, this meaning is lost. Suvi gave me the example of the bay where she lives. In Inari Sámi, its name is 'Siggávuonâ', which means 'Siggá Bay'. According to local legend, Siggá was a beautiful woman whose two suitors accidentally killed each other in an archery competition. In her grief, Siggá filled the bay with tears. In Finnish, the place is called

'Sikovuono', which translates as 'Pig's Bay', just because this sounded similar to the original name. The meaning is lost, replaced by a non-sensical name, because the bay has nothing to do with pigs.

Before I went to visit Suvi in Inari, I was of course impressed by her efforts to revive Inari Sámi, out of a general respect for linguistic diversity. But it didn't occur to me that this language might have a practical use.

This changed when I spent a week with Suvi and her family at the cottage where they lived at the time, on the shores of Lake Muddus-jävri, surrounded by endless forests. It was March. The timing was carefully chosen. The polar night, which had started in December and left the land in semi-darkness for weeks, had recently ended. The relentless, twenty-four-hour sun of the summer had not yet begun. Everything was covered in thick, rich snow. Lake Muddusjävri was frozen so solid that we drove across it with a snowmobile.

Every morning, I skied across the lake with Jieŋâ, the white dog. She belonged to Anna, Suvi's friend, who is from an Inari Sámi family. As I skied, Jieŋâ raced around me in wide loops. Once we reached the far side, I sat down on the snowy shore, opened my backpack, fed her a treat, and gave myself a restorative cinnamon bun and some coffee from a thermos. At some point, she started digging under my skis, her signal that it was time to head home.

I'd never felt so free, and so at peace with the world. I skied back, the dog running around me, the tiny red cottage in the distance growing larger and larger, until I could hear the voices of Suvi, Anna and the children.

During the day, we went ice-fishing, watched herders round up reindeer in a corral, or visited a Sámi cultural centre called Sajos in Inari, the nearest village. As vast and sparsely populated as the area was, there was a noticeable excitement over culture and languages. The centre was big, sleek and modern, and housed the Sámediggi, the Sámi Parliament of Finland, an archive and a library. One of the library's walls was covered with children's drawings of their homes, each capturing the essentials: a house with a snowmobile parked next to it, a smiling family, and a *lávvu*, a foldable, conical Sámi tent.

Little by little, I found myself shifting to a completely new perspective on what makes a language useful. For all the activities I enjoyed and observed that week, Inari Sámi was the perfect language. It can tell you everything you need to know about that frozen lake and the ice on it, about fishing and reindeer-herding, about berry-gathering, about Sámi arts and crafts. It can also, on a more basic level, help you to survive.

During the recent video call, I could see green grass and crocuses from my window. It was early spring in London. Suvi showed me the view from her own window: a snow-covered landscape, with conifers and fjells in the distance. The previous week, temperatures had dropped to minus thirty-six. This week, it was a balmy minus ten.

I'd called her just before midday, Arctic time. As we spoke, the sun rose. Suvi grew very excited. It was the first time she'd seen the sun in two months. Officially, the Arctic night had ended a couple of weeks before, but the sun had still been too low, hidden behind the fjells. Now, it appeared over them, bathing the living room in sunlight. As we talked, it went down again.

To an outsider, this part of the world can appear both stunningly beautiful and starkly inhospitable to humans. The Inari Sámi language tells a different story: that this is a good place to live, that humans can be happy here. Once you know this, it seems incredible that this hardy and useful language almost died out.

'We two ski'

Inari Sámi was never spoken by millions, simply because there aren't millions of people in the Arctic. Even in the early nineteenth century, when everyone in the Inari area spoke Inari Sámi, the population only amounted to about a thousand people.[4] This was therefore the total number of Inari Sámi speakers in the world. It was enough for the language to flourish, and to create a rich heritage of songs, stories, and specialist terms.

By the 1990s, that number had dramatically declined. There had been pressure on Inari Sámi since the mid-nineteenth century. First, North Sámi reindeer herders came to Inari and brought their mother tongue with them. The two Sámi languages share similarities, but they are different. 'Fish', for example, is *guolli* in North Sámi, and *kyeli* in Inari Sámi. The word for 'past' or 'done' is *meattá* in North Sámi, and *lappâd* in Inari Sámi. You can see how knowing one would certainly help you learn the other, but they're not identical.

In the early twentieth century, an increasing number of Finns moved to Inari from more southern regions, and brought Finnish. The Sámi languages are related to the Baltic Finnic family, which also includes Finnish and Estonian. They share certain similarities, but are ultimately distinct. For example, Inari Sámi has a dual form, used to refer to two people, a pair. *Čyeigeen* means 'we two ski', while *čuoigâm* means 'I ski', and *čuoigâp* means 'we ski'. Finnish may have had a dual in the past, but no longer does.

In this increasingly multilingual setting, Inari Sámi became a minority language. And then two brutal, traumatic events changed the fate of Inari Sámi, and the people who spoke it.

One was the Lapland War, fought between Finland and Nazi Germany from 1944 to 1945. During the fighting, almost all the inhabitants of Lapland were evacuated to southern Finland. As the Germans retreated, they pursued the scorched-earth tactic of destroying villages and laying landmines. Many Sámi learned Finnish during the evacuation. When they returned to their devastated homeland and slowly rebuilt their lives, they continued to speak

Finnish. They taught it to their children because they thought it would offer them better prospects in the world than Sámi.

The other historical wound was inflicted by boarding schools. Until the early twentieth century, Sámi children had been taught in mobile schools. The teachers, who usually knew Sámi languages, simply moved from one village or group of families to another. In the 1920s, the Finnish state ceased to fund those roaming schools, and instead set up boarding schools where Sámi children were taught in Finnish and banned from speaking Sámi. Children as young as seven were removed from their families and mother tongue, and housed in dormitories. When they returned home, the parents assumed that the native language was lost, and spoke Finnish with them.[5]

It was against this painful historical backdrop, with a dwindling language that seemed to be doomed, that a team of teachers, families and volunteers decided to revive Inari Sámi.

The revival

The fight to revive Inari Sámi started in the 1990s, thanks to a special type of nursery known by the lovely name of 'language nest' (*Kielâpiervâl* in Inari Sámi, *Kielâ* meaning language, and *piervâl*, bird's nest). Language nests are widely used to boost threatened languages, not just Sámi. The idea is to surround the children with their ancestral language, often with the support of elderly native speakers.

The first Inari Sámi nest was quite successful, in that it taught the language to forty children. However, to reach more children, and support them over a longer time span, the language needed adult teachers – and those were scarce. If Inari Sámi was to survive, it needed to be reclaimed by adults who'd grown up speaking Finnish. They were known as the lost generation: Inari Sámi people who no longer spoke their ancestral language.

The solution was a rather unusual language course.

The word 'course' doesn't really do it justice; it was a mission, a calling. With the support of various experts and volunteers, Marja-Liisa Olthuis, an Inari Sámi linguist, devised a year-long, intensive programme that would immerse a group of Finnish-speaking adults in Inari Sámi. The curriculum was put together from scratch, drawing on other efforts at language revitalization around the world. There was a core of conventional teaching: classes on grammar, pronunciation, vocabulary, Sámi literature and oral storytelling; homework and independent study. But the most interesting part of the course was its ambition to unleash the full potential of Inari Sámi, by organizing activities that showed the language at work: fishing, singing, cooking, and making things.

Suvi was one of the students on the programme. Her children were attending the Inari Sámi language nest, and she'd already learned North Sámi. But this was an entirely different experience, a true cultural, linguistic and historical immersion.

In a seminar series called 'Fishing I', 'Fishing II' and 'Fishing III', the students went out on the lake with their teachers, and older native speakers. They learned the traditional arts of net-making and winter fishing out on the lake, along with many fish-related words.

In another outing, they attended a reindeer round-up with an Inari Sámi female reindeer herder, and helped her turn a freshly butchered reindeer into sausages. They cooked soup from reindeer hooves, and made dumplings from reindeer blood, learning how to use all parts of this precious animal, and enriching their vocabulary.[6]

Fishing and reindeer-herding are fundamental to Inari Sámi life, and to understanding many other aspects of the language, such as its concept of time. The linguist Anna Idström has analysed Inari Sámi expressions around time, and found that many are defined by the rhythm of herding and fishing. For example, the Inari Sámi word for August literally means 'the month when the reindeer have new, soft hair'.[7] May is 'the month of the reindeer calf'. The phrase 'Cuckoo is choking on an unripe cloudberry' refers to the end of June, when the cuckoo stops calling.[8]

In Inari Sámi, time is generally not treated as a resource in itself, as something that can be had, wasted, invested, spent or stolen. These metaphorical concepts of time as a resource, or specifically as a kind of money, exist in both Finnish and English. *Tämä tekninen apuneuvo säästää aikaa*, for example, is Finnish for 'This gadget will save you time'.[9] In Inari Sámi, however, there are no common expressions around time being invested, spent, or saved. The closest term that Idström found is '*Ij must lah äigi vyelgið kiirkon*', 'I don't have time to go to church'.

An Inari Sámi speaker would be more likely to focus on the outcome of a given decision, rather than casting it as a wise allocation of a resource, time. Instead of saying 'This plan is a waste of time', they would say, for example, '*Tallet maid kal leibilase*', 'This plan will not bring us any bread', or '*Tallet maid kal mälisalgâ*', 'This plan will not put meat in our soup'.[10]

This is why fishing, cooking and other practical activities formed such an important part of the Inari Sámi course. They allowed the students to learn different technical terms and broaden their vocabulary, but on a deeper level they also allowed them to engage with Inari Sámi on its own terms, in its own territory, where life was defined by the passing of the seasons, and by plans that would, or would not, put meat in the soup.

Dried pike

As Suvi was drawn deeper into the Inari Sámi language, her home life changed. Her children's paternal grandmother was Inari Sámi, but had stopped using the language. Now, encouraged by the language nest, she was speaking it to her grandchildren, for the first time in decades.

Gradually, the teaching language of Suvi's course shifted from Finnish to Inari Sámi, until only Inari Sámi was spoken in the classroom. The students made Inari Sámi music videos, and documentaries. Suvi and her classmates founded a band called Koškepuško, 'Dried Pike', and translated Finnish folk and pop songs into Inari Sámi. While working on her fishing skills with the other students, Suvi picked up a useful Inari Sámi saying: 'There are always fish in the water if not in the net.'[11]

In a breakthrough moment for the whole family, her elder son uttered his first full sentence in Inari Sámi, gathering all his language skills to criticize hers: '*Mun jiem haalijd kuldâliđ tuu, ko tun sáárnuh nuuvt hitásávt*' – 'I don't want to listen to you because you talk so slowly.' One of Suvi's children asked at every meal: 'Who has killed this?' (In Inari Sámi, instead of the euphemistic 'to catch a fish', people say 'to kill a fish'.)

Older Inari Sámi speakers became the students' faithful allies in this language-saving battle. The programme paired the students with 'language masters', people who still spoke Inari Sámi, and still knew traditional skills and stories. An unintended effect was that the masters found their own Inari Sámi refreshed and reinvigorated. They liked chatting to younger people, talking about their childhood memories, teaching them traditional words, and even learning some new ones. The students enjoyed hearing the native sound and rhythm, and spending time with the masters.

One master asked Suvi why she was trying to learn the language, given that she wasn't Sámi. She'd been thinking about that, too, and had sometimes felt hesitant about revitalizing a language that wasn't hers. She explained her reasons: she lived here, her children were growing up here, their paternal ancestors were Inari Sámi. He reflected in silence for a bit, then said: 'I respect that. Hard-working people. For me it is an honour to be your master.'[12]

One day, Suvi and a classmate visited the home of a language master called Unto, a former reindeer herder and baker who was born in 1939, on the shores of Lake Inari. Suvi had been nervous about the visit, wondering if she'd find the right words. It turned out that Unto had been nervous, too. He hadn't spoken Inari Sámi since his father and brothers died, and worried that his skills were rusty. But as they sat and talked, everyone relaxed. Unto was thrilled by every word his visitors said in Inari Sámi, the sound of his childhood, of his family. Looking at the two students, he said: 'I feel like I've known you forever. Could it be the language? It must be the language.'[13]

Rapping in Inari Sámi

Can you revive a language? In the case of Inari Sámi, there are some signs that the experiment is working out. Before the revival took off in the 1990s, Inari Sámi as a home language was lost. Now the number of speakers is growing, the adult immersion course attracts new students every year, and the language nest is so packed that there's a waiting list. All over the world, rural communities struggle with depopulation, as young people move to the cities in search of better opportunities. In the Inari Sámi community, however, the language revival has created new jobs in radio broadcasting, teaching and research.

In the process, social attitudes to the language have changed.

Mikkal Morottaja, also known as Amoc, is a musician from Inari who started rapping in Inari Sámi in the late 90s. At the time, few listeners understood the lyrics, but he lured them in with his voice and catchy beats. 'When I was a kid there were only four children speaking Inari Sámi as a mother tongue,' he told me in an email. But that changed, he said, due to the revitalization campaign. It created a new generation of Sámi speakers. As he said: 'Back in the day, being Sámi was a shameful thing. Nowadays, I bet most of Sámis are proud of being a Sámi.'[14]

There are of course challenges, too. Suvi points out that in such a small language community, there are fewer specialists around to help children who need speech therapy or other support. Some Inari Sámi textbooks that are translated from Finnish don't really suit the Arctic environment.

The biggest threat to Inari Sámi isn't cultural, but environmental: climate change. Global warming is endangering the Sámi people's traditional way of life, and the environment that has sustained them for thousands of years. In warmer winters, snow thaws and refreezes as ice, which makes it impossible for reindeer to dig for lichen. Reindeer herders have suffered from climate-induced accidents, as snowmobiles crash through the thinning ice. Their deep knowledge of snow and ice, expressed through a rich vocabulary, no longer reliably guides them through the long winter.

Some years ago, I had the pleasure of hearing Anna sing. She sings in two traditional Sámi ways, a North Sámi form called *yoiking*, and an Inari Sámi form called *livđe*. Suvi and Anna had come to London for my wedding. At a party before the wedding, Anna stood on a roof terrace in London, and the sound of her powerful voice swept over the rooftops. A couple of days later, at the wedding itself, she yoiked to some disco beats, and we all jumped around and danced with abandon. We were very far from the Arctic, but the music was just as stirring as it would be on the shore of a lake. The Sámi languages emerged out of a specific environment, and a specific way of living. But like all languages, they are also infinitely adaptable, and can give joy in so many different situations. And so we danced to songs about reindeer and forests, in a language that carried within it the story of the north.

Walrus Asleep on Ice

Languages allow the mind to travel widely, even when the body is stuck. As I was finishing this book, the Covid-19 pandemic spread around the world. I stayed at home, trying to do my bit to slow the deadly contagion. The museums and libraries were shut, the inspiring displays and rare books completely out of reach. Travelling anywhere to hear the sound of a foreign language in its home environment was, of course, out of the question. I was grateful for online journals and dictionaries, and for my stacks of notes. Every word in another language felt like a link to a region I would not be able to visit in person any time soon.

Generations of researchers had painstakingly collected and transcribed these words. Now their efforts helped me recreate entire landscapes and cultures in my mind, and took me away from the unfolding catastrophe for an hour or two.

Among the most compelling dictionaries are those of the Eskimo-Aleut language family, which stretches from the Chukchi or Chukotka Peninsula east of Siberia, across the Aleutian Islands and Alaska, all the way to Greenland. In the past, outsiders used 'Eskimo' to refer to the people who spoke these languages, but this term was never used by the speakers themselves. 'Yupik' and 'Inuit' are now used to refer to the people. 'Eskimo' is still used in linguistics, as in 'Eskimo languages'. The Eskimo group subdivides into Yupic, which encompasses quite distinct languages, and Inuit, a collection of somewhat similar dialects.[1]

These languages describe such a specific landscape, such a long human tradition of observing and interacting with it, that I quickly found myself immersed in them. Before my inner eye, I watched seals and walruses clambering up onto ice floes, female polar bears digging dens in the snow, and whales swimming in pairs.

Just as Sámi languages are attuned to the rhythms of fishing and reindeer-herding, Inuit and Yupik express an awareness of and ability to describe fine, subtle phenomena related to this world of snow, ice and the sea. As Marie Greene, an Inuit leader, puts it in a foreword to one compendium: 'The words and meanings of this dictionary represent our unique world view which has evolved over thousands of years, as our ancestors have struggled to survive in order to leave this legacy to us.'[2]

Several highly specialized words from these languages have made it into English as loanwords. The English word igloo, for example, is rooted in the Inuit *iɣlu* (also spelled as *iglu*), meaning 'house'. In some regions, *iɣlu* refers specifically to a snow house, but in others it's a house made of sod (strips of soil).[3] An *iɣlu* can also be a non-human dwelling, such as a beaver dam.[4] As the word migrated into other languages, 'iglu' or 'igloo' came to be associated with just one type of building: the iconic dome-shaped house made of blocks of packed snow.

Kayak is another famous Inuit loanword in English. It's derived from the Inuit *qayaq* (also spelled *qajaq*), a slender boat used by hunters. Less well-known is the Inuit word *qayau*. It describes a common experience among first-time kayaers: 'to capsize in a kayak'.[5] Greenlandic Inuit adds a more tragic twist: *qayaa*, to 'capsize and drown from a kayak'.[6]

In the age of global warming, the landscapes and experiences encapsulated by Eskimo-Aleut languages are facing an existential threat. Knowing this makes reading an Eskimo dictionary a rather bittersweet experience. One wonders how many of the animals, natural features and hunting or fishing customs in it will still be there for future generations. On the other hand, every Eskimo dictionary is a call to action, a reminder of a whole world that will be lost when the snow and ice melt.

Seal warming itself on ice

One delightful mini-category of Inuit and Yupik words might be called 'animals interacting with ice and snow'. The Inuit word *kikkuliq*, for example, refers to a seal hole in the ice.[7] In Naukanski Siberian Yupik, the word *nunavaq* means 'walrus asleep on ice'.[8] This is not to be confused with another Naukanski Siberian Yupik word, *uxtaq*, which means 'walrus on an ice floe' (derived from *uuxte-*, to get up on something).[9] In Eastern Canadian Inuit and Greenlandic Inuit, the word *uuttuq* means 'seal warming itself on ice' or 'basking seal'.[10] In Inupiaq, a group of Alaskan Intuit dialects, *paamaguaq* refers to a 'creeping, crawling animal' such as a seal crawling on the ice, 'his breathing hole having frozen over'.[11]

In Western Canadian Inuit, *apitsiuvik* means a polar bear's den in a snowdrift.[12] This is similar to the North Alaskan Inuit word, *apitciq*. It refers to a female polar bear, which gives birth to its young in a hollow snowdrift. In the same dialect, *aniguyyaq* means snow hut or snow shelter, and also 'winter den of female bear'.[13]

Speaking of bears, as far as I know, Inuit and Yupik are the only languages in the world that have a word for 'polar bear'. Outside the Arctic, people tend to take their own word for 'bear' and then add *Arctic*, *polar*, *white*, *ice* and so on, to clarify the type of bear they mean. Thus the Russian word for polar bear is *Polyarnyy medved*, *medved* meaning bear. The Mandarin word is *běijíxióng*, literally, far-North-bear. The Dutch word is *ijsbeer*, ice-bear. But in Inuit and Yupik, this bear has a unique, specific name: *nanuq*. As in this sample sentence from an Inupiaq dictionary: '*Nanuq nanuigaqtuq aputmun*', 'the polar bear keeps rubbing himself against the snow'.[14]

As in many languages, Inuit and Yupik words to do with nature are also used metaphorically for humans and human behaviour.

The Inuit root word *alupaq* (or *alupak*) means 'to look after someone'. It can refer to a pair of whales swimming together. In Greenlandic Inuit, it also means to take one's wife along on a sledge, or to stick together all the time as a husband and wife, or a female seal and its pups.[15] Several Yupik languages have a specific word for kissing 'in the older style by pressing the nose against the face and sniffing softly'.[16] It is *cingar*.[17]

Hunting and fishing terms provide rich fodder for Inuit and Yupik metaphors, just like in English, where one can be snared or lured by a false promise, find oneself trapped, or rise to the bait. In Greenlandic Inuit, *tirlik* is a seal that 'lies safely in water and is easy to approach', while in Eastern Canadian Inuit, *tirli* is to 'be an unsuspecting victim' as well as 'game unaware of being hunted'.[18]

Amid the wealth of Arctic-specific words and expressions, there are some that have surprising parallels in English. In some Inuit languages, *aliuq* or *aliuqtuq* means to see a ghost. It can also mean to be amazed or astonished, be surprised by an unexpected sight – as someone told in English, 'you look like you've seen a ghost'.

How many words?

You may have heard that the Inuit have many words for snow. You may also have heard that this is a myth, and that this apparent glut of words is really just derived from a handful of basic roots.[19] So which is correct?

Firstly, it depends what you mean by 'word'. Both Yupik and Inuit are agglutinative languages, meaning that individual units can be strung together to form new expressions. Inuit speakers could therefore generate an infinity of words for snow (and for anything else they fancy describing) just by creating such new combinations from existing roots. As the anthropologist Laura Martin argues, 'the structure of Eskimo grammar means that the number of "words" for snow is literally incalculable'.[20]

On the other hand, even in languages where speakers can theoretically spend their days creating endlessly long and varied word chains, in practice they tend to draw from a core set of agreed-upon, commonly used words. These are the words collected in dictionaries, for example. Studying them can give us an idea of the general priorities of the language and its speakers, their areas of interest and expertise, even if on an individual basis people may invent additional words. That does not mean a language is eternally trapped in that one specialization. All languages can adapt to all circumstances. Eskimo languages could adapt to a landscape without snow. But so far, they have evolved to be particularly useful when talking about snow.

Asifa Majid, a specialist in cross-cultural perspectives on languages, has studied this phenomenon of linguistic specialization in the area of sensory perception. Certain languages have more agreed-upon words in specific areas, meaning they have developed a shared way of talking about some things or experiences. English has many such words in the visual domain. In experiments, different English speakers all tend to call a three-pointed shape a 'triangle', and a given colour as 'green'. Other languages, such as Lao, have an established, agreed-upon vocabulary for tastes. When given a bitter-tasting drink, all Lao speakers in an experiment described it as bitter. English speakers were more uncertain, and described it as sour or salty, or resorted to comparisons, saying it tasted like ear wax.[21] The reasons for such specialization are not always entirely clear. It may be that Lao cuisine favours a wider palette of flavours, including bitterness.

Speakers of agglutinative languages, which in theory can give rise to endless new word combinations, also tend to congregate around such agreed-upon words. The Internet abounds with examples of very long words in agglutinative languages, but those words are often artificial, created to entertain or make a point. In 2017, the multilingual Euronews channel in France held a competition to test which of its international journalists could come up with the longest word.

The winner was a Turkish word:

muvaffakiyetsizleştiricileştiriveremeyebileceklerimizdenmişsinizcesinesiniz.

According to an online article about this competition, it means: 'As though you are from those whom we may not easily be able to make into a maker of unsuccessful ones.' The article named 'anti-disestablishmentarianism' as one of the longest English words.[22]

It's debatable whether such grammatical acrobatics give a meaningful insight into these languages, or even into agglutination as used in everyday life. Unless you approach speech as an endurance sport, or are trying to win a game of Scrabble, you're unlikely to spend your days testing grammatical limits. Even in languages where endless words can be created, there tends to be a somewhat stable inventory of words that are actually used, that have a commonly understood meaning and a history.

The Inuit could in theory create all sorts of completely random words for snow. But they don't do that, at least not according to the dictionaries I've consulted. Instead, their snow-related terms very specifically reflect their environment, and their own relationship with it.

Lawrence Kaplan, a specialist in Eskimo languages, says this close attention to nature shouldn't be surprising. After all, it's critical to their hunting success and survival. As a result, 'linguists and others familiar with these languages have always taken it for granted that there is extensive vocabulary for the areas in question'.[23]

So how do the Inuit talk about snow?

Drifting, floating, falling

Some expressions are derived from words that originally had nothing to do with snow. Thus the verb *natirvik*, meaning 'drifting snow', is based on the noun *natiq*, meaning 'floor, bottom', according to Kaplan. *Puktaaq*, 'iceberg', is derived from *pukta*, 'to float'.[24]

Most Eskimo languages also have a number of common, basic words for different kinds of ice and snow. The Comparative Eskimo Dictionary mentions *qanik*, *qannik* or *qanniq*, for falling snow, snow-flake, snow in the air; *apun*: snow on the ground; *anigu* or *aniu* for fallen snow, which is also used to make water. The word *pukak* refers to granular, icy or crystallized snow.

Some Inuit snow words have an equivalent in English, but are arguably used in a more precise way. *Qinu* means slushy ice. In Eastern Canadian Inuit, it also refers to the thickening of the sea close to shore, before it freezes solid in autumn.[25] *Mauyak* is deep snow into which one may sink. *Aqilluqaq* is a bank of soft snow after a snowfall, from *aqit*, to be soft. Note that some of these words are derived from others, and may not strictly count as pure 'snow words'. But they still add up to an expressive, shared, agreed-upon way of describing and talking about snow.

Ciku or *siku* is a common Inuit word for ice. In West Canadian Inuit, *mituit* are small pieces of ice forming a thin cover on water. *Auniq* means 'rotten ice' in various Inuit dialects. It also refers to ground uncovered by melting snow in spring, or ice and snow that has become unsafe. In Eastern Canadian Inuit, *aukkaniq* means melted sea ice, while *illauyaq* is ice that forms sharp crystals when it breaks up in spring.[26]

These languages reveal a dynamic, finely calibrated relationship between humans and nature, as each adjusts and responds to the actions of the other. Fittingly, the Inuit word *sila* means weather, air, but also intelligence, or spirit.

As I looked up the different Yupik and Inuit words for this fragile landscape and the creatures in it, the disaster of the pandemic continued to unfold. It spread to even the most remote regions, to Arctic towns and villages that initially had seemed safe. The world ground to a halt. I read that in many countries, wild animals were roaming into areas that had only shortly before been teeming with humans, with walkers and swimmers. Then I returned to the Eskimo dictionaries, to a world that was still in balance, at least on the page. I had never visited Greenland or Alaska, and now wondered if I ever would, and if so, what these landscapes would look and feel like by the time I did.

One of my favourite words in Eskimo languages has nothing to do with snow. It's *qavlunaq*, a Yupik word, and refers to the ripple, wave or wake left by something swimming just below the surface of the water, such as a fish, or a seal.[27]

Kafka's Blue Notebook: Multilingual Creativity

In 1917, the year Franz Kafka was diagnosed with tuberculosis, he began studying Hebrew. Initially, he taught himself from books at his home in Prague. Later, he hired private teachers. He continued learning the language until his death from the side effects of tuberculosis in 1924. Why did Kafka pour so much of his dwindling energy into a language that for centuries had only been used in some scattered Jewish communities, and in religious worship?

One reason was a general love of languages. Kafka had grown up speaking and writing in German and Czech, with some traces of the Yiddish spoken by his ancestors. He studied Greek, Latin, French and some classical Hebrew at school, and continued to learn languages over the course of his life, fired by intellectual curiosity and a delight in new sounds and words.

Another was related to his quest to find a place in the world. Kafka thought deeply about his identity as a Jewish writer living with or between several cultures and languages. Despite being considered one of the greatest modern writers in the German language, he never felt fully at home in it. The idea of a newly invigorated language, tied to a Jewish homeland, was tempting in that context.

As assimilated Jews, his family in Prague had shrugged off Yiddish, confined Hebrew to religious settings, and embraced the prestigious German as one of their main languages, along with the practical

Czech. Kafka felt that the family's shift from Yiddish to German had come with a loss, in particular a loss of warmth and emotional closeness. The German word for mother, *Mutter*, sounded cold and distant to him. Nevertheless, he used it for his own mother, because those were the social norms of the educated middle-class at the time.[1] He wrote in his diary: 'Yesterday it occurred to me that I did not always love my mother as she deserved and as I could have done, because the German language hindered me. The Jewish mother is no "Mutter", the Mutter-term makes her a little strange.'[2]

He once wrote to a friend about the agonizing 'impossibility of not writing, the impossibility of writing in German, the impossibility of writing differently'.[3] His multilingual and multicultural essence was at odds with an increasingly nationalistic Europe that required people to pledge allegiance to one country, one culture, one language.

'The great space of one's own ignorance'

As was often the case with Kafka, his feelings about his own language skills were somewhat ambiguous, veering between optimism and spiralling anxiety. During one of several trips to Italy, he wrote in his diary that 'every Italian word addressed to one, penetrates the great space of one's own ignorance and therefore preoccupies one for a long time, regardless of whether it was understood or not understood. One's own uncertain Italian can't hold its own against the certainty of the Italians and therefore easily goes unheard, regardless of whether it's understood or not.'[4]

Referring to his Italian, he once called himself an inept 'Klotz', Yiddish for stupid or clumsy (in German, the word *Klotz* literally means 'wooden block'; in Yiddish, it's more commonly written as *Klutz*).[5] In the application form for his job with Assicurazioni

Generali, an insurance company, Kafka noted that he was proficient in German and Czech, as well as French and English, though the latter two were a little rusty.[6]

When Kafka took up Hebrew lessons as an adult, the language was bursting with new energy. At one point he even planned to emigrate to Palestine and contribute to the resurgence of Hebrew, a plan scuppered by his poor health.[7] Hebrew had always been used in some communities, such as the Jews of medieval Cairo, but in the late nineteenth century, it was revived by people who had never before spoken it in daily life. This was an intensely emotional process, as well as an enormous linguistic and educational challenge.

For the language to truly take off, children had to learn it as their mother tongue. This meant their parents had to leave behind their own languages and launch themselves into Hebrew.

The pioneers among them were Eliezer Ben-Yehuda, a Lithuanian, and his wife, Deborah. In the early 1880s, they moved to Jerusalem and had a son, Ithamar. They raised him only in Hebrew. Ben-Yehuda banned all other languages from the home, though Deborah secretly sang to the boy in Russian, her mother tongue. Ithamar would remember one of her lines for the rest of his life, from a poem by Mikhail Lermontov, a Russian poet: 'A single sail a blaze of white through haze on a pale blue sea.'[8] (In his memoir, Ithamar remembers the line as: 'across the waves of the blue sea'.)

Ithamar became the first child to be raised in modern Hebrew, and the first native speaker of the language in its modern form. His parents coined the Hebrew words for objects, plants and animals that had no name in the language, such as doll (*bouba*), violet (the flower: *segoulit*) and butterfly (*parpar*, from an Aramaic word meaning 'agitated').[9]

*

Chatting about carpets

The vigour and youth of Hebrew seemed to appeal to Kafka. He is sometimes thought of as a morose and inward person, but he had a lively and humorous side that is evident from his letters and his diary. In 1923, during a spa retreat, he delightedly wrote to a friend about meeting a group of 'healthy, cheerful, Hebrew-speaking children'. He corresponded with young Hebrew-speakers, and read new Hebrew literature.[10] During an earlier holiday in Meran, an Alpine spa town, he wrote to a friend that he'd met 'a Turkish-Jewish carpet dealer, with whom I exchanged my few words in Hebrew'.[11]

At that point, he'd only recently started teaching himself, and yet seemed to feel less anxious about speaking Hebrew than in his previous struggles with conversational Italian. It may have helped that this was a language in progress, meaning he did not have to feel automatically inferior to native speakers. After all, modern native speakers in Hebrew had only come into existence quite recently. The language offered the possibility of 'writing differently', as he had once put it, of finding a different linguistic and cultural identity.

Kafka experimented with Hebrew as a literary language. In 1923, he wrote a letter to his Hebrew teacher, a woman called Puah Ben-Tovim, who was having a disagreement with her parents about her academic plans. She was waiting for a letter from them with their final thoughts on the matter. Kafka's letter to her, written in Hebrew, contains some striking metaphors and conveys his characteristic empathy tinged with despair:

'I understand the confusion one feels when waiting for a decisive letter that's straying around somewhere. How many times in my life have I burnt through such fear. One is surprised that one doesn't turn into ash even earlier than is the case in reality. I'm very sorry that you too are suffering that way, my dear Puah.'[12]

Around that time, Kafka read only Hebrew literature. A shabby, thin blue notebook from 1922, which he'd filled with line after line of obscure German words and their Hebrew translation, suggests that Kafka saw literary potential in it for himself, too.[13] The notebook reads almost like a parody of a Kafka story, with very specific words related to matters of health, bugs, legal and administrative processes, and soul-wrenching emotions.[14]

One entry that jumps out is the German word *Verleumdung* (defamation or denunciation), translated into Hebrew.[15] This also appears in the opening line of one of Kafka's greatest novels, *Der Proceß*, 'The Trial': '*Jemand mußte Josef K. verleumdet haben, denn ohne daß er etwas Böses getan hätte, wurde er eines Morgens verhaftet.*' ('Someone must have denounced Josef K, for one morning, without having done anything bad, he was arrested.')[16]

Continuing the theme of betrayal and punishment, Kafka noted down the Hebrew words for the German *Spott* (mockery), *Treubruch* (breach of trust), *Verabscheuen* (to despise), *Betrügen* (to betray), *Niederträchtigkeit* (baseness, vileness, trickery), *Rechtsentscheidung* (legal decision), *Frevel* (sacrilege), *Religionsverfolgung* (religious persecution), *Richter* (judge), *Vertilgung* (extermination), and other transgressions and punishments.

Another category relates to bugs and health. Kafka looked up the Hebrew words for *Schabe* (a kind of cockcoach or bug), *Erholungsheim* (sanatorium), *Schwindsucht* (consumption, as in the disease), *verschmachten* (to waste away), *Heilmittel* (remedy).

Judging by some pages, Kafka may have been either reading or planning to write a Hebrew story set in a seaside sanatorium. On one page are *Brühe* (broth), *Frühstück* (breakfast), *Tau* (dew), *Verlangen* (desire), among other words; on the next are *Leuchtturm* (lighthouse), *Meereswoge* (sea-wave), *klatschen* (the sound of waves splashing against rocks or a lighthouse), *Kühle* (cool air), *Schönheit* (beauty), but also *Pflege* (care) and *gesund machen* (to heal). Reading the words, my mind could not help but picture a coughing young man arriving at his seaside retreat, waking up the next morning to a breakfast of broth, then walking through the dewy sea grass to a beach where he listened to the waves wash against a lighthouse.

Writing in tongues

Does multilingualism make a person more creative? I doubt it. There are infinite examples of people who are not particularly good at languages, but who do astonishing things with the one language in which they feel confident. Albert Einstein famously struggled with English, even after living in the United States. He once wrote a (German) poem for his American translator and interpreter, Helen Porter-Lowe, after she moved away: '*Dass Du schiedst ist fürchterlich / Denn was mach' ich ohne Dich/ Wenn auf Englisch man mich quält / Und das rechte Wort (mir fehlt)*' (That you left is terrible / For what am I going to do without you / When they torture me in English / and I can't find the right word).[17]

Mixing languages on the page, can, however, be both artistically and emotionally fulfilling. It can create friction and energy, and fashion a space where these languages interact and enrich each other. Just as Kafka searched for a language of his own, one that would feel like home, so many present-day writers continue to build themselves multilingual sanctuaries.

For the French-Congolese writer Alain Mabanckou, layering languages is a way of shaping the French canon rather than trying to fit into it. As he told an interviewer in 2010: 'I learned French when I was six. This means that before six I was speaking five or six African languages: Bembé, Lingala, Laari, Munukutuba, Vili, Kamba. I was shocked to see later on that there was no literature in these languages. Nothing is *written* in Bembé or in Lingala – they're oral languages. The only way to reach any knowledge about writing was by learning French literature in school.' He felt frustrated by having to write in a colonial language, and eventually remodelled French to fit his purpose. His novel *Broken Glass* is 'written in French, but if you feel the rhythm of the prose, it's like the Congolese way of speaking... I'm proud that I now finally found a way to deal with the French.'[18]

In Raymond Antrobus's poem 'Conversation with the Art Teacher (a Translation Attempt)', a Somali-born deaf teacher tells him about her life, using British Sign Language (BSL). He writes her words down in English, which is different from BSL. At some point she questions whether it is even possible to write in sign language:

> I still know some Somali sign. Wait, you write down what I say, how? You know BSL has no English grammar structure? How you write me when I am visual? Me, into fashion, expression in colour. How will someone reading this see my feeling?[19]

Transcribing the signs forces the English language to adapt, to accept BSL on its own terms. Something similar happens in this passage from Salman Rushdie's novel *The Ground Beneath Her Feet*, in which English is reworked into a multilingual dialect:

> ... she could prattle on in Bombay's garbage argot, *Mumbai ki kachrapati baat-cheet*, in which a sentence could begin in one language, swoop through a second and even a third and then swing back round to the first. Our acronymic name for it was Hug-me. Hindi Urdu Gujarati Marathi English. Bombayites like me were people who spoke five languages badly and no language well.

I can see the scribes of ancient Qatna, who started their sentences in Akkadian and ended them in Hurrian, nodding along in agreement, familiar with the idea of cramming the maximum number of languages into a text.

Kafka arguably dreamed of a language that would be the European equivalent of Rushdie's Hug-me. Meanwhile, his linguistic discomfort resulted in a new and different kind of German. He cut a fresh path through the language.

Take the opening of *Die Verwandlung*, 'Metamorphosis': '*Als Gregor Samsa eines Morgens aus unruhigen Träumen erwachte, fand er sich in seinem Bett zu einem ungeheueren Ungeziefer verwandelt.*' In English, this means something like: 'As Gregor Samsa woke one morning from fitful dreams, he found himself in his bed, transformed into a monstrous bug.' But it also doesn't, because in German, Gregor doesn't just find himself in his bed. Instead, he wakes up and realizes that while he was sleeping, right there in his bed, he was transformed into a … well, the '*ungeheueres Ungeziefer*', the monstrous bug, can't be translated either. In terrifyingly vague terms, it conjures up an image of something very big, unclean and uncanny.

As much as Kafka wrestled with his languages and agonized over them, he couldn't escape them. And sometimes, reading his stories and letters and diary entries and even that blue notebook, I have a feeling that he's in on the joke. He knows he's being self-indulgent, tearing his hair out over the soul-invasive experience of ordering a coffee in Italian. But he also feels that his intense experiences with languages are worth recording, and worth sharing with others. This was, after all, a writer who sent letters to friends about his '*Mäuse-furcht*' (mouse phobia) and '*Ungezieferangst*' (vermin phobia) after surviving a '*Mäusenacht*' (night of the mice) during which countless mice scurried all around him, a 'terrible silent noisy tribe'. In the morning, he felt such disgust and sadness that he was unable to get up, and spent the morning in bed. Even his bread tasted '*mäusig*', 'mousy'.[20] None of these words – *mäusig, Mäusenacht, Mäuseangst* – exist in standard German. Or rather, now they do, because of Kafka.

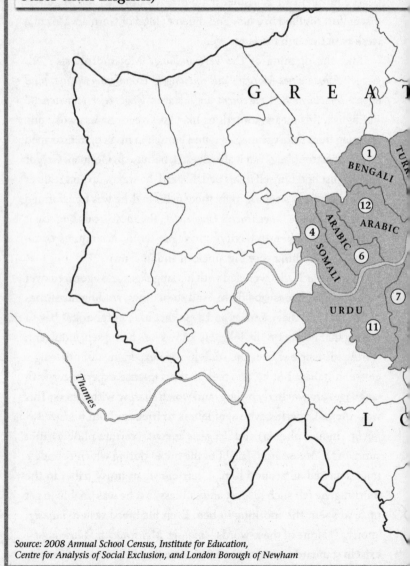

Main home language spoken by pupils at state schools in London, other than English (showing the language most widely spoken by pupils at home in each borough other than English)

GREAT

BENGALI

TURK

① BENGALI

⑫ ARABIC

④ ARABIC

SOMALI ⑥

⑦

URDU

⑪

L O

Thames

Source: 2008 Annual School Census, Institute for Education, Centre for Analysis of Social Exclusion, and London Borough of Newham

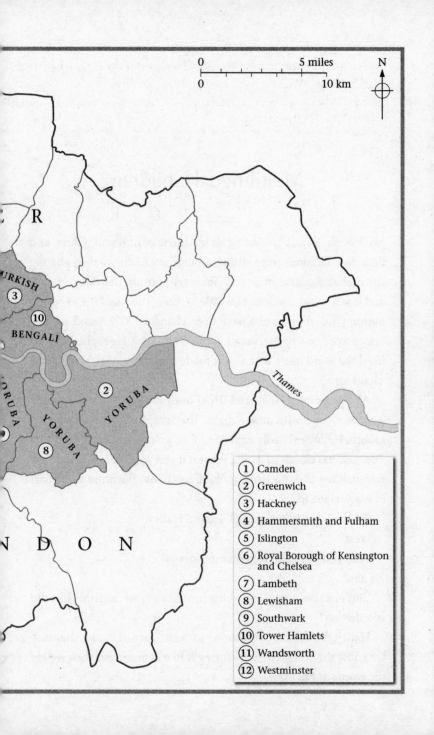

Map legend:

1. Camden
2. Greenwich
3. Hackney
4. Hammersmith and Fulham
5. Islington
6. Royal Borough of Kensington and Chelsea
7. Lambeth
8. Lewisham
9. Southwark
10. Tower Hamlets
11. Wandsworth
12. Westminster

Multilingual Children

My Korean friend Jae Young, her American husband, Chris, and their two children were sitting around my kitchen table, sharing their favourite Korean words. Their six-year-old daughter, Hailey, said it was *satang*, sweetie. Her little brother, Theo, said it was *omma*, mummy (all their names have been changed). Chris said his favourite word was *ppang*, bread. I asked him why. He replied that he liked the word itself, and also it made him think of *guleum ppang*, 'cloud bread'.

At this point, Hailey and Theo both jumped up and shouted '*guleum ppang!*' with utter delight. Theo snapped at the air with his mouth. Hailey excitedly explained that '*guleum ppang* is bread that flies, and has clouds in it, and you eat it and you fly'. I gathered they were talking about a Korean children's book, featuring some sort of magical bread.

'So the book is in Korean?' I asked Hailey.

'Yes!'

'And you all read it together in Korean?'

'Yes.'

'But just now, you were telling me the story in English. How did you do that?'

Hailey thought about it for a moment. Then she said: 'Because we know the story. We're picturing it in our head, and then we say the words in English.'

This was a very impressive answer and, actually, a neat summary of a process that's often described in more complex terms. Here's the same argument in the words of the writer and critic John Berger: 'True translation is not a binary affair between two languages but a triangular affair. The third point of the triangle being what lay behind the words of the original text before it was written.'[1]

This was exactly what Hailey was saying. She translated the Korean words into pictures, into a preverbal or non-verbal mental narrative. Then she told the story she could see, using English words.

Apart from being amazed by her analytical skills, I also knew exactly what she meant. Walking around London, where people speak in so many different languages, I sometimes understand what someone is talking about before identifying the language they said it in. It's as if my brain, immersed in so much noise, picks out meaningful sounds, without always bothering to label them with a language.

I have noticed a similar phenomenon in multilingual families. When I ask people which food words they remember in their parents' language, or which language they spoke on a given occasion or to specific relatives, they often pause and assume a kind of inward expression, as if replaying words and conversations, in order to consciously assign them to one language or another. Clearly, our internal language inventories aren't quite like books lined up on a shelf. Instead, they're more like a sort of magical library that has a life of its own. There are books in it, yes, and word lists. But sometimes, a story just unfolds as a play you can watch, or a voice you can hear, or even as a feeling. Hailey, for example, was watching the story of the cloud bread, and then helpfully narrated it for me in English.

The ability to translate and interpret is often taken for granted in multilingual children, but it's actually a sophisticated and very variable skill. Not all multilingual children can easily translate between their languages, even if they are fully proficient in them, separately. Indeed, many of the things multilingual children can do are far from automatic or innate. They are not just little sponges who passively absorb languages, as if all it takes is dropping them into a cauldron and fishing them out as perfect multilinguals. Multilingual children work very hard at their language skills, but in ways that can be easy to overlook. In that, they're similar to all language-learners. There's something else they have in common with all language-learners: their proficiency really fluctuates.

Children don't automatically become fluent in all the languages spoken in the home. Even within the same family, proficiency levels can vary dramatically between siblings. That proficiency can also change over time. A child may be completely native-like in language A in their early years, but later prefer language B, and even forget language A. Conversely, a child may grow up being not particularly fluent in one family language, but then claim that language for themselves by studying it at university, moving to the ancestral country for work, and so on.

As with all language-learning, time is a crucial ingredient. For all learners, the question is not so much how quickly you can learn a language. It's how you can ensure that you stick with it over time, because if you do, you will get better and better at it, and acquire an ever richer and deeper proficiency. This goes for adults enrolling in evening classes or downloading apps, and it goes for children in families where several languages are spoken. As inspiring and fascinating as multilingual children are, they are in some ways not that different from the rest of us, whose language acquisition seems so much more laborious. And because of these similarities, there's a lot we can learn from them. So how do they do it?

★

Language-learning

I used to think multilingual children had it easy. They simply inherited their parents' languages, then floated through life as effortless polyglots. Then I had my son, and realized how much behind-the-scenes work goes into the seemingly automatic process. Dan and I kept things simple by generally sticking to our own mother tongues, presenting German as Mama's language and English as Daddy's language. Still, keeping both languages going required by constant effort by all of us.

Rather than passively absorbing languages, children put an enormous amount of effort into learning them. This starts at birth, when they organize the languages around them by their prosodies, their different underlying melodies. Later, they assign sounds, words and grammatical patterns to each of these streams.

When you observe a bilingual child, you can sometimes witness that process in real time.

My son was almost two when he developed a great love of word lists. They were mostly about cars and other things with wheels. He recited them with the precision of a Sumerian scribe working on a cuneiform tablet: *Kipplaster* (dump truck), *Schubkarre* (wheelbarrow), *Rasenmäher* (lawnmower), and so on. One night, I was woken by a little voice in the dark, exclaiming joyfully: *Rasenmäher! Schubkarre, maybe wheelbarrow! Kipplaster!*

This was the start of a bilingual list phase. One by one, he matched up German words with their possible English equivalents. Sometimes he also added 'German' or 'English' after each word, in a hit-and-miss attempt to categorize them. *Kipplaster* was German, but, to his mind, so was 'washing machine'. The lists gave way to sentences. One day my son stood in the garden, pointed at a rose bush, and said: 'How do you say spiky plant in German?' After some reflection, he suggested the answer himself: 'Maybe, Piekpflanze' (literally, sting-plant). For a second, it was like being in someone else's mind, seeing a process that is usually silent and hidden. I realized that he was forming these sorts of hypotheses and guesses all the time, that all children do this, constantly updating their linguistic inventory to incorporate new ideas and observations.

Another time, he showed me a little toy mixer. I told him: '*Damit kannst du Kaffee mahlen*' (You can grind coffee with this). He stared at me, confused, and it occurred to me that he'd probably heard an exact homonym, '*Damit kannst du Kaffee malen*', *malen* meaning 'to paint'. I was about to clear up the misunderstanding, but he'd already run off to get some crayons, then sat down and began drawing on the side of his mixer. The phrase 'you can paint coffee with this' doesn't really make sense, but he was giving meaning to it as best he could. Moreover, he didn't even seem surprised that I'd said something nonsensical. It occurred to me that toddlers must think adults say weird things all the time. All they can do is take in our baffling instructions and try to convert them into meaningful actions.

In the past, it was thought that multilingual children learned to speak later than monolinguals, because they needed to figure out all these strange patterns and meanings in several languages. Research has shown that this is not the case. Speech delays do occur among multilinguals, but not at a higher rate than for monolinguals. However, while multilingual children develop at the same pace, they do so in a slightly different way.

Monolingual children typically produce their first word around the age of one, and start putting two words together between the ages of 1.5 and 2.2. This tends to apply to all languages, including sign language. Babies who acquire sign languages also sign their first word around one, and so on.[2]

Multilingual children hit those milestones at the same time, too. They even do this when they learn a spoken language and a sign language. In a Canadian study of babies who learned spoken

English and American Sign Language, or French and Langue des Signes Québécoise, all met the linguistic milestones of the first word, the first fifty words, and the first two-word combinations, 'on a timetable that was fundamentally similar to that of the mono-lingual babies.'[3]

In the case of multilingual children, those words are, however, distributed across two or more languages. This may sometimes give the impression that they are slower to speak.[4] Thus a monolingual child may know fifty words in, say, Spanish. A bilingual child of the same age will typically know twenty-five words in Spanish and twenty-five in English. Later, once the bilingual child acquires a full repertoire of countless words in both languages, that discrepancy tends to become less noticeable.

One might think that this intensive but ultimately satisfying cognitive process simply continues until the child is completely fluent in all the languages in the home, and that's it: they're multi-lingual.

Unfortunately, this is not the case. In many families, the day the child starts school or nursery marks an important turning point in their multilingual journey. Until then, all the languages in the home are equal. Once the children are out in the world, other, social factors start to affect which languages they will end up speaking, and how well.

Language strategies

Parents who want to raise their child bilingually will quickly learn a number of acronyms that pop up in online chats, books and videos for such families. They refer to different methods families can use to give their children the best chance of becoming fluent in two or more languages.

One of them is OPOL, short for 'one parent, one language'. With this strategy, each parent will speak to the child in their own native language (for example, Dan speaks English to our son, and I speak German to him). OPOL is very popular, because it allows each parent to use the language that comes to them naturally. Unfortunately, the method has some weaknesses, most of them linked to the family's wider linguistic environment.

In the home, all languages may be equal. Outside, however, one language will probably be the majority language, spoken by most people in daily life, as English is in the UK. The other will be a minority language, as German is in the UK. Once a child starts school, they will start using the majority language more and more. Children can adapt very quickly to these environmental shifts. My son speaks noticeably more English when he comes home from nursery, and more German after a day spent with me.

After a while, children may start using the majority language at home, too. One typical consequence is that the parent will speak in their own mother tongue, and the child will reply in the language spoken by everyone else. I hear these two-stream conversations all over London, in homes, on buses, in shops. Once, I walked past an older woman scolding her grown-up grandson in a language I couldn't identify. He replied in English: 'Oh my days, Granny, we're not in Cyprus any more!' His tone was a mixture of fondness and exasperation. I have no idea what their conversation was about, but I still think of this man as the voice of a whole second generation. Whenever my son answers back in English, I hear its echo. *Oh my days, we're not in your country, why should we still follow your ways?* It's an entirely reasonable reaction.

Conversations held in two or more languages are not necessarily detrimental to fluency. Many multilinguals can separate or merge their various languages depending on the situation. But in families using 'one parent, one language', the longer-term consequence may be that the second language is used less and less. Eventually, the child may become used to replying in the majority language, and rarely speak the other one. François Grosjean, a specialist in bilingualism, describes how 'little by little, the majority language will start taking over, much to the distress of the parent who uses the minority language'.[5] A study of close to two thousand families showed that one in four children raised with OPOL did not speak the minority language.[6]

Parents tend to be aware of this risk. There are a number of ways to promote the weaker language. Play groups, holidays in the old country, Skype sessions with relatives, books and cartoons can all help counter the slide into insignificance. Ideally, they fulfil two functions. They allow the child to hear the language more frequently and in many different contexts, thereby enriching their vocabulary. They also have a subtle propaganda effect, presenting the language as fun, varied and valuable, rather than just a strange sound made by one person.

'I still cherish it'

MLAH, or 'minority language at home', is another common method. It simply means that the whole family speaks the language of their ancestors. According to Grosjean, MLAH is much more effective than OPOL. Most children will learn to speak the family's language with this method.[7] This is perhaps not surprising. If a language is constantly spoken by all the parents or other carers in the home, the children are likely to speak it too, even if the outside world moves to a different sound. However, even in these families, many factors can affect the children's level of proficiency. One is how the parents feel about their language, and how keen they are to transmit it to the next generation.

My friend Alona grew up in a MLAH family. She came to the UK from Israel with her family when she was five. Their parents spoke only Hebrew at home. Alona and her siblings spoke English at school and with their friends. Alona's parents read Hebrew books, watched Hebrew TV, and conveyed their deep love of the language to their children. As Alona's dad, Daniel, told me, it was always precious to him, even as a boy.

'When I went to school in the 1950s, everybody made a big effort to speak good Hebrew,' he recalled. 'It has a lot to do with the beauty of the language. I think I was very proud of my good Hebrew. I can still remember teachers who taught me Hebrew when I was six, seven years old, and how much I appreciated and loved their Hebrew teaching. I still cherish it.'

Such commitment to a language is known to boost the chances of its survival. Children who are read to in the minority language, and who see their parents reading books or magazines in it, are more likely to become literate in it.[8] Family ties to the old country and a sense that the language is treasured also have a positive effect.[9]

On the other hand, even in families where both parents speak the minority language, the outside world may make its influence felt. Older siblings will often use the majority language at school and with their friends, making it more attractive to the younger siblings. This is one reason why proficiency tends to decline from one sibling to another (also, parents may run out of energy and give up on trying to promote their language as the family grows). In a study of Korean-American children, almost 80 per cent of first-borns spoke Korean with their parents before they started school, but only some 66 per cent of second-borns, and 43 per cent of third-borns.[10]

Other factors are completely outside the control of parents. When a language is tinged with shame, derided by other children and teachers, and associated with poverty or an undesirable cultural background, children may refuse to learn it. And parents may refrain from teaching it to them, fearing it will only bring trouble. Such social hostility to a language is known to make its transmission less likely.[11]

In Latin America, the use of indigenous languages tends to decline sharply as a person's income and education rise. Switching to Spanish can be an expression of moving up the social ladder, and leaving behind indigenous cultures that still face stigma and prejudice. Mainstream education is largely in Spanish. Younger, educated people tend to move to the cities, where Spanish is the dominant language. Even in communities where indigenous languages are still spoken by most people, the percentage of speakers dives to 5.3 per cent among those who have finished secondary school, and to less than 2 per cent among university graduates.[12]

Never too late

Studies of bilingual children often measure their proficiency in the early years. This can give the impression that if a child is not fluent in their home language by age five, or ten, or fifteen, they will never master it. What these childhood studies fail to take into account is that people can learn languages at any point in their lives. Even people who grew up monolingually can do this.

A study of native English speakers from the UK, Ireland and the United States who had moved to France at an average age of 28.6 years showed that all had learned French to the extent that they 'regularly passed for native speakers of French'.[13] Older adults can learn words at the same pace as younger adults.[14] Those who find language-learning hard actually benefit from it more than any others, in terms of brain growth. According to one study, 'struggling learners showed stronger increase of grey matter in middle frontal areas compared to more successful learners'.[15]

The speed at which children learn languages is often due to a mixture of factors. Children moving to a new country tend to be fully immersed in the language through school and friends, and have strong social incentives for mastering it. Adults may be able to choose jobs that don't require language skills, and may socialize with other immigrants.

Just as monolingual speakers can learn languages later in life, bilingual children can do many things to boost their proficiency as adults. Alona moved to Israel as an adult and came back to the UK with a firmer grasp of the language.

Another friend, Yukari, moved back and forth between Japan and the United States as a child, and worked in both places as an adult. Her parents are both Japanese, and followed the MLAH strategy of always using the language at home. Yukari speaks fluent Japanese and English, with a wide vocabulary in both because she supplemented her childhood exposure to those languages with new experiences in adulthood. She also uses Japanese in ways her parents probably didn't envisage when they taught it to their children. As a teenager at an American high school, she started learning French. She used *katakana*, a Japanese script of syllables, to spell out some of the French words phonetically, as an informal pronunciation guide for herself. More recently, she used the same shortcut to remind herself how Italian consonants were pronounced in different contexts. She added little *katakana* signs to her Italian notebook to remind herself that the Italian *ci* was pronounced チ ('tchi'), while *ca* was pronounced カ ('ka').

In my conversations with parents raising multilingual children, several saw their goal as providing options rather than ensuring native-like proficiency. They tried to work their different languages into daily routines, supplementing them with holidays in the old country, play groups and singalongs, cartoons and extra lessons. Many also followed an essential ritual of the modern bilingual parenting experience: Saturday school.

Saturday school

Every weekend, parents all over the UK dutifully usher their children to a community centre, church hall or private home where they sing and chat, and, later, read and write. These extra lessons are generally known as Saturday school or Sunday school. Some are run by places of worship, but many are organized by the families themselves. The informal Saturday and Sunday classes add up to a considerable educational movement when considered across language groups.

In Manchester alone, there are about a hundred such supplementary schools, teaching classes to some eight thousand schoolchildren.[16] Researchers from the University of Manchester visited twenty-three of them, which taught languages as diverse as Armenian, Tigrinya, Bosnian, Arabic, and many others. Some were tiny, others as large as a mainstream school. The Igbo Language Society consisted of a teacher and two pupils who met at a library. At the Huaxia Chinese School, a whole faculty of staff taught Mandarin to 400 children.

All these different groups faced very similar hopes and challenges. The parents and teachers commonly expressed a wish to instil a sense of cultural pride in the children, along with language skills. As staff at the Sudanese Supplementary School put it: 'It doesn't mean we don't want to integrate into the [British] community; it's just that we want the kids to understand their history because if you don't have a history you don't have a future.'[17]

Staff at a Somali school said that some decades ago, 'a lot of the parents were more concerned about pushing their children toward the mainstream language, to learn English. And it was the main concern for them that their children can be effective communicators. But now, a lot of parents are realizing the importance of the mother tongue.'[18]

At the Ensemble French School, set up by Francophone African families, the head teacher said they wanted the children to understand that African culture was not a 'second-class thing'. Teaching them French was part of that: 'We're not French, but we are French African.' A girl at the Ukrainian Saturday School expressed a very similar sentiment: 'It's good to try and keep it up, because it's where you're from.'[19]

Across cultures, there was a common concern: as much as the adults wanted the children to speak the ancestral language, the children often switched to English at the first opportunity.

The teachers at the Ukrainian Saturday School in Manchester said avoiding English was hard, since it was the children's main language. The Chinese teachers reported that the children preferred to speak English, even though many of the parents spoke Cantonese to them. The Bosnian teacher said that these days, many children came from mixed families, making English the dominant language in the home. A teacher at the Iranian Cultural Society sighed that 'most of the time, students speak to each other in break time in English, and then when they see me, they change to speaking Persian.'[20]

Some of the staff blamed the parents. One Panjabi teacher was particularly vexed by what he saw as a lack of cooperation: 'One of the children asked how to tell his mum he was hungry. In the following week, when the child came, he said: I did [ask my mum in Panjabi], but she answered in English "what do you want?"'

London children

In London, multilingual families have changed the soundscape of an entire city. In London's schools, more than two hundred different languages are spoken.[21] A survey of a million schoolchildren in

London, published in 2008, shows the whole world squeezed into the UK's capital. It lists the main languages spoken by the children at home, and breaks them down by borough.[22]

The most prominent language is of course English, spoken as a main language by more than six hundred thousand schoolchildren in Greater London (and presumably by all of them as a second language).

Among the other languages, the most widespread is Bengali, spoken by more than forty thousand children in Greater London. About half of them live in the borough of Tower Hamlets. South Asian languages generally make a strong showing in the survey, including Urdu, Panjabi, Gujarati, Tamil, Hindi, Malayalam, Nepali, Sinhala, Konkani, Telugu, Marathi, Pahari, Balochi. One of the less common South Asian languages in London is Sindhi, from Pakistan. It's spoken by all of sixty children in Greater London.

Then there are East Asian languages: Chinese, Tagalog, Vietnamese, Japanese, Korean, Thai, Malay, Mongolian, Burmese. And West and Central Asian tongues: Turkish, Farsi, Pashto, Kurdish, Hebrew and Aramaic. Aramaic, the language Jesus spoke, is still the home language of 180 children in London. Arabic, its successor, is of course much more strongly represented.

There are schoolchildren whose home languages come from different regions of Britain and Ireland, such as Welsh, Irish and Scots Gaelic. European languages are well represented, too, such as Polish, Greek, Italian, Lithuanian, German, Dutch/Flemish, French, Portuguese, Spanish, Romanian, Slovak, Czech, Hungarian, Romany, Maltese, Slovenian, Albanian, Russian, Serbian/Croatian/Bosnian, Bulgarian, Ukrainian, Armenian, Latvian, Macedonian, Georgian and Nordic languages.

Somali is spoken by more than twenty-four thousand children in London. Ethiopian languages, such as Tigrinya and Amharic, are also reported by the survey.

Some thirteen thousand children in London speak Yoruba, one of the main languages of Nigeria. The other West African languages spoken in London are Akan, Igbo, Ga, Krio, Edo/Bini, Wolof, Ebira, Hausa, Ewe, Urhobo/Isoko, Efik-Ibibio, Manding, Fula/Fulfulde-Pulaar, Mende, Esan/Ishan and Temne.

There are languages from East, Southern and Central Africa: Lingala, spoken in the Democratic Republic of Congo and the Republic of Congo, and Luganda, spoken in Uganda. Swahili, Shona, Acholi, Katchi, Afrikaans, Ambo, Ndebele, Bemba, Tigre, Zulu, Kikuyu/Gikuyu, Luo, Dinka/Jieng, Kinyarwanda, Chichewa/Nyanja, Xhosa and Lango have also found a foot-hold in London.

Sign languages and Creole languages are also mentioned, completing the impression of a city filled with almost every imaginable form of communication.

Some of these children will grow up fully proficient in their family's languages. Others will let the ancestral sound fade away. Their multilingual heritage may form a vast repertoire of stories and songs, or it may amount to only a handful of words. Some may even end up describing themselves as speaking only English. But when they think back to their childhood, they may find themselves in a place where a grandparent lets them sniff a fragrant brown spice called jeera, or where a parent cooks them a bowlful of atole.

Languages can affect us in ways that go far beyond rough measures such as fluency and grammar tests. One common sentiment I heard from parents of multilingual children was that they wanted them to feel part of a lineage. That lineage is independent of the broader usefulness of a language. It is, perhaps, about giving your children something to remember you by; a sound that will always remind them of home. My late friend George, born in Brooklyn before the Great Depression, was in his eighties when he told me that he still remembered his mother standing in the kitchen, singing songs in Russian.

Epilogue

After finding about a hundred god signs in the Louvre, I was so thrilled by my success that I looked for an online Sumerian course. I found an excellent series of free video seminars on Sumerian grammar for beginners, run by a husband-and-wife team, Joshua Bowen and Megan Lewis, who go by the name 'Digital Hammurabi'.[1] I learned the words for mighty, hero, Lagash, ruler, and other interesting battle- and power-related terms. Armed with a notebook full of cuneiform signs and words from the course, and a laptop to look up more signs and words if necessary, I went to the Mesopotamian section of the Ashmolean Museum in Oxford.

At first, the visit wasn't very promising. I passed tablet after tablet, slab after slab, and could just about make out the god sign.

But then I saw a clear, short, sharp cuneiform text, cut into stone, perfect for a beginner. Not just that, but it featured the words warrior, mighty, ruler, Lagash, hero. How was that possible? My online video course had materialized as a cuneiform tablet!

It took me a moment to realize that it was the other way round. Josh and Megan had probably chosen the core vocabulary for their course because there were many inscriptions about mighty heroes, and Lagash.

I squatted down to see the signs better. This inscription was about four thousand years old. Someone had carved the words 'mighty' and 'hero' into a stone, four thousand years ago, in a faraway place, in a language that fell out of use more than two thousand years ago. And yet I could recognize them. An idea had just leaped from one human mind into another, across that vast time span.

I opened my laptop, got out my biro and notebook, and set to work, driven by an intense curiosity. The riddle felt strangely urgent, as if I were solving a present-day mystery, not one from ancient history. After a while, I had come up with the following translation:

The god Ningirsu
Mighty hero
Of Enlil
His king
Gudea
Ruler of
Lagash
The wall of Girsu (?)
[some place] kill/turn?

I tidied this up so it read: *The god Ningirsu, mighty hero of Enlil. His king Gudea, ruler of Lagash. The wall of Girsu (?) [some place] kill/turn?*

It wasn't exactly flowing prose, but it wasn't gibberish either. Assuming I'd interpreted the signs correctly, this seemed to be a meaningful text about Gudea of Lagash, who was dedicating something to the god Ningirsu. Was it real, though? Was this actually what the inscription said, more or less? And what was Gudea doing to that wall?

I couldn't ask anyone around me to check my translation. But I so desperately wanted to know! I wanted to know if my translation was right, and I also wanted to know about the wall business. So I emailed Megan to ask if she would kindly take a look. She agreed and I sent her my lines, along with a picture of the inscription. She replied with an enthusiastic: 'You did a great job with that translation, well done!' (which already made my day), followed by the full translation:

> For Ningirsu, mighty hero of Enlil, his king, Gudea, ruler of Lagash, restored the wall of Girsu (literally 'returned it to its place').

I know that such short, formulaic texts are as far as my Sumerian will ever go. I'll never be able to read a full tablet of dense signs. But cuneiform has become quite an enjoyable part of my life. In its home country, Iraq, it is also finding new followers. The cuneiform sign for 'freedom', *ama-gi* in Sumerian, was used by an Iraqi graffiti artist as part of a mural during protests in 2019.[2] It literally means 'return to mother', and is based on the liberation of enslaved people in the ancient world who were then free to return to their homelands.

Every time I learn a new language, I feel the walls of my mind push back a little. Suddenly, life feels more spacious. I can see things from a new perspective. I can discover thoughts and experiences that weren't there before.

I wrote this book during an anxious time for foreigners in the UK. Neither foreign languages, nor the people who spoke them, seemed particularly welcome here. But wherever I interviewed people for this book, in universities, museums, archives or private homes, there was a sense of openness, curiosity and generosity towards other cultures. It reminded me why I'd come to the UK in the first place, and why I'd long experienced it as inspiring and intellectually stimulating. These conversations gave me hope. There was a feeling of connection, of being together.

It made me think of those words from the Inari Sámi man, speaking his mother tongue for the first time in years: 'I feel I have known you forever. Is it the language? It must be the language.'

Acknowledgements

I would like to thank my editor, Neil Belton, for entrusting me with his brilliant idea for a book about the joy of languages. His expert guidance, advice and support made this book what it is. I am also very grateful to Clare Gordon, my agent Mark 'Stan' Stanton, my copy-editor Jenni Davis and the team at Head of Zeus for all their enthusiasm and hard work. Christian Duck and Jessie Price kept the publication process moving while much of the world was on standstill.

Writing this book would not have been possible without the generous support of many specialists who have devoted their lives to scripts and languages. They let me sit in on seminars and workshops, taught me how to read an ancient tablet, patiently answered my never-ending questions, and reviewed the resulting chapters for accuracy. Their comments have helped me greatly improve the manuscript; any remaining errors are all my own.

For the chapter dealing with early sounds and prosody, I am particularly grateful to Kathleen Wermke, Janet Werker, Krista Byers-Heinlein, Danijela Trenkic and Judit Gervain for their time and expertise.

Eleanor Robson shared her vast knowledge of cuneiform cultures with me and helped me understand the more puzzling aspects of the ancient world. Megan Lewis not only supported my cuneiform translation efforts, but reviewed two long chapters in the midst of a pandemic. Émilie Pagé-Perron kindly guided me through online databases, lexical lists and spice-related Sumerian and Akkadian vocabulary.

I began sending out drafts for review just as Covid-19 spread around the globe, and one country after another went into lockdown. One of my readers was trapped in a foreign city, midway to a cancelled conference. Another was just recovering from the virus itself, and still weakened by high fevers. Others were scrambling to help their friends, families, colleagues and students, while looking after children or elderly relatives. It was terrible timing to ask people for the big favour of commenting on draft chapters, and yet everyone helped. Many sent additional references, including online links to chapters, aware that I could no longer look them up in libraries. I am so grateful for this extraordinary generosity.

Cécile Michel kindly reviewed the chapter on the multilingual families of Kanesh, and helped me gain a more nuanced perspective of this fascinating community. Ben Outhwaite did the same for the section on the Cairo Genizah, providing specialist knowledge that improved the draft. Philippa Steele generously invited me to her seminars and drew me into the world of the ancient eastern Mediterranean. I could not have written the chapter on Cypro-Minoan without her and the CREWS team, especially Cassandra Donnelly and Philip Boyes. Anna Judson expertly answered my detailed questions on Linear B and provided precious references that I would not have been able to find on my own. Philip Boyes gave me one of the most generous gifts of them all: he redrew the Cypro-Minoan text on a tablet from Enkomi for this book, allowing us all to enjoy the beauty of these ancient signs.

Alexandra Croom, Senior Keeper of Archaeology and Curator of Arbeia Roman Fort, helped me understand the history and context of the Regina Stone. I am deeply grateful for her explanations of the Latin inscription and Roman-era family structures and relationships, her generous guidance on finding further resources, and the time she took to look at the stone with me and discuss possible meanings and interpretations. Staff at the Arbeia Roman Fort went out of their way to let me visit the museum outside of the official season.

The librarians at The Word Library, at the National Centre for the Written Word in South Shields, kindly provided access Robert Blair's original notes and scrapbook, which revealed fascinating insights into the Victorians' analysis and interpretations of the Regina Stone.

Alexander West shared his expertise on spices and languages, provided very helpful comments and pointed me towards excellent resources. John Gallagher's insightful feedback helped me improve the section on being 'well languaged'. Camilla Townsend kindly reviewed the chapter on Malinche's languages and helped me with her expertise, and Craig Volker did the same for the chapter on Unserdeutsch. The team around Péter Maitz created a comprehensive online archive of Unserdeutsch materials and research papers; without these, it would not have been possible for me to piece together the story of the children who invented a language.

In Tokyo, Elizabeth Andoh and Ann Tashi Slater read my chapters on Japanese food and the Japanese language, and contributed valuable insights and inspiration. In Inari, Suvi Kivelä (Suvi King) and Anna Morottaja shared their knowledge of Inari Sámi. Their love and passion for this beautiful language continues to inspire me.

Friends and family generously talked about their own linguistic heritage. Marlène Bensimon-Lerner's stories and memories of her multilingual family have been a wonderful part of my life for many years now. James Regan, Yukari Iwatani Kane, Jake Gonzalez and Laura Gonzalez Gray, Alona and her father Daniel, K and Michael, Ninni, Türküler, Vinay, Sabeeha, Raisa, Elad and family, Yifan, Olof, Jonathan and Peter, Ceri, Halima and many others have contributed to this book with much-appreciated advice, conversations and personal stories. Thank you.

I would like to thank Iwona Wysocka for her kindness, patience and support. Above all, I am grateful to Dan and Aaron, my treasured collaborators, for enabling this project and filling my life with joy.

Notes

Prologue

1 References William W. Hallo, *Origins: The Ancient Near Eastern Background of Some Modern Western Institutions* (Brill, 1996), p. 158.

2 Nora Ellen Groce, *Everyone Here Spoke Sign Language: Hereditary Deafness on Martha's Vineyard* (Cambridge, Mass.; London: Harvard University Press, 1997), pp. 2–3.

3 Groce, pp. 64–66.

4 Julien Meyer, B. Gautheron and Keith Brown, 'Whistled Speech and Whistled Languages', in *Encyclopedia of Language & Linguistics, Second Edition* (Oxford: Elsevier, 2006), XIII, pp. 573–76 (p. 574).

5 Julien Meyer, *Whistled Languages: A Worldwide Inquiry on Human Whistled Speech* (Springer, 2015), pp. 23–24.

6 Meyer, p. 11.

7 See for example: Nicholas Ostler, *Empires of the Word: A Language History of the World* (London, New York, Toronto, Sydney: Harper Perennial, 2006), p. 162; Christopher Goscha, *The Penguin History of Modern Vietnam* (London: Penguin Books, 2017), pp. 5, 25.

Early Sounds

1 Kathleen Wermke and Werner Mende, 'From Emotion to Notion: The Importance of Melody', in *The Oxford Handbook of Social Neuroscience*, ed. by Jean Decety and John Cacioppo (Oxford: Oxford University Press, 2011); Daniela Dobnig and others, 'It All Starts with Music – Musical Intervals in Neonatal Crying', *Speech, Language and Hearing*, 2017.

2 Denis Querleu and others, 'Fetal Hearing', *European Journal of Obstetrics & Gynecology and Reproductive Biology*, 29 (1988), pp. 191–292 (p. 205).

3   Amandine Michelas and Mariapaola d'Imperio, 'Durational Cues and Prosodic Phrasing in French: Evidence for the Intermediate Phrase', *Speech Prosody*, 2010 <https://hal.archives-ouvertes.fr/hal-00463205>.

4   Birgit Mampe and others, 'Newborns' Cry Melody Is Shaped by Their Native Language', *Current Biology*, 19 (2009).

5   Kathleen Wermke and others, 'Fundamental Frequency Variation within Neonatal Crying: Does Ambient Language Matter?', *Speech, Language and Hearing*, 2016.

6   Karl Grebe, 'The Domain of Noun Tone Rules in Lam Nso' (The University of Calgary, 1984), p. 7–8 <https://www.sil.org/system/files/reapdata/39/68/99/39689999909557748802691309123780886576/lamnso_grebe1984_0987_p.pdf>.

7   Matt Malzkuhn, 'What Type Are You? The Typography of Fingerspelling', *Motion Light Lab, Gallaudet University* <https://www.motionlightlab.com/new-page-4>.

8   Susanne Mohr, 'The Linguistic Setup of Sign Languages – The Case of Irish Sign Language (ISL)', in *Mouth Actions in Sign Languages: An Empirical Study of Irish Sign Language* (Boston/Berlin: De Gruyter, 2014), pp. 4–30 (p. 25) <https://www.jstor.org/stable/j.ctvbkjxov.9>.

9   'British Sign Language: Non-Manual Features (Video Series)', Dot Sign Language, University of Surrey <https://bsl.surrey.ac.uk/principles/f-non-manual-features>.

10   'Making Sign Interesting to Watch', *BabyHearing* <https://www.babyhearing.org/language-learning/making-sign-language-interesting>.

11   Annie M. Sullivan, 'How Helen Keller Acquired Language', *American Annals of the Deaf*, 37.2 (1892), pp. 127–154 (p. 129).

12   Annie M. Sullivan, p. 130.

13   Meyer, p. 15.

14   Mampe and others; Wermke and others; Wermke and Mende.

15   Dobnig and others.

16   Krista Byers-Heinlein, Janet F. Werker and Tracey Burns, 'The Roots of Bilingualism in Newborns', *Psychological Science*, 2010.

17   Judit Gervain, Marina Nespor and Reiko Mazuka, 'Bootstrapping Word Order in Prelexical Infants: A Japanese-Italian Cross-Linguistic Study', *Cognitive Psychology*, 57.1 (2008), pp. 56–74.

18   Janet F. Werker and Richard C. Tees, 'Cross-Language Speech Perception: Evidence for Perceptual Reorganization during the First Year of Life', *Infant Behavior and Development*, 7.1 (1984), pp. 49–63; Janet F.

Werker, 'Becoming a Native Listener: A Developmental Perspective on Human Speech Perception', *American Scientist*, 77.1 (1989), pp. 54–59.

19 Patricia Kuhl, 'Effects of Language Experience on Speech Perception: American and Japanese Infants' Perception of /Ra/ and /La/', *The Journal of the Acoustical Society of America*, 102.5 (1997).

20 Laura Ann Petitto and Paula Marentette, 'Babbling in the Manual Mode: Evidence for the Ontogeny of Language', *Science*, 251 (1991), pp. 1493–96.

Language on Clay

1   Anonymous, 'Clay Bulla (Clay Ball Impressed with Tokens)' (Cuneiform Digital Library Initiative, 3500) <https://cdli.ucla.edu/P274836>.

2   Robert K. Englund, 'Accounting in Proto-Cuneiform', in *The Oxford Handbook of Cuneiform Culture*, ed. by Eleanor Robson and Karen Radner (Oxford: Oxford University Press, 2011), pp. 32–50 (pp. 33–34).

3   Englund, p. 38.

4   'Emeĝir (Sumerian Language; Akkadian: Akk. Šumeritum; Šumerû)', ed. by Steve Tinney, Åke Sjöberg and Erle Leichty, *The Pennsylvania Sumerian Dictionary (Electronic Version)* (Philadelphia: The University of Pennsylvania Museum of Anthropology and Archaeology, 1974) <http://psd.museum.upenn.edu>.

5   Englund, p. 38.

6   Annette Zgoll, *Der Rechtsfall Der En-Hedu-Ana Im Lied Nin-Me-Sara* (Münster: Ugarit-Verlag, 1997), p. 13; Jeremy Black and others, 'The Exaltation of Inana' (The Electronic Text Corpus of Sumerian Literature, Oxford, 1998–2006) <http://etcsl.orinst.ox.ac.uk/cgi-bin/etcsl.cgi?text=t.4.07.2#>.

7   Jeremy Black and others, 'Enmerkar and the Lord of Aratta' (The Electronic Text Corpus of Sumerian Literature, Oxford, 1998-2006) <http://etcsl.orinst.ox.ac.uk/cgi-bin/etcsl.cgi?text=t.1.8.2.3#>.

8   Black and others, 'Enmerkar and the Lord of Aratta'.

9   Black and others, 'Enmerkar and the Lord of Aratta'.

10 'Dingir, Diĝir (God, Deity; Akkadian Ilu)', ed. by Steve Tinney, Åke Sjöberg and Erle Leichty, *The Pennsylvania Sumerian Dictionary (Electronic Version)* (Philadelphia: The University of Pennsylvania Museum of Anthropology and Archaeology, 1974) <http://psd.museum.upenn.edu>.

11   'Inanna (Translation)', trans. by Douglas R. Frayne (Cuneiform Digital
      Library Initiative, 2000), composite text, based on fragments from Larsa
      <https://cdli.ucla.edu/P448426>.

12   Karenleigh Overmann, 'Beyond Writing: The Development of Literacy
      in the Ancient Near East', *Cambridge Archaeological Journal*, 26.2 (2015),
      pp. 285–303 (p. 300).

13   Tinney, Sjöberg and Leichty, 'Emeĝir (Sumerian Language; Akkadian:
      Akk. Šumeritum; Šumerû)'.

14   Tinney, Sjöberg and Leichty, 'Dingir, Diĝir (God, Deity; Akkadian
      Ilu)'.

15   *Beyond Babylon: Art, Trade and Diplomacy in the Second Millennium
      B.C.*, ed. by Joan Aruz, Kim Benzel and Jean M. Evans (New Haven and
      London: Yale University Press, 2008), pp. 248–49.

16   *JPS Hebrew-English Tanakh*, 2nd edn (Philadelphia: The Jewish Publi-
      cation Society, 1999).

17   *Biblia, Das Ist, Die Gantze Heilige Schrifft (Digital Copy)*, trans. by Martin
      Luther (Wittemberg: Lufft, 1534), Digitale Sammlungen der Herzogin
      Anna Amalia Bibliothek <https://haab-digital.klassik-stiftung.de>.

18   William Tyndale, 'Pentateuch, The Fyrst Boke (Digital Copy)' (Antwerp:
      Martin de Keyser, Joannes Grapheus, Hans Luft, 1530), p. 22 <https://
      dpul.princeton.edu/wa/catalog/0r9677704>.

19   Eric Cline, 1177 B.C.: *The Year Civilization Collapsed* (Princeton Univer-
      sity Press, 2015), p. 19; 'Laws of Hammurapi (Image and translation)',
      trans. by Douglas R. Frayne (Cuneiform Digital Library Initiative, 1750)
      <https://cdli.ucla.edu/P464358>.

20   *The El-Amarna Correspondence: A New Edition of the Cuneiform Letters
      from the Site of El-Amarna Based on Collations of All Extant Texts*, ed. by
      William Schniedewind and Ziporah Cochavi, trans. by Anson Rainey
      (Brill, 2015), pp. 93 (EA 9); p. 97 (EA 10).

21   'Salamu (Akkadian: Peace, Wellbeing, Friendly Relations)', ed. by Martha
      Roth, *The Assyrian Dictionary of the Oriental Institute of the University of
      Chicago* (Chicago: Oriental Institute, The University of Chicago, 2006)
      <https://oi.uchicago.edu/research/publications/assyrian-dictionary-
      oriental-institute-university-chicago-cad>.

22   Jeremy Black and others, 'A Drinking Song: Translation' (The Electronic
      Text Corpus of Sumerian Literature, Oxford, 1998–2006) <http://etcsl.
      orinst.ox.ac.uk/section5/tr55a.htm>; Miguel Civil, 'A Hymn to the Beer
      Goddess and a Drinking Song', *Studies Presented to A. Leo Oppenheim*
      (Chicago: The Oriental Institute of the University of Chicago, 1964).

23 R. Campbell Thompson, *Late Babylonian Letters* (London: Luzac and Co, 1906), p. 75.

24 Jeremy Black and others, 'A Lullaby for a Son of Šulgi' (The Electronic Text Corpus of Sumerian Literature, Oxford, 1998–2006) <http://etcsl.orinst.ox.ac.uk/cgi-bin/etcsl.cgi?text=t.2.4.2.14#>.

25 Cline, p. 9.

26 Leo Oppenheim, *Letters from Mesopotamia* (The University of Chicago Press, 1967), p. 85.

27 Jack M. Sasson, 'Texts, Trade and Travelers', in *Beyond Babylon: Art, Trade and Diplomacy in the Second Millennium B.C.*, ed. by Joan Aruz, Kim Benzel and Jean M. Evans (New Haven and London: Yale University Press, 2008), pp. 95–100 (p. 99).

28 Oppenheim, p. 85.

29 Anonymous, *Serabit Sphinx with Proto-Sinaitic Inscription, c.1800 BCE*, The British Museum <https://www.bl.uk/collection-items/serabit-sphinx-with-proto-sinaitic-inscription#>.

30 Jeremy Black and others, 'A Praise Poem of Shulgi (Shulgi B): Translation' (The Electronic Text Corpus of Sumerian Literature, Oxford, 1998–2006) <http://etcsl.orinst.ox.ac.uk/section2/tr24202.htm>.

31 Jeremy Black and others, 'The Marriage of Martu: Translation' (The Electronic Text Corpus of Sumerian Literature, Oxford, 1998–2006) <http://etcsl.orinst.ox.ac.uk/section1/tr171.htm>.

32 Nele Ziegler, 'Music, the Work of Professionals', in *The Oxford Handbook of Cuneiform Culture*, ed. by Eleanor Robson and Karen Radner (Oxford: Oxford University Press, 2011); Sasson, p. 96; *The Investiture of the King of Mari (Mural); Bread Tins and Other Artefacts from the Palace at Mari (Permanent Exhibition)*, Musée du Louvre, Paris.

33 Nele Ziegler and Dominique Charpin, 'Amurritisch Lernen', *Wiener Zeitschrift Für Die Kunde Des Morgenlandes*, 97 (2007), pp. 55–77 (p. 76).

34 Sasson, p. 97.

35 Cline, p. 18.

36 Ziegler and Charpin, p. 74.

37 Gwendolyn Leick, *Mesopotamia: The Invention of the City* (London: Allen Lane, 2001), p. 204.

38 Ziegler and Charpin, p. 70.

39 Ziegler and Charpin, p. 62.

40 Ziegler and Charpin, p. 62.

41 Black and others, 'A Praise Poem of Shulgi (Shulgi B): Translation'.

The Secrets of House F

1   Eleanor Robson, 'The Tablet House: A Scribal School in Old Baby-
    lonian Nippur', *Revue d'assyriologie et d'archéologie orientale*, 95.1 (2001),
    pp. 39–66.

2   Dominique Charpin, *Reading and Writing in Babylon* (Cambridge, Mass:
    Harvard University Press, 2010), p. 27.

3   Charpin, *Reading and Writing in Babylon*, pp. 27–28.

4   Donald McCown and Richard Haines, *Nippur I: Temple of Enlil, Scribal
    Quarter, and Soundings (Excavations of the Joint Expedition to Nippur
    of The University Museum of Philadelphia and The Oriental Institute of
    the University of Chicago)* (Chicago: The University of Chicago Press,
    1967), p. 148.

5   Robson, p. 60.

6   Konrad Volk, 'Über Bildung Und Ausbildung in Babylonien Am Anfang
    Des 2. Jahrtausends v. Chr.', *Orientalia*, 80.3 (2011), pp. 269–99 (pp. 290–
    91).

7   Dominique Charpin, *Le Clergé d'Ur Au Siècle d'Hammurabi* (Geneva:
    Droz, 1986), p. 432.

8   Charpin, *Reading and Writing in Babylon*, p. 39.

9   Charpin, *Le Clergé d'Ur au Siècle d'Hammurabi*, p. 431.

10 All details from: Charpin, *Le Clergé d'Ur au Siècle d'Hammurabi*.

11 Leonard Woolley and Max Mallowan, *Ur Excavations, The Old Babylon-
    ian Period* (London: British Museum Publications, 1976), p. 111.

12 Brigitte Lion, 'Literacy and Gender', in *The Oxford Handbook of Cunei-
    form Culture*, ed. by Karen Radner and Eleanor Robson (Oxford; New
    York: Oxford University Press, 2011), p. 99.

13 Lion, p. 99.

14 Lion, p. 99.

15 Lion, p. 99.

16 Brigitte Lion and Eleanor Robson, 'Quelques textes scolaires paléo-
    babyloniens rédigés par des femmes', *Journal of Cuneiform Studies*, 57
    (2005), pp. 37–54 (p. 51).

17 Charpin, *Reading and Writing in Babylon*, p. 64.

18 S. D. Goitein, 'Nicknames as Family Names', *Journal of the American
    Oriental Society*, 90.4 (1970), pp. 517–24 (p. 518).

19 Goitein, p. 518.

20 Daniel A. Foxvog, *Introduction to Sumerian Grammar* (CreateSpace
    Independent Publishing Platform, 2014), p. 18.

21 'Old Babylonian list incl. interpreter, ca. 2350–2250 BCE', trans. by Mohammed Lahlouh and Amalia Catagnoti (Cuneiform Digital Library Initiative), National Museum of Syria, Idlib, Syria <https://cdli.ucla.edu/P242433>.

22 'Old Babylonian list incl. dragon, ca. 1900–1600 BCE', trans. by Niek Velduis, (Cuneiform Digital Library Initiative), composite text based on fragments from Nippur <https://cdli.ucla.edu/P461397>.

23 'Old Babylonian list incl. snake charmer, ca. 1900–1600 BCE', trans. by Jonathan Taylor (Cuneiform Digital Library Initiative), source: private; anonymous, Canada <https://cdli.ucla.edu/P349945>.

24 'Old Babylonian list incl. trees, ca 1900-1600 BCE', trans. by Mark Wilson (Cuneiform Digital Library Initiative), Cotsen Collection of Cuneiform Tablets, Special Collections, UCLA, Los Angeles, California, USA <https://cdli.ucla.edu/P388265>.

25 Charpin, *Reading and Writing in Babylon*, p. 44.

26 'Dub (Tablet, Akk. Tuppu); Edubba'a (Scribal School, Akk. Bīt Tuppi)', ed. by Steve Tinney, Åke Sjöberg and Erle Leichty, *The Pennsylvania Sumerian Dictionary (Electronic Version)* (Philadelphia: The University of Pennsylvania Museum of Anthropology and Archaeology, 1974) <http://psd.museum.upenn.edu>.

27 'Sar (to Write; Akkadian Šatāru)', ed. by Steve Tinney, Åke Sjöberg and Erle Leichty, *The Pennsylvania Sumerian Dictionary (Electronic Version)* (Philadelphia: The University of Pennsylvania Museum of Anthropology and Archaeology, 1974) <http://psd.museum.upenn.edu>.

28 'Dubsar (Scribe; Akkadian Tupšarru); Munus Dubsar, Female Scribe; Dubsartur, Junior Scribe.', ed. by Steve Tinney, Åke Sjöberg and Erle Leichty, *The Pennsylvania Sumerian Dictionary (Electronic Version)* (Philadelphia: The University of Pennsylvania Museum of Anthropology and Archaeology, 1974) <http://psd.museum.upenn.edu>.

29 'Bītu, Bīt, Bētu (Akkadian: House, Shelter, Temple, Palace, Household, Family, Place, Tomb)', ed. by Martha Roth and others, *The Assyrian Dictionary of the Oriental Institute of the University of Chicago* (Chicago: Oriental Institute, The University of Chicago, 2006) <https://oi.uchicago.edu/research/publications/assyrian-dictionary-oriental-institute-university-chicago-cad>.

30 'Bīt Dīni (Akkadian: Court of Judgment); Dīnu (Akkadian: Decision, Verdict, Judgment, Punishment, Law, Lawsuit, Claim)', ed. by Martha Roth and others, *The Assyrian Dictionary of the Oriental Institute of the University of Chicago* (Chicago: Oriental Institute, The University

of Chicago, 2006) <https://oi.uchicago.edu/research/publications/assyrian-dictionary-oriental-institute-university-chicago-cad>.

31 Charpin, *Reading and Writing in Babylon*, p. 15.

32 Konrad Volk, 'Über Bildung Und Ausbildung in Babylonien Am Anfang Des 2. Jahrtausends v. Chr.', *Orientalia*, 80.3 (2011), pp. 269–99 (p. 294).

33 Samuel Noah Kramer, *The Sumerians: Their History, Culture and Character* (The University of Chicago Press, 1963), p. 241.

34 Jeremy Black and others, 'The Debate between the Hoe and the Plough: Translation' (The Electronic Text Corpus of Sumerian Literature, Oxford, 1998–2006) <http://etcsl.orinst.ox.ac.uk/cgi-bin/etcsl.cgi?text=t.4.07.2#>.

35 Kramer, pp. 237–39.

36 Kramer, p. 240.

37 Anonymous, '"Why do you curse me?" (A bilingual short story set in Nippur; composite text assembled from fragments, ca. 626–539 BCE)', trans. by Dylan M. Guerra (Cuneiform Digital Library Initiative) <https://cdli.ucla.edu/P499718>.

38 'Egal (Palace; Akkadian: Ekallu)', ed. by Steve Tinney, Åke Sjöberg and Erle Leichty, *The Pennsylvania Sumerian Dictionary (Electronic Version)* (Philadelphia: The University of Pennsylvania Museum of Anthropology and Archaeology, 1974) <http://psd.museum.upenn.edu>.

39 'Tablet incl. dragon woman, ca. 2500–2340 BCE', trans. by Douglas R. Frayne (Cuneiform Digital Library Initiative (Also in: Th. Jacobsen, OIP 058, 291, no. 9) <https://cdli.ucla.edu/P431028>.

Cumin: A Travelogue

1 'Ur III accounting tablet incl. crushed gamun, coriander', trans. by Marcos Such-Gutiérrez, (Cuneiform Digital Library Initiative), Oriental Museum, University of Durham, UK <https://cdli.ucla.edu/P361739>.

2 'Old Babylonian list incl. kamuna for asu disease, ca. 1900–1600 BCE', trans. by Antoine Cavigneaux and Farouk Al-Rawi (Cuneiform Digital Library Initiative), National Museum of Iraq, Baghdad, Iraq <https://cdli.ucla.edu/P355732>.

3 A. Kirk Grayson, 'Neo-Assyrian list, donkey-load of gamun, ca. 900–600 BCE' (Cuneiform Digital Library Initiative) <https://cdli.ucla.edu/P463664>.

4 Federico Poole, '"Cumin, Set Milk, Honey": An Ancient Egyptian

Medicine Container', *The Journal of Egyptian Archaeology*, 87 (2001), pp. 175–80 (p. 176).

5   Poole, p. 176.

6   Anna Morpurgo-Davies, *A Companion to Linear B, Vol 1*, 2008, p. 288.

7   *Medieval Arab Cookery*, ed. by Maxime Rodinson and A. J. Arberry (Devon, England: Prospect Books, 2006).

8   Rodinson and Arberry, pp. 78–79.

9   Susan Francia, 'The Spice of Life? The Multiple Uses of Cumin in Medieval England', *The Local Historian*, 41.3 (2011), pp. 203–15 (p. 206).

10 Goitein, p. 524.

11 Gerrit Bos and Fabian Käs, 'Arabic Pharmacognostic Literature and Its Jewish Antecedents: Marwān Ibn Ǧanāḥ (Rabbi Jonah), Kitāb al-Talḫīṣ', *Aleph*, 16.1, pp. 145–229.

12 Francia, p. 203.

13 Francia, p. 206.

14 Paul Freedman, *Out of the East: Spices and the Medieval Imagination* (New Haven and London: Yale University Press, 2008), p. 4.

15 Francia, pp. 209, 210–11.

16 Francia, p. 210.

17 Francia, p. 207.

18 Florent Quellier, *Gourmandise: Histoire d'un Péché Capital* (Paris: Armand Collin, 2010), p. 26.

19 Quellier, pp. 47, 50, 53.

20 Quellier, p. 43.

21 Quellier, p. 53.

22 Quellier, p. 53.

23 Quellier, p. 13.

24 Olivia Remie Constable, 'Food and Meaning: Christian Understandings of Muslim Food and Food Ways in Spain, 1250–1550', *Viator: Medieval and Renaissance Studies*, 44.3, pp. 199–235 (p. 205).

25 Constable, p. 208.

26 'Lozano, Lozana', *Diccionario de La Lengua Española* (Real Academia Española) <https://dle.rae.es/lozano?m=form>.

27 Constable, p. 218.

28 'Indicadores básicos por agrupación lingüística' (Gobierno de México, 2010) <https://site.inali.gob.mx/Micrositios/estadistica_basica/estadisticas2015/index_indicadores_basicos_agrupacion_linguistica_2015.html>.

29 Anonymous, *The Codex Zouche-Nuttall*, ca. 1200–1521, The British

Museum <https://www.britishmuseum.org/collection/object/E_Am1902-0308-1>.

30 Esther Katz, 'La influencia del contacto en la comida campesina Mixteca', in *Conquista y comida: Consecuencias del encuentro de dos mundos*, ed. by Janet Long (Mexico: Universidad Nacional Autónoma de Mexico, 1996), p. 344.

31 Katz, pp. 346, 349, 352.

32 Katz, p. 346.

33 Priya Krishna, 'A Texas Border Town's Booming Trade in Great Tacos', *New York Times* (New York, 25 February 2020) <https://www.nytimes.com/2020/02/25/dining/tacos-brownsville-texas.html>.

34 Cemal Pulak, 'The Uluburun Shipwreck and Late Bronze Age Trade', in *Beyond Babylon: Art, Trade and Diplomacy in the Second Millennium B.C.* (New Haven and London: Yale University Press, 2008), pp. 289–385 (pp. 295–96).

The God Sign

1 Tinney, Sjöberg and Leichty, 'Emeĝir (Sumerian Language; Akkadian: Akk. Šumeritum; Šumerû)'.

The Narrow Track

1 Cécile Michel, 'Les malheurs de Kunnanīya, femme de marchand', p. 248; Cécile Michel, 'Femmes au foyer et femmes en voyage. Le cas des épouses des marchands assyriens au début du IIe millénaire Av. J.-C.', *Clio. Femmes, Genre, Histoire*, 28 (2008), pp. 17–38 (p. 34).

2 Klaas Veenhof and Jesper Eidem, *Mesopotamia: The Old Assyrian Period*, ed. by Markus Wäfler (Fribourg: Academic Press Fribourg, 2008), p. 43 <https://www.zora.uzh.ch/id/eprint/151184/1/Veenhof_Eidem_2008_Mesopotamia.pdf>.

3 Veenhof and Eidem, p. 56.

4 Cécile Michel, 'The Private Archives from Kanis Belonging to Anatolians', *Altorientalische Forschungen*, 2011, pp. 94–115 (p. 111).

5 Ewen Callaway, 'Siberia's Ancient Ghost Clan Starts to Surrender Its Secrets', *Nature*, 27 February 2019 <https://www.nature.com/articles/d41586-019-00672-2>.

6 Veenhof and Eidem, p. 82.

7 Veenhof and Eidem, p. 32.

8   Oppenheim, p. 74.

9   Cécile Michel, 'Women Work, Men are Professionals in the Old Assyr-
     ian Private Archives', in B. Lion & C. Michel (eds), *The Role of Women
     in Work and Society in the Ancient Near East*, Studies in Ancient Near
     Eastern Records 13, 2016, pp. 199–214 (pp. 202–3). <https://halshs.
     archives-ouvertes.fr/halshs-01674010>.

10   Cécile Michel, 'Women and Real Estate in the Old Assyrian Texts', *Orient,
     The Society for Near Eastern Studies in Japan*, 51 (2016), p. 85 <https://
     halshs.archives-ouvertes.fr/halshs-01674007/document>.

11   Michel, 'Women Work, Men Are Professionals in the Old Assyrian Pri-
     vate Archives', p. 197.

12   Cécile Michel, 'Ecrire et compter chez les marchands assyriens du
     début du IIe millénaire av. J.-C.', in T. Tarhan, A. Tibet and E. Konyar
     (eds), *Muhibbe Darga Armağanı*, Istanbul: Sadberk Hanım Müzesi,
     2008, pp. 345–364 (pp. 353–354) <http://halshs.archives-ouvertes.fr/
     halshs-00443900/fr/>.

13   Veenhof and Eidem, p. 48.

14   Veenhof and Eidem, p. 113.

15   Cécile Michel, 'The Private Archives from Kaniš Belonging to Ana-
     tolians', *Altorientalische Forschungen*, 2011, pp. 94–115 (p. 111) <http://
     halshs.archives-ouvertes.fr/halshs-01186438>.

16   'Targumannum, Eme-Bala', Martha Roth and others (eds) *The Assyrian
     Dictionary of the Oriental Institute of the University of Chicago* (Chicago:
     Oriental Institute, The University of Chicago, 2006), Vol 18, p. 229
     <https://oi.uchicago.edu/research/publications/assyrian-dictionary-
     oriental-institute-university-chicago-cad>; 'Eme-Bala (Digital Images
     of all tablets mentioning Eme-Bala)', *Cuneiform Digital Library Initia-
     tive* <https://cdli.ucla.edu/search/search_results.php?SearchMode
     =Text&PrimaryPublication=&MuseumNumber=&Provenience=&
     Period=&TextSearch=eme-bala&ObjectID=&requestFrom=Subm
     it>; 'Eme-Bala, Eme-Bal', *The Pennsylvania Sumerian Dictionary Project
     (Digital)* (The University of Pennsylvania Museum of Anthropology and
     Archaeology) <http://psd.museum.upenn.edu/nepsd-frame.html>.

17   Hallo, p. 158.

18   Stefano Seminara, 'Beyond the Words. Some Considerations about the
     Word "to Translate" in Sumerian.', *Vicino Oriente*, XVIII (2014), pp. 7–13.

19   Hallo, p. 158; Annelies Kammenhuber, *Hippologia Hethitica* (Wiesbaden:
     Otto Harrassowitz, 1961), p. 91; Hasan Peker, 'A Funerary Stele from
     Yunus (Karkemish)', *Orientalia*, 82.2 (2014), pp. 189–93 (pp. 190–91).

20 Cécile Michel and others, 'Considerations on the Assyrian Settlement at Kanesh', in *Current Research at Kültepe-Kanesh* (Lockwood Press, 2014), pp. 69–84 (p. 77); Michel, 'The Private Archives from Kanis Belonging to Anatolians', pp. 110–11.

21 Sasson, p. 95; Aruz, Benzel and Evans, p. 4.

22 Aruz, Benzel and Evans, p. 4.

23 Ronald L. Eisenberg, *The JPS Guide to Jewish Traditions* (Philadelphia: The Jewish Publication Society, 2004), p. 453.

24 Elliott Colla, 'Dragomen and Checkpoints', *The Translator*, 21. Issue 2: Translating in the Arab World (2015), pp. 9–10 <https://static1. squarespace.com/static/52dc0cc7e4b0e34b862ece81/t/568ffa28d8af10 8f9a8caaa5/1452276280589/Colla-Dragomen+and+Checkpoints.pdf>.

25 Colla, p. 10.

26 Francesco Balducci Pegolotti, 'La Pratica Della Mercatura Scritta Da Francesco Balducci Pegolotti', Capitolo II, p. 3. <https://archive.org/details/bub_gb_IRIxirmx9JAC/page/n3/mode/2up>; also: John Keay, *The Spice Route: A History* (London: Murray, 2005), p. 114.

27 Pegolotti, p. 2.

28 Helen Cooper, 'Going Native: The Caxton and Mainwaring Versions of Paris and Vienne', *The Yearbook of English Studies*, 41.1 (2011), pp. 21–34; *The Oxford Dictionary of English Etymology*, ed. by Charles T. Onions (Oxford: Oxford University Press, 1996), p. 945; Colla, p. 12.

29 Colla, p. 12.

30 Patricia Palmer, 'Interpreters and the Politics of Translation and Traduction in Sixteenth-Century Ireland', *Irish Historical Studies*, 33.131 (2003), pp. 257–277.

31 'Trujamán, Na', *Diccionario de La Lengua Española* (Real Academia Española) <https://dle.rae.es/trujamán>; 'Lengua', *Diccionario de La Lengua Española* (Real Academia Española) <https://dle.rae.es/lengua?m=form>.

32 Anonymous, *The Family of a Court Interpreter (Dragoman)*, Watercolour portrait, 1750, V&A <http://collections.vam.ac.uk/item/O154583/the-family-of-a-court-watercolour-unknown/>.

33 Jenny Randall, 'The Dragoman and his Garden', *Historic Gardens Review*, 18 (2007), pp. 21–23.

34 *Suaheli-Dragoman* (Leipzig, 1891) <https://archive.org/stream/suahelidragomanoonettgoog#page/n5/mode/2up>.

35 Jeremy Black, 'Amethysts', *Iraq*, Vol. 63 (2001), pp. 183–86.

36 Pulak, p. 293.

Naming the World

1   Kammenhuber, pp. 141, 354.

2   Cline, p. 30.

3   Kammenhuber, p. 45.

4   Johannes Potratz, 'Hippologica Hethitica (Review)', *Zeitschrift Der Deutschen Morgenländischen Gesellschaft*, 113.1 (1963), pp. 181–86 (p. 182).

5   Kammenhuber, p. 55.

6   Gil Stein, 'Sweet Honey in the Rocks', *The University of Chicago Magazine*, Fall 2015 <https://mag.uchicago.edu/arts-humanities/sweet-honey-rocks#>.

7   Titima Suthiwan 'Thai vocabulary: "àtsawá, horse (Sanskrit: ashva); aachaa (Pali: assa) (2009)', in World Loanword Database, ed. by Haspelmath, Martin & Tadmor, Uri (Leipzig: Max Planck Institute for Evolutionary Anthropology) <http://wold.clld.org/vocabulary/23>.

8   Kammenhuber, p. 151.

9   Kammenhuber, p. 91.

10   John F. Hartmann, 'The Spread of South Indic Scripts in Southeast Asia', *Crossroads: An Interdisciplinary Journal of Southeast Asian Studies* 3, no. 1 (1986), pp. 6–20, (p. 7).

11   Hartmann, p. 7.

12   Thomas W. Gething, 'Selective Development of the Thai Lexicon', *Crossroads: An Interdisciplinary Journal of Southeast Asian Studies* 3, no. 1 (1986), pp. 118–22 (p. 119).

13   Uri Tadmor, 'Indonesian vocabulary: "bahasa, language, from Sanskrit bhāṣā" (2009)', in World Loanword Database, ed. by Martin Haspelmath and Uri Tadmor (Leipzig: Max Planck Institute for Evolutionary Anthropology) <http://wold.clld.org/vocabulary/27> and Titima Suthiwan, 'Thai vocabulary: "phaasǎa, language, from Sanskrit bhāṣā" (2009)', in World Loanword Database, ed. by Martin Haspelmath and Uri Tadmor (Leipzig: Max Planck Institute for Evolutionary Anthropology) <http://wold.clld.org/vocabulary/23>.

14   Uri Tadmor, 'Indonesian vocabulary' and Titima Suthiwan 'Thai vocabulary'.

15   Titima Suthiwan 'Thai vocabulary: "àtsawá, horse (Sanskrit: ashva); aachaa (Pali: assa) (2009)'.

16   Titima Suthiwan, 'Thai vocabulary: "máa, horse", (2009)', in World Loanword Database, ed. by Martin Haspelmath and Uri Tadmor (Leipzig:

Max Planck Institute for Evolutionary Anthropology) <http://wold. clld.org/vocabulary/23>.

17 Thekla Wiebusch, 'Mandarin Chinese vocabulary: "ma3, horse" (2009)', in World Loanword Database, ed. by Martin Haspelmath and Uri Tadmor (Leipzig: Max Planck Institute for Evolutionary Anthropology) <http://wold.clld.org/vocabulary/22>; Titima Suthiwan 'Thai vocabulary: "máa, horse" (2009)'.

18 Henry G. Schwarz, 'Animal Words in Mongolian and Uyghur, *Mongolian Studies*, vol. 24 (2001), pp. 1–6 (p. 1–2).

19 Thilo Schadeberg, 'Swahili vocabulary: "farasi, horse; from Arabic faras" (2009)', in World Loanword Database, ed. by Martin Haspelmath and Uri Tadmor (Leipzig: Max Planck Institute for Evolutionary Anthropology) <http://wold.clld.org/vocabulary/1>.

20 Zarina Estrada Fernández, 'Yaqui vocabulary (2009)' <http://wold. clld.org/vocabulary/32>; Søren Wichmann, Kerry Hull, 'Q'eqchi' vocabulary (2009)' <http://wold.clld.org/vocabulary/34>, both in World Loanword Database, ed. by Martin Haspelmath and Uri Tadmor.

21 Jorge A. Gómez Rendón, 'Imbabura Quechua vocabulary (2009)', in World Loanword Database, ed. by Martin Haspelmath and Uri Tadmor <http://wold.clld.org/vocabulary/37>.

22 Lyle Campbell and Veronica Grondona, 'Linguistic Acculturation in Nivaclé and Chorote', *International Journal of American Linguistics*, 78.3 (2012), pp. 335–67 (p. 340).

23 Peter Mitchell, *Horse Nations: The Worldwide Impact of the Horse on Indigenous Societies Post-1492* (Oxford; New York: Oxford University Press, 2015), p. 151.

24 Mitchell, p. 184.

25 Vincent Collette, 'Nakota Linguistic Acculturation', *Anthropological Linguistics*, 59.2 (2017), pp. 117–62 (p. 147).

26 Mitchell, p. 22.

27 Václav Blažek, 'Indo-European "Bear"', *Historische Sprachforschung / Historical Linguistics*, 130 (2017), pp. 148–92 (pp. 148–49).

28 Interview de Jean Sola, traducteur du TDF, par la Garde de Nuit <https://www.lagardedenuit.com/wiki/index.php?title=Interview_ de_Jean_Sola,_traducteur_du_TDF,_par_la_Garde_de_Nuit>.

29 Bénédicte Mathieu, 'Jean-François Ménard, "Harry Potter" en VF', *Le Monde*, 5 October 2005 <https://www.lemonde.fr/culture/article/ 2005/10/05/jean-francois-menard-harry-potter-en-vf_695928_3246. html>.

30 Meera Sodha, 'Meera Sodha's Vegan Recipe for Nam Jim Aubergine Salad with Wild Rice', *Guardian* <https://www.theguardian.com/food/2019/nov/30/vegan-recipe-nam-jim-aubergine-salad-wild-rice-meera-sodha>.

31 María Ángeles Pérez Samper, 'The Early Modern Food Revolution', in *Global Goods and the Spanish Empire, 1492–1824: Circulation, Resistance and Diversity*, ed. by Bethany Aram and Bartolomé Yun Casalilla (Houndmills, Basingstoke, Hampshire: Palgrave Macmillan, 2014), p. 24.

32 My thanks to Similolu Ojelade for the translation.

33 Yoruba Proverbs, Twitter message, April 10 2012, @yoruba_proverbs

34 Lizzy Collingham, *Curry: A Biography* (London: Chatto & Windus, 2005).

35 'Indicadores básicos por agrupación lingüística'.

36 Thelma D. Sullivan, 'Nahuatl Proverbs, Conundrums, and Metaphors, Collected by Sahagun', p. 134 <http://www.historicas.unam.mx/publicaciones/revistas/nahuatl/pdf/ecn04/046.pdf>.

37 Adela Blay-Brody, 'Rx. Pepper Soup', *Gastronomica*, 9.4 (2009), pp. 62–65.

38 Francisco Javier Clavijero, *The History of Mexico*, trans. by Charles Cullen (Richmond, Virginia: William Prichard, 1806), p. 254.

39 'Comalli (Nahuatl: griddle)', Stephanie Wood (ed), *Nahuatl Dictionary* (Wired Humanities Projects, 2000) <https://nahuatl.uoregon.edu/content/comalli>.

40 Clavijero, p. 254.

The Book Cemetery

1 S. D. Goitein, *A Mediterranean Society: The Jewish Communities of the Arab World as Portrayed in the Documents of the Cairo Geniza* (Berkeley: University of California Press, 1967), pp. I–VI.

2 'Taylor-Schechter Genizah Research Unit, Cambridge University Library' <https://www.lib.cam.ac.uk/collections/departments/taylor-schechter-genizah-research-unit>.

3 'Magical amulet to protect against scorpions (T-S AS 143.26)', 11th–12th-century, University of Cambridge Digital Library / Cairo Genizah.

4 Ben Outhwaite, 'Lines of Communication: Medieval Hebrew Letters of the Eleventh Century', in *Scribes as Agents of Language Change*, ed. by Ben Outhwaite, Esther-Miriam Wagner and Bettina Beinhoff (Boston/Berlin: De Gruyter, 2013), pp. 184–85.

5   Outhwaite, p. 196.

6   Rainey, Schniedewind and Cochavi, p. 33 (EA34).

7   Sidney Smith, C. J. Gadd and Eric Peet, 'A Cuneiform Vocabulary of Egyptian Words', *The Journal of Egyptian Archaeology*, 11.3/4 (1925), pp. 230–40.

8   Rainey, Schniedewind and Cochavi, p. 361 (EA 41).

9   Robert R. Stieglitz, 'A Physician's Equipment List from Ugarit', *Journal of Cuneiform Studies*, 33.1 (1981), pp. 52–55.

10   Sasson, p. 96.

11   Aruz, Benzel and Evans, p. 311.

12   Pulak.

13   Pulak, pp. 358, 359, 368.

14   'London Medical Papyrus', 14th century BCE, British Museum <https://www.britishmuseum.org/collection/object/Y_EA10059-1>.

15   Evangelos Kyriakidis, 'Indications on the Nature of the Language of the Keftiw from Egyptian Sources', *Ägypten und Levante / Egypt and the Levant*, 12 (2002), pp. 211–19 (p. 211).

16   Kyriakidis, p. 213.

17   Kyriakidis, p. 213.

18   Kyriakidis, p. 214.

19   Richard Steiner, 'Northwest Semitic Incantations in an Egyptian Medical Papyrus of the Fourteenth Century B.C.E.', *Journal of Near Eastern Studies*, 51.3 (1992), pp. 191–200 (p. 198).

20   Steiner, p. 198.

21   J. N. Adams, *Bilingualism and the Latin Language* (Cambridge: Cambridge University Press, 2003), p. 112.

22   Adams, p. 114.

23   Katherine McDonald, *Oscan in Southern Italy and Sicily: Evaluating Language Contact in a Fragmentary Corpus* (Cambridge: Cambridge University Press, 2015), p. 133.

24   Katherine McDonald, 'SALAVS – Learn Oscan Online', Oscan <https://katherinemcdonald.net/teaching-2/teaching-current/salavs-learn-oscan-online/>.

25   Francesca Murano, 'The Oscan Cursing Tablets: Binding Formulae, Cursing Typologies and Thematic Classification', *The American Journal of Philology*, 133.4 (2012), p. 639.

26   Adams, pp. 127–45.

27   Alderik Blom, 'Linguae Sacrae in Ancient and Medieval Sources', in *Multilingualism in the Graeco-Roman Worlds*, ed. by Alex Mullen and

Patrick James (Cambridge: Cambridge University Press, 2012), p. 136.

28 Janis Winehouse, *Loving Amy: A Mother's Story*, 2015, p. 89.

29 'Any ghost stories from your NS days?' (Reddit, 2018) <https://www. reddit.com/r/singapore/comments/86syoy/any_ghost_stories_fron_ your_ns_days/>.

30 Nicholas J. Long, 'Haunting Malayness: The Multicultural Uncanny in a New Indonesian Province', *The Journal of the Royal Anthropological Institute*, 16.4, pp. 874–91 (p. 884).

31 Sofi Oksanen, *Purge* (London: Atlantic, 2011), p. 164.

Rosetta Riddles

1 Cristelle Baskins, 'Lost in Translation: Portraits of Sitti Maani Gioerida Della Valle in Baroque Rome', *Early Modern Women*, Arizona State University, 7.Fall 2012, 241–60.

2 Richard Parkinson, *Cracking the Code: The Rosetta Stone and Decipherment* (London: British Museum Press, 1999), p. 28; Neil MacGregor, *A History of the World in 100 Objects* (London: Penguin Books, 2012), p. 178.

3 Parkinson, pp. 29–30.

4 Parkinson, p. 20.

5 Parkinson, pp. 21–22.

6 Parkinson, p. 25.

7 Parkinson, p. 31.

8 Andrew Robinson, *Lost Languages: The Enigma of the World's Undeciphered Scripts* (New York: McGraw-Hill, 2002), p. 13.

9 Parkinson, p. 41.

10 Arthur John Booth, *The Discovery and Decipherment of the Trilingual Cuneiform Inscriptions* (London: Longmans, Green & Co, 1902), p. 169; Charpin, *Reading and Writing in Babylon*, pp. 4–6.

11 Georg Grotefend, 'Erläuterung Des Anfangs Der Babylonischen Inschrift Aus Behistun', *Zeitschrift Der Deutschen Morgenländischen Gesellschaft*, 7.2 (1853), pp. 156–61 (p. 344).

12 W. H. Fox Talbot and others, 'Comparative Translations', *The Journal of the Royal Asiatic Society of Great Britain and Ireland*, 18 (1861), pp. 150–290 (p. 156).

13 Kevin Cathcart, 'The Earliest Contributions to the Decipherment of Sumerian and Akkadian', *Cuneiform Digital Library Journal*, 1 (2011), p. 6.

14 Cathcart, p. 8.

Cakes and Islands

1   Philippa M. Steele, *A Linguistic History of Ancient Cyprus* (Cambridge: Cambridge University Press, 2013).

2   Sylvia Ferrara, 'Writing without Reading: The Cypro-Minoan Script between the Linear and Cuneiform Traditions', *Bulletin of the Institute of Classical Studies*, 52 (2009), pp. 259–60.

3   Arthur Evans, *Scripta Minoa: The Written Documents of Minoan Crete, with Special Reference to the Archives of Knossos*, ed. by John Linton Myres (Oxford: Clarendon Press, 1909), pp. 8–9.

4   Homer, *The Odyssey*, trans. by E. V. Rieu and D. C. H. Rieu, Penguin Classics (London; New York: Penguin Books, 2003), p. 254.

5   Philippa M. Steele, 'CREWS Display: Replica Linear A Tablet', *CREWS Project*, 2018.

6   Steele, *A Linguistic History of Ancient Cyprus*, pp. 51, 56.

7   Ilse Schoep, 'Building the Labyrinth: Arthur Evans and the Construction of Minoan Civilization', *American Journal of Archaeology*, 122.1 (2018), pp. 5–32 (p. 11).

8   Arthur Evans, p. 10.

9   Joan Evans, *Time and Chance: The Story of Arthur Evans and His Forebears* (London, New York, Toronto: Longmans, Green & Co, 1943), p. 317.

10 Arthur Evans, pp. 17–18; John Chadwick, *The Decipherment of Linear B*, 2nd ed (Cambridge University Press, 1992), pp. 12–14, London Library.

11 Maurice Pope, *The Story of Decipherment: From Egyptian Hieroglyphic to Linear B* (London: Thames and Hudson, 1975), p. 129.

12 Chadwick, p. 35.

13 'Alice Kober to Franklin Daniels', Alice E. Kober Papers, The University of Texas at Austin <https://repositories.lib.utexas.edu/handle/2152/15875>.

14 Margalit Fox, *The Riddle of the Labyrinth: The Quest to Crack an Ancient Code and the Uncovering of a Lost Civilisation* (London: Profile Books, 2013), p. 185.

15 Jean-Pierre Olivier, *Édition Holistique Des Textes Chypro-Minoens* (Rome: Fabrizio Serra Editore, 2007).

16 Steele, *A Linguistic History of Ancient Cyprus*, pp. 67–70.

17 Philippa M. Steele, 'Tolkien and Elvish Writing', *CREWS Project*, 2019 <https://crewsproject.wordpress.com/2019/07/29/tolkien-and-elvish-writing/>.

18   Anna P. Judson, Cake, in *Understanding Relations Between Scripts: The Aegean Writing Systems*, ed. by Philippa M. Steele (Oxford: Oxbow Books, 2017).

19   *Cuneiform Tablet: Student Exercise Tablet ca. 20th–16th Century B.C.*, The Metropolitan Museum of Art, New York <https://www.metmuseum.org/art/collection/search/321878>.

20   Sylvia Ferrara, *Cypro-Minoan Inscriptions* (Oxford: Oxford University Press, 2012), p. 269.

21   André Bataille, *Pour Une Terminologie En Paléographie Grecque* (Paris, 1954), p. 60.

22   Anna P. Judson, 'Clay Play Day and Baking Double Bill: Cypro-Minoan', *It's All Greek to Anna*, 2019 <https://itsallgreektoanna.wordpress.com/2019/06/13/clay-play-day-and-baking-double-bill-cypro-minoan/>.

23   *Cuneiform tablet: student exercise tablet ca. 20th–16th century B.C.* <https://www.metmuseum.org/art/collection/search/321878>.

Love in South Shields

1   Paul T. Bidwell, *Roman Forts in Britain* (Stroud: Tempus, 2007), pp. 101, 104–6, 82–83.

2   Robert Blair, 'Robert Blair's Scrapbook: Excavation Reports, Drawings, Newspaper Clips', 1878, 'The Word', Central Library, South Shields, p. 173.

3   Blair, Nov 1878, p. 173.

4   'Roman Inscriptions of Britain, RIB 1065. Funerary Inscription for Regina', South Shields, Arbeia <https://romaninscriptionsofbritain.org/inscriptions/1065>; Mary Beard, *SPQR: A History of Ancient Rome*, 2016, pp. 509–10.

5   Bidwell, p. 22.

6   M. Gawlikowski, 'Palmyra as a Trading Centre', *Iraq*, 56 (1994), pp. 27–33 (p. 29).

7   Keay, p. 45.

8   Tali Erickson-Gini and Yigal Israel, 'Excavating the Nabataean Incense Road', *Journal of Eastern Mediterranean Archaeology & Heritage Studies*, 1.1 (2013), pp. 24–53 (p. 39).

9   Gawlikowski, pp. 27–28, 32.

10   Maura K. Heyn, 'Gesture and Identity in the Funerary Art of Palmyra', *American Journal of Archaeology*, 114.4 (2010), p. 638.

11   Heyn, p. 639.

12   Eleonora Cussini, 'Regina, Martay and the Others: Stories of Palmyrene Women', *Orientalia*, 73.2, p. 240.

13   Heyn, p. 632.

14   Cussini, pp. 238–39.

15   'Roman Inscriptions of Britain, RIB 1064. Funerary Inscription for Victor', South Shields, Arbeia <https://romaninscriptionsofbritain.org/inscriptions/1064>.

16   Adams, pp. 248–58.

17   Blair, p. 173.

18   'Three Types of Freedom', *Jewish World* <https://www.jpost.com/Jewish-World/Judaism/Three-types-of-freedom-351681>.

19   Steinsaltz, 'Bat Horin' <https://steinsaltz.org/daf/gittin86/>.

20   Matt Nosanchuk, 'Celebrating Passover at the White House', *The White House, President Barack Obama*, 2015 <https://obamawhitehouse.archives.gov/blog/2015/04/03/celebrating-passover-white-house>.

21   Marc Lacey, 'Heir to Power and to Kenya's Great Name', *New York Times* (New York, 15 October 2002) <https://www.nytimes.com/2002/10/15/world/heir-to-power-and-to-kenya-s-great-name.html>.

22   David Curwin, 'Herut and Uhura', *Balashon – Hebrew Language Detective*, 2007 <http://www.balashon.com/2007/03/herut-and-uhura.html>; Simon Hattenstone, 'Star Trek's Nichelle Nichols: "Martin Luther King Was a Trekker"', *The Guardian* (London, 18 October 2016) <https://www.theguardian.com/tv-and-radio/2016/oct/18/star-trek-nichelle-nichols-martin-luther-king-trekker>; 'Nichelle Nichols on How Star Trek's "Uhura" Got Her Name', *FoundationInterviews* (YouTube, 2011) <https://www.youtube.com/watch?v=cfLNZBjc5bY>.

'Well Languaged': The British Art of Language-Learning

1   John Gallagher, *Learning Languages in Early Modern England* (Oxford: Oxford University Press, 2019), p. 101.

2   Elizabeth Tyler, 'Introduction: England and Multilingualism: Medieval and Modern', in *Conceptualizing Multilingualism in Medieval England, c.800–c.1250*, ed. by Elizabeth Tyler (Turnhout: Brepols, 2011), pp. 6–7.

3   Tyler, 'Introduction: England and Multilingualism: Medieval and Modern', pp. 6–7.

4   Patrizia Lendinara, 'The Germanic Background', in *A Companion to*

Anglo-Saxon Literature, ed. by Phillip Pulsiano and Elaine M. Treharne, Blackwell Companions to Literature and Culture (Oxford; Malden, MA: Blackwell Publishers, 2001), pp. 119–34 (p. 126).

5   All examples from: *The Oxford Dictionary of English Etymology*, ed. by Charles T. Onions (Oxford: Oxford University Press, 1996).

6   Seamus Heaney, *Beowulf* (London: Faber and Faber, 2000), p. ix.

7   Heaney, pp. ix, 6.

8   Heaney, p. xxii.

9   *Beowulf*, ed. by Michael Alexander, Penguin Classics (London; New York: Penguin Books, 1995), p. 167.

10 Alexander, p. 101.

11 Matthew Townend, 'Cnut's Poets: An Old Norse Literary Community in Eleventh-Century England', in *Conceptualizing Multilingualism in Medieval England, c.800–c.1250*, ed. by Elizabeth Tyler, Studies in the Early Middle Ages, v. 27 (Turnhout: Brepols, 2011), p. 205.

12 Bruce O'Brien, 'Translating Technical Terms in Law-Codes from Alfred to the Angevins', in *Conceptualizing Multilingualism in Medieval England, c.800–c.1250*, ed. by Elizabeth Tyler, Studies in the Early Middle Ages, v. 27 (Turnhout: Brepols, 2011), p. 60.

13 Felix, 'Life of Guthlac, Manuscript (Vita S Guthlaci) with Commentary', 10th century, British Library <https://www.bl.uk/collection-items/felixs-life-of-guthlac>.

14 Helen Fulton, 'Negotiating Welshness: Multilingualism in Wales Before and After 1066', in *Conceptualizing Multilingualism in Medieval England, c.800–c.1250*, ed. by Elizabeth Tyler, Studies in the Early Middle Ages, v. 27 (Turnhout: Brepols, 2011), p. 153.

15 Joseph P. McGowan, 'An Introduction to the Corpus of Anglo-Latin Literature', in *A Companion to Anglo-Saxon Literature*, ed. by Phillip Pulsiano and Elaine M. Treharne, Blackwell Companions to Literature and Culture, 11 (Oxford; Malden, MA: Blackwell Publishers, 2001), pp. 11–49 (p. 17).

16 McGowan, p. 19.

17 Alban Gautier, 'Cooking and Cuisine in Late Anglo-Saxon England', *Anglo-Saxon England*, 41 (2013), 373–406 (p. 396); Alison Ray, 'Silence Is a Virtue: Anglo-Saxon Monastic Sign Language', *British Library Blog*, 2016 <https://blogs.bl.uk/digitisedmanuscripts/2016/11/silence-is-a-virtue-anglo-saxon-monastic-sign-language.html>.

18 McGowan, p. 28.

19 Lendinara, p. 124.

20 Thomas A. Bredehoft, 'Multiliteralism in Anglo-Saxon Verse Inscriptions', in *Conceptualizing Multilingualism in Medieval England, c.800–c.1250*, ed. by E. M. Tyler, Studies in the Early Middle Ages, v. 27 (Turnhout: Brepols, 2011), p. 28.

21 *The Franks Casket / The Auzon Casket, c.* 8th century, The British Museum <https://www.britishmuseum.org/collection/object/H_1867-0120-1>.

22 Michelle P. Brown, 'Anglo-Saxon Manuscript Production: Issues of Making and Using', in *A Companion to Anglo-Saxon Literature* (2017), pp. 102–117 (p. 108).

23 McGowan, pp. 29, 32.

24 Elizabeth Tyler, 'Crossing Conquests: Polyglot Royal Women and Literary Culture in Eleventh-Century England', in *Conceptualizing Multilingualism in Medieval England, c.800–c.1250*, ed. by Elizabeth Tyler, Studies in the Early Middle Ages, v. 27 (Turnhout: Brepols, 2011), p. 172.

25 Tyler, 'Crossing Conquests: Polyglot Royal Women and Literary Culture in Eleventh-Century England', p. 172.

26 O'Brien, p. 58.

27 Eadmer, *Eadmer of Canterbury: Lives and Miracles of Saints Oda, Dunstan, and Oswald*, ed. by Bernard James Muir and Andrew J. Turner, Oxford Medieval Texts (Oxford: New York: Clarendon Press: Oxford University Press, 2006), p. 185.

28 Eadmer, p. 187.

29 Eadmer, p. 189.

30 Ordericus Vitalis, *The Ecclesiastical History of Orderic Vitalis*, trans. by Marjorie Chibnall, Oxford Medieval Texts (Oxford: Clarendon Press, 1969), Vol.II Book III, p. 256.

31 Ordericus Vitalis, Vol.II Book III, pp. 184–85.

32 Ordericus Vitalis, Vol.II Book III, pp. 184–85.

33 Stephen Baxter, 'The Making of Domesday Book and the Languages of Lordship in Conquered England', in *Conceptualizing Multilingualism in Medieval England, c.800–c.1250*, ed. by Elizabeth Tyler, Studies in the Early Middle Ages, v. 27 (Turnhout: Brepols, 2011), pp. 272–74.

34 Baxter, p. 308.

35 Paul Russell, 'Externarum Linguarum Excellens: The Rhetoric and Reality of the Languages of Gruffudd Ap Cynan, Ruler of Gwynedd', in *Multilingualism in Medieval Britain, (c. 1066–1520): Sources and Analysis*, ed. by Judith Anne Jefferson, Medieval Texts and Cultures of Northern Europe, 15 (presented at the Conference 'Multilingualism in Medieval Britain', Turnhout: Brepols, 2013), p. 83.

36 Gallagher, pp. 142, 75.

37 Gallagher, p. 123.

38 Gallagher, pp. 187–88.

39 Gallagher, pp. 33–34.

40 Gallagher, p. 152.

41 Gallagher, p. 202.

42 William Caxton, *The Recuyell of the Historyes of Troye (Digitized Copy, Harvard University Library)* (London: David Nutt in The Strand, 1894), p. 708.

43 'Caxton's "egges" Story (William Caxton, Eneydos, 14900)', *British Library, Learning English Timeline* <https://www.bl.uk/learning/timeline/item126611.html>.

44 David Steinsaltz, 'The Politics of French Language in Shakespeare's History Plays', *Studies in English Literature, 1500–1900*, 42.2 (2002), pp. 317–34; William Shakespeare, *Henry V* (Penguin Classics, 2015).

45 Henry Yule and A. C. Burnell, *Hobson-Jobson: A Glossary of Colloquial Anglo-Indian Words and Phrases, and of Kindred Terms, Etymological, Historical, Geographical and Discursive*, ed. by William Crooke (London: John Murray, 1903), p. 748.

46 Bruno Gonçalves, Lucía Loureiro-Porto, José J. Ramasco and David Sánchez, 'Mapping the Americanization of English in Space and Time', PLoS ONE 13 (5) (2018) <https://doi.org/10.1371/journal.pone.0197741>.

Global Trade, Global Languages

1 Keay, p. 33.

2 Keay, p. 19.

3 Keay, p. 92.

4 Keay, pp. 126–27.

5 Keay, pp. 108–9.

6 Alexander West, 'Indonesian Commodities in the Codex Cumanicus', Medium, 2019 <https://medium.com/@siwaratrikalpa/indonesian-commodities-in-the-codex-cumanicus-496e419c942e>.

7 Keay, pp. 25–26.

8 Chien Y. Ng and Shahrim Ab. Karim, 'Historical and contemporary perspectives of the Nyonya food culture in Malaysia', *Journal of Ethnic Foods*, Vol 3 Issue 3 (2016), pp. 93–106.

9   John U. Wolff, 'Peranakan Chinese Speech and Identity', *Indonesia*, 64 (1997), pp. 29–44.

10   Tan Chee-Beng, 'Baba Malay Dialect', *Journal of the Malaysian Branch of the Royal Asiatic Society* 53, no. 1 (237) (1980), pp. 150–66 (p. 150).

11   Tan Chee-Beng, 'Baba Malay Dialect' (p. 153).

The Languages of Soy, Rice and Fish

1   Erino Ozeki, 'Fermented Soybean Products and Japanese Standard Taste', in *The World of Soy*, ed. by Christine du Bois, Chee-Beng Tan and Sidney Mintz (Urbana, Illinois: University of Illinois Press, 2008), p. 146.

2   Elizabeth Andoh, *Kansha: Celebrating Japan's Vegan and Vegetarian Traditions* (Berkeley: Ten Speed Press, 2010), pp. 73–76.

3   Naomichi Ishige, *The History and Culture of Japanese Food* (London: Kegan Paul, 2001), p. 37.

4   Ishita Saha, 'A–Z of Bengali Fish', IshitaUnblogged, 2018 <https://ishitaunblogged.com/2018/03/26/a-z-of-bengali-fish/>.

5   Dan Jurafsky, *The Language of Food: A Linguist Reads the Menu* (New York, London: W. W. Norton, 2015), p. 50.

6   Ishige, p. 40.

7   Ishige, p. 42.

8   Ishige, pp. 226–27.

9   Ishige, p. 227.

10   Ozeki, p. 149.

11   Robert Hass, *The Essential Haiku: Versions of Basho, Buson and Issa*, 2013, p. 57.

12   Hass, p. 12.

13   Hass, p. 46.

14   Ann Tashi Slater, 'Summer in Tokyo: Rain Women, Cicadas, and Visits from the Dead', *Catapult*, 2019 <https://catapult.co/stories/column-tokyo-journal-summer-in-tokyo-rain-women-cicadas-visits-from-the-dead>.

15   Andoh, p. 91.

16   Christopher Goscha, *The Penguin History of Modern Vietnam* (London: Penguin Books, 1017), p. xxiii, p. 5.

17   Mark Alves, 'Vietnamese vocabulary, nam, south (Chinese nan, south)', in World Loanword Database, ed. by Martin Haspelmath and Uri Tadmor (Leipzig: Max Planck Institute for Evolutionary Anthropology, 2009) <http://wold.clld.org/vocabulary/24>.

18   Goscha, p. xxiii, p. 5.

19   Timothy Allen, Introduction, in *The Song of Kieu* by Nguyen Du (Penguin Classics 2019), p. xiv.

20   Goscha, p. 29–30.

21   Alves.

22   All examples from Alves, 'Vietnamese vocabulary'.

23   Hong Lien Vu, *Rice and Baguette: A History of Food in Vietnam* (London: Reaktion Books, 2016), pp. 68, 76.

24   Vu, p. 193.

25   Goscha, p. 381.

26   Vu, p. 119.

27   Vu, p. 119.

28   Alves.

29   Vu, p. 119.

30   Vu, p. 143.

31   Vu, p. 155.

32   Vu, p. 153.

33   Sandra C. Taylor, *Vietnamese Women at War* (Lawrence: University Press of Kansas, 1999).

34   Michael Morris, 'When American Soldiers Met Vietnamese Cuisine', *New York Times* (New York) <https://www.nytimes.com/2018/01/12/opinion/when-american-soldiers-met-vietnamese-cuisine.html>.

35   Vu, p. 155.

'La Lengua': Interpreters in the Colonial Age

1   Ostler, p. 333.

2   Ostler, p. 343.

3   Ostler, pp. 342–44.

4   Thelma D. Sullivan, p. 94.

5   *The Four Voyages of Christopher Columbus (Excerpts from His Log-Book, Letters and Historical Accounts by Others)*, ed. & trans. by J. M. Cohen, The Penguin Classics (Harmondsworth: Penguin, 1969), p. 53.

6   Cohen, pp. 55–56.

7   Cohen, p. 59.

8   Cohen, p. 62.

9   Cohen, p. 76.

10   Cohen, p. 80.

11   Cohen, p. 98.

12   MacGregor, p. 355.

13   MacGregor, p. 359.

14   'Rodríguez, Cristóbal. La Lengua. España, c. 1475, intérprete', *Diccionario Biográfico* (La Real Academia de la Historia) <http://dbe.rah.es/biografias/42650/cristobal-rodriguez>.

15   Ostler, p. 342.

16   Ostler, p. 355.

17   José Vargas Sifuentes, 'Felipillo, ¿traidor o Héroe?', *El Peruano*, 27 October 2018 <https://elperuano.pe/noticia-felipillo-¿traidor-o-heroe-i-72311.aspx>.

18   Mary Louise Pratt, '"Yo Soy La Malinche": Chicana Writers and the Poetics of Ethnonationalism', *Callaloo*, 16.4 (1993), pp. 859–73 (p. 867).

Malinche's Languages

1   Camilla Townsend, *Malintzin's Choices: An Indian Woman in the Conquest of Mexico* (Albuquerque: University of New Mexico Press, 2006), pp. 12–13.

2   Townsend, p. 13.

3   Ostler, p. 351.

4   Ostler, pp. 354–55.

5   'Indicadores básicos por agrupación lingüística'.

6   Thelma D. Sullivan, pp. 103, 111, 137, 165.

7   Thelma D. Sullivan.

8   Thelma D. Sullivan.

9   Thelma D. Sullivan.

10   Townsend, p. 28.

11   Townsend, p. 16.

12   Townsend, pp. 22–24.

13   'The Dresden Maya-Codex' (Sächsische Landesbibliothek – Staats- und Universitätsbibliothek Dresden, 1200) <https://www.slub-dresden.de/en/collections/manuscripts/the-dresden-maya-codex/>.

14   Terry G. Powis and others, 'Cacao Use and the San Lorenzo Olmec', *PNAS*, 108.21 (2011) <https://www.pnas.org/content/108/21/8595>.

15   Thelma D. Sullivan.

16   Terrence Kaufman and John Justeson, 'The History of the Word for Cacao in Ancient Mesoamerica', *Ancient Mesoamerica*, 18.2 (2007), pp. 193–237 (p. 217).

17   Townsend, pp. 30–31.

18   Townsend, p. 34.

19   Bernal Díaz del Castillo, *Historia verdadera de la conquista de la Nueva España* (Bal Harbour: Plaza Editorial, 2011), p. 31.

20   Díaz del Castillo, p. 33.

21   Díaz del Castillo, p. 76.

22   Díaz del Castillo, pp. 98, 101.

23   *The Oxford Encyclopedia of Food and Drink in America*, ed. by Andrew F. Smith and Bruce Kraig, 2nd ed (New York, NY: Oxford University Press, 2013), p. 372.

24   Díaz del Castillo, p. 49.

25   Townsend, pp. 43, 45.

26   Townsend, pp. 66–71.

27   Díaz del Castillo, pp. 106–7.

28   Díaz del Castillo, p. 108.

29   Díaz del Castillo, p. 108.

Translator, Traitor?

1   Rachel Mairs, 'Translator, Traditor: The Interpreter as Traitor in Classical Tradition', *Greece & Rome*, 58.1 (2011), 64–81 (p. 65).

2   Mairs, pp. 68–69.

3   Mairs, pp. 64–65.

4   Patricia Palmer, 'Interpreters and the Politics of Translation and Traduction in Sixteenth-Century Ireland', *Irish Historical Studies*, 33.131 (2003) pp. 257–277 (p. 257).

5   Palmer, p. 273.

6   Palmer, p. 271.

7   'Krotoa !Goa/Gõas Translator, Negotiator & Peacemaker 1642–1674' (Cape Town Museum) <https://capetownmuseum.org.za/wp-content/uploads/Krotoa.pdf>.

8   Julia Wells, 'Eva's Men: Gender and Power in the Establishment of the Cape of Good Hope, 1652–74', *The Journal of African History*, 39.3 (1998), pp. 417–37 (p. 421).

9   Hilde Gunnink, Bonny Sands, Brigitte Pakendorf and Koen Bostoen, 'Prehistoric language contact in the Kavango-Zambezi transfrontier area: Khoisan influence on southwestern Bantu languages', *Journal of African Languages and Linguistics*, Vol 36 Issue 2 (2015) pp. 193–232.

10   'Krotoa !Goa/Gōas Translator, Negotiator & Peacemaker 1642–1674'; Wells.

11   Nicola Daniels, 'Special Role of Krotoa, Khoi Matriarch of Resistance', 30 August 2019 <https://www.iol.co.za/capetimes/news/special-role-of-krotoa-khoi-matriarch-of-resistance-31529587>.

12   Diana Ferrus, 'I've Come to Take You Home: A Tribute to Sarah Baartman' (Poetry for Life) <http://www.poetryforlife.co.za/index.php/anthology/south-african-poems/130-i-ve-come-to-take-you-home-a-tribute-to-sarah-baartman>.

13   Nicolas About, 'Proposition de loi autorisant la restitution par la France de la dépouille mortelle de Saartjie Baartman, dite "Vénus Hottentote", à l'Afrique du sud', 2001 <https://www.senat.fr/leg/ppl01-114.html>.

14   Denver Toroxa Breda, '#MotherLanguageDay: How Did We Let the Khoekhoe Language Die without Trying to Save It?', Cape Argus, 21 February 2019.

15   Mae M. Ngai, '"A Slight Knowledge of the Barbarian Language": Chinese Interpreters in Late-Nineteenth and Early-Twentieth-Century America', Journal of American Ethnic History, 30.2 (2011), pp. 5–32 (pp. 13–14).

16   'Icxiyoyomocaliztli (restlessness and anxiety of a wanderer with itchy feet; from Alonso de Molina)', Stephanie Wood (ed), Nahuatl Dictionary (Wired Humanities Projects, 2000) <https://nahuatl.uoregon.edu/content/icxiyoyomocaliztli>.

The Children Who Invented a Language

1   Péter Maitz and Craig A. Volker, 'Documenting Unserdeutsch. Reversing Colonial Amnesia', Journal of Pidgin and Creole Languages, 32.2 (2017), pp. 365–397 (p. 391).

2   Peter Mühlhäusler, 'Varieties of Language Policies and Their Consequences in the German Colonies of the Pacific Area', Language and Linguistics in Melanesia. Journal of the Linguistic Society of Papua New Guinea, Special Issue: Language Contact in the German Colonies: Papua New Guinea and beyond (2017), pp. 13–14.

3   Mühlhäusler, 'Varieties of Language Policies and Their Consequences in the German Colonies of the Pacific Area', pp. 13, 22.

4   Mühlhäusler, 'Varieties of Language Policies and Their Consequences in the German Colonies of the Pacific Area', p. 16.

5   Peter Mühlhäusler, 'Samoan Plantation Pidgin English and the Origins of New Guinea Pidgin: An Introduction', *The Journal of Pacific History*, 11.2.

6   Peter Mühlhäusler and Ulrike Mosel, 'New Evidence of a Samoan Origin of New Guinea Tok Pisin (New Guinea Pidgin English)', *The Journal of Pacific History*, 17.3 (1982).

7   Mühlhäusler, 'Samoan Plantation Pidgin English and the Origins of New Guinea Pidgin: An Introduction', p. 169.

8   Françoise Vergès, 'Creolization and Resistance', in *Creolizing Europe: Legacies and Transformations*, ed. by Encarnacion Gutierrez Rodriguez and Shirley Anne Tate (Liverpool University Press, 2016), pp. 42–43.

9   Mühlhäusler and Mosel, p. 174.

10   Maitz and Volker, p. 378.

11   Craig A. Volker, 'The Birth and Decline of Rabaul Creole German', *Language and Linguistics in Melanesia*, 22 (1991), pp. 143–56 (p. 145).

12   Maitz and Volker, p. 374.

13   Maitz and Volker, p. 374.

14   Maitz and Volker, p. 375.

15   Volker, 'The Birth and Decline of Rabaul Creole German', p. 146.

16   Maitz and Volker, p. 376.

17   Maitz and Volker, p. 376.

18   Rebekka Endler, 'Pippi und das Unserdeutsch – Auf den Spuren der Heimkinder von Papua-Neuguinea' (WDR, 30.06.2019).

19   Maitz and Volker, p. 391.

20   *Pippi & Der König: Auf den Spuren von Efraim Langstrumpf*, ed. by Joakim Langer and Hélena Regius (Berlin: List, 2005), p. 199.

21   Endler, 'Pippi und das Unserdeutsch – Auf den Spuren der Heimkinder von Papua-Neuguinea'; Rebekka Endler, 'Pippi und die vergessenen Kinder Papua-Neuguineas' (Deutschlandfunk, 04.01.2019).

22   Gerald Florian Messner, 'The Shark-Calling Ceremony in Paruai, New Ireland, Papua New Guinea', *The World of Music*, Vol. 32. No. 1, Oceania (1990), pp. 49–83 (p. 50).

23   Messner, p. 49.

24   Messner, p. 66.

25   Messner, p. 70.

26   Messner, p. 54.

27   Endler, 'Pippi und das Unserdeutsch – Auf den Spuren der Heimkinder von Papua-Neuguinea'; Endler, 'Pippi und die vergessenen Kinder Papua-Neuguineas'.

28 Craig A. Volker, 'The Relationship between Traditional Secret Languages and Two School-Based Pidgin Languages in Papua New Guinea', *Horizons. Journal of Asia-Pacific Issues*, 3 (1989), pp. 19–24 (p. 20).

29 Volker, 'The Relationship between Traditional Secret Languages and Two School-Based Pidgin Languages in Papua New Guinea', p. 20.

30 Siegwalt Lindenfelser and Péter Maitz, 'The Creoleness of Unserdeutsch (Rabaul Creole German): A Typological Perspective', *Language and Linguistics in Melanesia. Journal of the Linguistic Society of Papua New Guinea*, Special Issue 2017.

31 Maitz and Volker, p. 372.

32 Lindenfelser and Maitz, pp. 107–10.

33 Maitz and Volker, p. 377.

34 Lindenfelser and Maitz, pp. 107–10.

35 Maitz and Volker, p. 382.

36 Endler, 'Pippi und das Unserdeutsch – Auf den Spuren der Heimkinder von Papua-Neuguinea'; Endler, 'Pippi und die vergessenen Kinder Papua-Neuguineas'.

37 Maitz and Volker, p. 390.

38 Péter Maitz, Siegwalt Lindenfelser and Craig A. Volker, 'Unserdeutsch (Rabaul Creole German), Papua New Guinea', in *Varieties of German Worldwide* (Oxford: Oxford University Press, In prep.).

39 Angelika Götze and others, 'Documenting Unserdeutsch (Rabaul Creole German): A Workshop Report', *Language and Linguistics in Melanesia*, Special Issue 2017 <http://www.langlxmelanesia.com/LLM%20S%20 2017_Workshop_Report.pdf>.

40 'Unserdeutsch (Rabaul Creole German): Official Website of the Unserdeutsch Research Team, University of Bern' <https://www.germanistik. unibe.ch/research/projects/unserdeutsch_rabaul_creole_german/ index_eng.html>.

41 'Unserdeutsch (Rabaul Creole German): Official Website of the Unserdeutsch Research Team, University of Bern'.

42 Péter Maitz, 'Unserdeutsch (Rabaul Creole German): Eine Vergessene Koloniale Varietät Des Deutschen Im Melanesischen Pazifik', in *German Abroad: Perspektiven Der Variationslinguistik, Srachkontakt- Und Mehrsprachigkeitsforschung*, ed. by Alexandra Lenz (Vienna: Vienna University Press), p. 236.

43 Endler, 'Pippi und das Unserdeutsch – Auf den Spuren der Heimkinder von Papua-Neuguinea'; Endler, 'Pippi und die vergessenen Kinder Papua-Neuguineas'.

Cinderella and the Innkeeper's Daughter

1   Heinz Rölleke, 'Alt Wie Der Wald': Reden und Aufsätze zu den Märchen der Brüder Grimm' (Trier: Wissenschaftlicher Verlag Trier, 2006), p. 189.

2   Wilhelm Grimm and Jacob Grimm, Brüder Grimm: Kinder- und Hausmärchen (Ausgabe letzter Hand mit den Originalanmerkungen der Brüder Grimm), ed. by Heinz Rölleke (Reclam, 1857), p. Band 1 p. 150.

3   Heiner Boencke and Phoebe Alexa Schmidt, Marie Hassenpflug: Eine Märchenerzählerin der Brüder Grimm (Darmstadt: wbg Philipp von Zabern, 2013), p. 24.

4   Boencke and Schmidt, pp. 23–24.

5   Boencke and Schmidt, p. 28.

6   Boencke and Schmidt, pp. 44–45.

7   Grimm and Grimm, p. Band 1 p. 246.

8   Rölleke, 'Alt Wie Der Wald': Reden und Aufsätze zu den Märchen der Brüder Grimm', pp. 10–11.

9   Rölleke, 'Alt Wie Der Wald': Reden und Aufsätze zu den Märchen der Brüder Grimm', p. 11.

10 Heinz Rölleke, Es war einmal… : Die Wahren Märchen der Brüder Grimm und wer sie ihnen erzählte (Die Andere Bibliothek, 2011), p. 284.

11 Grimm and Grimm, p. Band 1 p. 150.

12 Heinz Rölleke, 'Die Kinder- und Hausmärchen der Brüder Grimm und ihre Beiträger', in Märchen, Mythen Und Moderne: 200 Jahre Kinder- Und Hausmärchen Der Brüder Grimm (Frankfurt: Peter Lang Edition, 2015), p. 26.

13 Rölleke, Es War Einmal… : Die Wahren Märchen Der Brüder Grimm Und Wer Sie Ihnen Erzählte, p. 106.

14 Heinz Rölleke, 'Die Kinder- und Hausmärchen der Brüder Grimm und ihre Beiträger', in Märchen, Mythen Und Moderne: 200 Jahre Kinder- Und Hausmärchen der Brüder Grimm (Frankfurt: Peter Lang Edition, 2015), p. 26.

15 Märchen, Mythen Und Moderne: 200 Jahre Kinder- Und Hausmärchen Der Brüder Grimm, ed. by Holger Ehrhardt, Hans-Heino Ewers, and Annekatrin Inder (Frankfurt: Peter Lang Edition, 2015), p. 26.

16 Rölleke, Es war einmal… : Die Wahren Märchen der Brüder Grimm und wer sie ihnen erzählte, pp. 103–4.

17 Rölleke, Es war einmal… : Die Wahren Märchen der Brüder Grimm und wer sie ihnen erzählte, pp. 117–18.

18   Rölleke, *Es war einmal...* : *Die Wahren Märchen der Brüder Grimm und wer sie ihnen erzählte*, pp. 117–18.

19   Rölleke, *Es war einmal...* : *Die Wahren Märchen der Brüder Grimm und wer sie ihnen erzählte*, pp. 117–18.

20   Grimm and Grimm, p. Band 1 p. 131.

21   Grimm and Grimm, p. Band 1 p. 132.

22   Grimm and Grimm, p. Band 3 p. 34–35.

23   'Ashypet', 'Ashiepattle', Dr. Jamieson's Scottish Dictionary, Vol. 3 (Edinburgh: William Tait, 1825) p. 29 Online edition: <http://www.scotsdictionary.com>.

24   Grimm and Grimm, p. Band 3 p. 46.

25   A. K. Ramanujan, 'Food for Thought: Towards an Anthology of Hindu Food-Images', in *The Table Is Laid: The Oxford Anthology of South Asian Food Writing*, ed. by John Thieme and Ira Raja (New Delhi: Oxford University Press, 2009), p. 18.

26   Grimm and Grimm, p. Band 1 p. 19.

The Sound of Snow

1   Inger Marie Gaup Eira and others, 'Traditional Sámi Snow Terminology and Physical Snow Classification – Two Ways of Knowing', *Cold Regions Science and Technology*, 85 (2013), pp. 117–30.

2   Eira and others, pp. 8–9.

3   Ante Aikio, 'An Essay on Saami Ethnolinguistic Prehistory', in *A Linguistic Map of Prehistoric Northern Europe* (Helsinki: Mémoires de la Société Finno-Ougrienne, 2012), pp. 63–117.

4   Marja-Liisa Olthuis, Suvi Kivelä and Tove Skutnabb-Kangas, *Revitalising Indigenous Languages: How to Recreate a Lost Generation* (Bristol: Multilingual Matters, 2013), p. 25.

5   Olthuis, Kivelä and Skutnabb-Kangas, pp. 32–34.

6   Olthuis, Kivelä and Skutnabb-Kangas, p. 75.

7   Anna Idström, 'What Inari Saami Idioms Reveal about the Time Concept of the Indigenous People of Inari', *Yearbook of Phraseology*, 1 (2010), p. 172.

8   Idström, p. 170.

9   Idström, p. 166.

10   Idström, p. 166.

11   Marja-Liisa Olthuis, Suvi Kivelä and Tove Skutnabb-Kangas, *Revital-*

ising Indigenous Languages: How to Recreate a Lost Generation (Bristol: Multilingual Matters, 2013), p. 71.

12   Olthuis, Kivelä and Skutnabb-Kangas, p. 89.

13   Olthuis, Kivelä and Skutnabb-Kangas, p. 84.

14   Jouni Jaakkola, Suvi Juntunen and Klemetti Näkkäläjärvi, 'The Holistic Effects of Climate Change on the Culture, Well-Being, and Health of the Saami, the Only Indigenous People in the European Union', *Current Environmental Health Reports*, 2018, 5:401–417.

Walrus Asleep on Ice

1   Michael D. Fortescue, Steven Jacobson and Lawrence Kaplan, *Comparative Eskimo Dictionary: With Aleut Cognates*, 2nd ed (Fairbanks, AK: Alaska Native Language Center, University of Alaska Fairbanks, 2010), p. x.

2   Donald Webster and Wilfried Zibell, *Iñupiat Eskimo Dictionary* (Fairbanks, AK: University of Alaska, 1970), p. 5 <https://library.alaska.gov/hist/hist_docs/docs/anlm/200078.pdf>.

3   Fortescue, Jacobson and Kaplan, p. 123.

4   Webster and Zibell, p.26.

5   Fortescue, Jacobson and Kaplan, p. 319.

6   Fortescue, Jacobson and Kaplan, p. 319.

7   Fortescue, Jacobson and Kaplan, p. 191.

8   Fortescue, Jacobson and Kaplan, p. 263.

9   Fortescue, Jacobson and Kaplan, p. 393.

10   Fortescue, Jacobson and Kaplan, p. 263; 'Uqausiit: The Inuktut Grammar Dictionary' (Pirurvik Centre for Inuit Wellbeing, Language and Culture) <https://uqausiit.ca>.

11   *Iñupiatun Eskimo Dictionary*, ed. by Wolf A. Seiler, Language and Culture Documentation and Description, 16 (SIL International, 2012).

12   Fortescue, Jacobson and Kaplan, p. 40.

13   Fortescue, Jacobson and Kaplan, p. 31.

14   Seiler, p. 127.

15   Fortescue, Jacobson and Kaplan, p. 22.

16   Fortescue, Jacobson and Kaplan, p. 88.

17   'Yup'ik Eskimo Dictionary', ed. by Steven Jacobson (Alaska Native Language Center, 2012) <https://uafanlc.alaska.edu/Online/CY972J2012/YED_2012_smaller.pdf>.

18   Fortescue, Jacobson and Kaplan, p. 375.

19   See for example: Martin Pullum, 'The Great Eskimo Vocabulary Hoax', *Natural Language and Linguistic Theory*, 7 (1989), pp. 275–281.

20   Laura Martin, '"Eskimo Words for Snow": A Case Study in the Genesis and Decay of an Anthropological Example', *American Anthropologist*, 88.2 (1986), pp. 418–23 (p. 419).

21   Asifa Majid and others, 'Differential Coding of Perception in the World's Languages', *PNAS*, 115.45 (2018), 11369–11376; Sophie Hardach, 'How Your Language Reflects the Senses You Use', *BBC Future*, 27 February 2019 <https://www.bbc.com/future/article/20190226-how-your-language-reflects-the-senses-you-use>.

22   'Turkish Tongue-Twister Wins Longest Word Competition', *Daily Sabah*, 2017 <https://www.dailysabah.com/turkey/2017/06/13/turkish-tongue-twister-wins-longest-word-competition>.

23   Lawrence Kaplan, 'Inuit Snow Terms: How Many and What Does It Mean?', in *Building Capacity in Arctic Societies: Dynamics and Shifting Perspectives. Proceedings from the 2nd IPSSAS Seminar. Iqaluit, Nunavut, Canada*, ed. by François Trudel (Montreal: Alaska Native Language Center, 2003) <https://www.uaf.edu/anlc/resources/inuit_snow_terms.php>.

24   Kaplan.

25   Fortescue, Jacobson and Kaplan, p. 325.

26   Fortescue, Jacobson and Kaplan, p. 140.

27   Fortescue, Jacobson and Kaplan, p. 319.

Kafka's Blue Notebook: Multilingual Creativity

1   Marek Nekula, 'Franz Kafkas Sprachen Und Sprachlosigkeit', *Brücken – Germanistisches Jahrbuch Tschechien-Slowakei*, 15.1–2 (2007), p. 101.

2   Nekula, p. 101.

3   Nekula, p. 99.

4   Nekula, p. 107.

5   Nekula, p. 107.

6   Nekula, p. 105.

7   Nekula, p. 112.

8   Eliézer Ben-Yéhouda and Ithamar Ben-Avi, *La Renaissance de l'hébreu*, trans. by Gérard Haddad (Paris: Desclée de Brouwer, 1998), p. 200; Mikhail Lermontov, 'Sail, in: After Lermontov: Translations for the

Bicentenary', ed. by Peter France and Robyn Marsack (Carcanet, Manchester, 2014), Scottish Poetry Library website <https://www.scottishpoetrylibrary.org.uk/poem/sail/>.

9   Ben-Yéhouda and Ben-Avi, p. 207.

10   Nekula, p. 111.

11   Nekula, p. 109.

12   Nekula, p. 110.

13   Franz Kafka, 'Booklet filled with Hebrew-German vocabulary in Kafka's own hand, possibly 1922 (Digital)', The National Library of Israel, Jerusalem   <https://beta.nli.org.il/en/archives/NNL_ARCHIVE_AL003561085/NLI>.

14   Chen Malul, 'Kafka's "Blue Notebook" Revealed', 2019, The National Library of Israel, Jerusalem <https://blog.nli.org.il/en/kafkas-blue-notebook-revealed/>.

15   Kafka, 'Booklet filled with Hebrew-German vocabulary in Kafka's own hand, possibly 1922'.

16   Franz Kafka, *Der Proceß: Roman; in Der Fassung Der Handschrift*, ed. by Hans-Gerd Koch (Frankfurt am Main: Fischer-Taschenbuch-Verl, 2008).

17   Einstein, Albert, '"Dass du schiedst ist fürchterlich": Humorous poem for Helen Porter-Lowe', 1946, Albert Einstein Archives Online, The Hebrew University of Jerusalem <http://alberteinstein.info/vufind1/Record/EAR000055515>.

18   Alain Mabanckou, *Alain Mabanckou interviewed by Binwavanga Wainaina*, 2010, BOMB Magazine <https://bombmagazine.org/articles/alain-mabanckou/>.

19   Raymond Antrobus, *The Perseverance* (London: Penned in the Margins, 2018), p. 47.

20   Franz Kafka, 'Brief an Felix Weltsch, Zürau, Mitte November 1917, Sowie an Max Brod, Zürau, 4. Dezember 1917' <http://www.franzkafka.de/franzkafka/fundstueck_archiv/fundstueck/457430>.

Multilingual Children

1   John Berger, 'Writing is an off-shoot of something deeper', *Guardian*, 12 Dec 2014.

2   Laura Ann Petitto and Siobhan Holowka, 'Evaluating Attributions of Delay and Confusion in Young Bilinguals: Special Insights from Infants Acquiring a Signed and a Spoken Language'. *Sign Language Studies*,

vol. 3, no. 1, Fall 2002, pp. 4–33. (p. 9) <https://www.jstor.org/stable/pdf/26204891.pdf?refreqid=excelsior%3Ac7ff421994818f84a3032d1bf591f5ba>.

3   Petitto, p. 10.

4   Petitto, p. 11.

5   François Grosjean, *Bilingual* (Cambridge, Mass.; London: Harvard University Press, 2010), p. 208.

6   Grosjean, p. 208.

7   Grosjean, p. 209.

8   David Singleton and Simone Pfenninger, 'Bilingualism in Midlife', in *The Cambridge Handbook of Bilingualism*, ed. by Lourdes Ortega and Annick De Houwer (Cambridge, United Kingdom; New York, NY: Cambridge University Press, 2018), pp. 76–100 (p. 39).

9   Singleton and Pfenninger, pp. 39–40, 47.

10   Sarah Shin, 'Birth Order and the Language Experience of Bilingual Children', *Teachers of English to Speakers of Other Languages*, 36.1 (2002), pp. 103–13 (p. 105).

11   Singleton and Pfenninger, p. 47.

12   Freire, Schwartz and Steven, p. 85.

13   Singleton and Pfenninger, p. 90.

14   Mira Goral, 'Language and Older Bilinguals', in *The Cambridge Handbook of Bilingualism*, ed. by Lourdes Ortega and Annick De Houwer (Cambridge, United Kingdom; New York, NY: Cambridge University Press, 2018), pp. 106–16 (p. 112).

15   Singleton and Pfenninger, p. 95.

16   Leonie Gaiser and Philippa Hughes, *Language Provisions in Manchester's Supplementary Schools* (School of Arts, Languages and Cultures, The University of Manchester, 2015), p. 10 <http://mlm.humanities.manchester.ac.uk/wp-content/uploads/2015/12/Language-provisions-in-Manchester-supplementary-schools.pdf>.

17   Gaiser and Hughes, p. 21.

18   Gaiser and Hughes, p. 19.

19   Gaiser and Hughes, p. 51.

20   Gaiser and Hughes, pp. 32–34.

21   Greater London Authority, *Languages Spoken by Pupils, Borough & Middle Super Output Area (Data from the 2008 Annual School Census)*, 2008 <https://data.london.gov.uk/dataset/languages-spoken-pupils-borough-msoa>.

22   Greater London Authority.

Epilogue

1   Joshua Bowen and Megan Lewis, *Learn to Read Ancient Sumerian: An Introduction for Complete Beginners* (Digital Hammurabi Press, 2020).

2   Moudhy Al-Rashid @Moudhy, 'Cuneiform in Iraqi street art.' Twitter message, 7 Nov 2019; Osama Sadiq @osama_sadiq1, Iraqi graffiti, Instagram, 2019. Eva von Dassow, 'Freedom in Ancient Near Eastern Societies', in *The Oxford Handbook of Cuneiform Culture*, ed. by Eleanor Robson and Karen Radner (Oxford: Oxford University Press, 2011), pp. 205–224 (p. 208).

Index

Illustrations are in *italic*.

Cover key
The writing in the bubbles spells out the word for 'language' in:

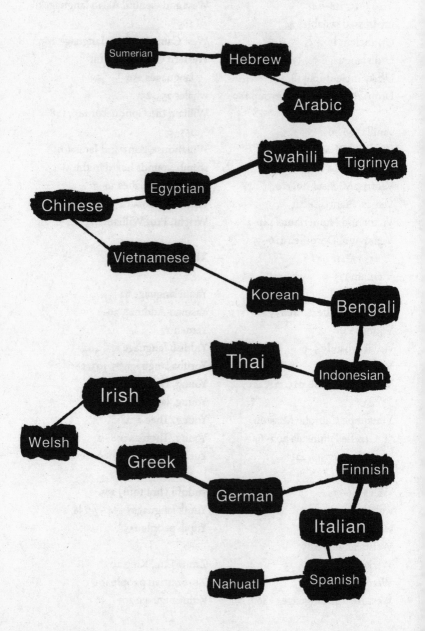